THE EASTER BOOK
OF LEGENDS AND STORIES

THE EASTER BOOK OF LEGENDS AND STORIES

Selected by
ALICE ISABEL HAZELTINE
and ELVA SOPHRONIA SMITH

Illustrated by PAMELA BIANCO

NEW YORK
LOTHROP, LEE AND SHEPARD CO.

Republished by Omnigraphics • Penobscot Building • Detroit • 1992

Copyright, 1947 by

Lothrop, Lee & Shepard Company, N. Y.

All Rights Reserved

~~2113~~

9189

Library of Congress Cataloging-in-Publication Data

The Easter book of legends and stories/selected by Alice Isabel Hazeltine and Elva Sophronia Smith.
    p. cm.
  ISBN 1-55888-857-8 (lib. bdg.: alk. paper)
   1. Easter—Literary collections. I. Hazeltine, Alice Isabel, b. 1878. II. Smith, Elva Sophronia, 1871-
PN6071.E2H3   1990
808.8'033—dc20   89-63107
                                                           CIP

∞

This book is printed on acid-free paper meeting the ANSI Z39.48 Standard. The infinity symbol that appears above indicates that the paper in this book meets that standard.

Printed in the United States of America

ACKNOWLEDGMENTS

The compilers wish to thank the following publishers for permission to reprint selections or quotations:

The American Book Company for "A Song of Praise: Words Adapted from an Ancient Canticle" from the *Sixth Book of Songs* edited by Robert Foresman.

G. Bell & Sons for "A Lesson of Faith" from *Parables from Nature* by Margaret Gatty.

Expression Company for "Easter Morning" from *Choral Speaking Arrangements for the Upper Grades* by Louise Abney.

Friends General Conference and the author for "Ivan's Easter Service" from *The Observance of Easter* by Amelia W. Swayne.

Great Britain. The Controller of H. M. Stationery Office for the use of material from *The Tripartite Life of Patrick*, edited by Whitley Stokes, in the story "Saint Patrick at Tara."

Harper & Brothers for "The Fountain of Youth" from *Plays of the Pioneers* by Constance D'Arcy Mackay; and for "Easter Flowers" by Margaret E. Sangster.

Hodder & Stoughton for "The Alleluiatic Sequence" from the *Collected Hymns, Sequences and Carols* by John Mason Neale.

Henry Holt and Company for "A Prayer in Spring" from *Collected Poems* by Robert Frost; "The Lent Lily" and "Loveliest of Trees" from *Collected Poems* by A. E. Housman; and "The Sacred Flame" from *Christ Legends* by Selma Lagerlöf.

v

Houghton Mifflin Company for "The Butterfly" from *A Marriage Cycle* by Alice Freeman Palmer; "The First Te Deum" from *Colonial Ballads, Sonnets and Other Verse,* by Margaret J. Preston; "A Song of Easter" from *Stories and Poems for Children* by Celia Thaxter; and "Elena's *Ciambella*" from *Friends in Strange Garments* by Anna Milo Upjohn.

Little, Brown & Company for "A Fuzzy Fellow" and "The Waking Year" from *Poems* by Emily Dickinson; and for "Easter-Time" from *In My Nursery* by Laura E. Richards.

Longmans, Green and Company for lines quoted in "Apollon, a Gardener" by Katharine Gibson from the "Sun Song" of St. Francis as found in *St. Francis of Assisi* by Johannes Jorgensen.

The Macmillan Company for "April" and "The Sun Comes Dancing" from *Twelve Months Make a Year* by Elizabeth Coatsworth; and for "Brendan" from *Old Pastures* by Padraic Colum.

Macmillan & Co., London, and Miss Pamela Hinkson for "Love at Easter" from *Collected Poems* by Katharine Tynan Hinkson; also Macmillan & Co. for "An Easter Carol" from *Poetical Works* by Christina Georgina Rossetti.

The Parish Choir for "Ye Happy Bells of Easter Day," from *Carols Old and Carols New.*

Patrick Geddes Colleagues, The Outlook Tower, Edinburgh, for the "Rune of St. Patrick" quoted in "Saint Patrick at Tara."

G. P. Putnam's Sons for "Ponce de Leon Finds the Land of Flowers," adapted from *The Spanish Settlements, 1513-1561,* by Woodbury Lowery.

Fleming H. Revell Company for "The Easter People" abridged from the book with the same title by Winifred Kirkland; and for "Easter Flowers are Blooming Bright" by Mary A. Nicholson from the *New Church Hymnal* edited by H. Augustine Smith.

Charles Scribner's Sons for "Easter Morning: A Play of the Resurrection" from *Adam's Dream and Two Other Miracle Plays for Children* by Alice Corbin Henderson.

The Society for Promoting Christian Knowledge for the greater part of the text of "Saint Patrick at Tara," taken from *Saint Patrick, his Writings and Life,* by Newport J. D. White.

Willett, Clark & Company for "An Easter Wish" from *1000 Quotable Poems, v. 1.* compiled by Thomas Curtis Clark and Esther A. Gillespie.

Acknowledgment is also made for the following selections:

"An Easter Processional" is reprinted from *An Easter Processional* by Helen Gray Cone, from St. Nicholas Magazine, copyright 1891, 1919 by the Century Company, by permission of D. Appleton-Century Company, Inc. "An Easter Carol" by Emily D. Chapman from *St. Nicholas Songs* by Waldo S. Pratt is also reprinted by permission of D. Appleton-Century Company, Inc.

"Easter Lambs" by Anne D. Kyle, copyright 1925 by the Methodist Publishing Company, and "Easter Candle" by Anne D. Kyle, copyright 1928 by the Methodist Publishing Company, are reprinted by permission of Brandt & Brandt.

"An Easter Greeting" from *Russian Lyrics* by Martha Gilbert Dickinson Bianchi; "Daffodil's Return" from *Poems* by Bliss Carman; and "Easter Again" from *Silver Saturday* by Nancy Byrd Turner are reprinted by permission of Dodd, Mead & Company, Inc.

"Ys and Her Bells" from *Once in France* by Marguerite Clement, copyright 1927; "Aniela's Easter" from *Up the Hill,* by Marguerite De Angeli, copyright 1942; and "Easter" from *Trees and Other Poems* by Joyce Kilmer, copyright 1914; are reprinted by courtesy of Doubleday & Company, Inc.

"Easter" from *Poems by a Little Girl* by Hilda Conkling, copyright 1920, is reprinted with permission of J. B. Lippincott Company.

"The World Itself" by John Mason Neale; also "Easter Carol," "Flower Carol," and "Hilariter," are reprinted from the *Oxford Book of Carols* by permission of the Oxford University Press. Also, "Sing, All Ye Christian People!" by Jan Struther is reprinted from *Enlarged Songs of Praise* by permission of the author and the Oxford University Press.

"Easter Rabbit," by Mary Root Kern, from the *Progressive Music Series, Book Two,* copyright 1915, is reprinted by permission of the author and by special permission of the publishers, Silver Burdett Company, New York.

The following selections are reprinted by permission of the Viking Press, Inc., New York

"Easter."
From *Nino,* by Valenti Angelo.
Copyright 1938 by Valenti Angelo.

"Easter Eggs."
From *The Good Master* by Kate Seredy.
Copyright 1935 by Kate Seredy.

For permission to reprint the following selections the compilers wish to thank:

Miss Catherine Annable, Co-Executor of the Estate of Margaret Deland, for "Easter Music: Jonquils" from *The Old Garden and Other Verses* by Margaret Deland.

Mrs. Carol Ryrie Brink for "In All Things Beautiful," published in the Elementary Magazine for March, 1929; for "Waking-Up Time," published in the Elementary Magazine for April, 1931; and for "Daffodils Out of the Dark" published in Queens Gardens, April 15, 1933.

Miss Katharine Gibson for "Apollon, a Gardener" written for this book.

Miss Pamela Hinkson for "Daffodil" by Katharine Tynan Hinkson.

Miss Erica Oxenham for "Risen" by John Oxenham.

Miss Helene Pelzel for "A Happy Easter" written for this book.

Miss Jessie B. Rittenhouse, Literary Executor, for "A Canticle" by Clinton Scollard.

Mr. Charles Hanson Towne for "An Easter Canticle" from his *Selected Poems.*

Mrs. Agnes Sligh Turnbull for "The Maid of Emmaus" from her *Far Above Rubies.*

Miss Helen Waddell for "Saint Brendan and the White Birds" from her *Beasts and Saints.*

Miss Margaret Widdemer for "A Child's Easter Song."

Miss Ella Young and the Horn Book Magazine for "Pasque."

The sources of other selections are as follows:

"A Child's Easter" by Annie Trumbull Slosson is from *Easter Dawn* edited and published by A. D. F. Randolph, 1880.

"Tell Us, Gard'ner, Dost Thou Know?" by Arthur Cleveland Coxe; and "Smile Praises, O Sky," a Latin hymn translated by Mrs. Elizabeth Charles are taken from *Resurgit: a Collection of Hymns and Songs of the Resurrection,* edited by Frank Foxcroft and published by Lee and Shepard in 1879.

"Rise, Flowers, Rise" by Mary A. Lathbury may be found in her *Poems* published by the Nunc Licet Press in 1915. The poem, "Easter Song," is customarily attributed to Miss Lathbury, but its original source is not known.

CONTENTS

FOREWORD

THE FIRST EASTER

Very Early in the Morning . . . *St. Mark XVI: 1–3. St. Matthew XXVIII: 2–6. St. Mark XVI: 7. St. Luke XXIV: 8, 9, 11–12. St. John XX: 11–18. St. Matthew XXVIII: 16, 18–20*	3
Tell Us, Gard'ner, Dost Thou Know?—*Arthur Cleveland Coxe*	6
The World Itself—*John Mason Neale*	9
Risen—*John Oxenham*	11
Easter Morning: a Play of the Resurrection for Children—*Alice Corbin Henderson*	15
The Maid of Emmaus—*Agnes Sligh Turnbull*	24
Hallelujah—*from the Messiah by George Frederick Handel*	38

THE WAKING YEAR

Easter Again—*Nancy Byrd Turner*	41
The Waking Year—*Emily Dickinson*	42
Pasque—*Ella Young*	44
Loveliest of Trees—*A. E. Housman*	45
Rise, Flowers, Rise—*Mary A. Lathbury*	46
Easter Flowers—*Margaret E. Sangster*	48
Flower Carol—*translated from the Latin*	50
Easter Flowers are Blooming Bright—*Mary A. Nicholson*	52
Easter-Time—*Laura E. Richards*	54

xi

Daffodil's Return—*Bliss Carman*	56
Daffodil—*Katharine Tynan Hinkson*	57
The Lent Lily—*A. E. Housman*	59
Easter Music: Jonquils—*Margaret Deland*	61
Easter Song—*Author Unknown*	62
A Child's Easter Song—*Margaret Widdemer*	64

THE WHOLE BRIGHT WORLD REJOICES

Smile Praises, O Sky—*translated from the Latin by Elizabeth Charles*	67
Hilariter—*translated from the German*	69
An Easter Carol—*Christina Georgina Rossetti*	70
An Easter Greeting—*translated from the Russian of Maikow by Martha Gilbert Dickinson Bianchi*	72
Ye Happy Bells of Easter Day—*Author Unknown*	73
An Easter Processional—*Helen Gray Cone*	75
Easter—*Joyce Kilmer*	76
The Sun Comes Dancing—*Elizabeth Coatsworth*	77
A Canticle—*Clinton Scollard*	78
Love at Easter—*Katharine Tynan Hinkson*	80
Easter Morning—*Louise Abney*	82
An Easter Carol—*Emily D. Chapman*	83
A Song of Praise—*adapted from an Ancient Canticle*	85
Easter—*Hilda Conkling*	86
Easter Rabbit—*Mary Root Kern*	87

A LESSON OF FAITH

An Easter Canticle—*Charles Hanson Towne*	91
Easter Carol—*written for a French Carol Tune*	93
A Fuzzy Fellow—*Emily Dickinson*	95
A Lesson of Faith—*Margaret Gatty*	97
The Butterfly—*Alice Freeman Palmer*	105
A Prayer in Spring—*Robert Frost*	107
Sing, All Ye Christian People!—*Jan Struther*	109
A Song of Easter—*Celia Thaxter*	111

"STILL IS THE STORY TOLD"

Ys and Her Bells—*Marguerite Clement*	115
Apollon, a Gardener—*Katharine Gibson*	130
The First Te Deum—*Margaret J. Preston*	146
Saint Patrick at Tara—*adapted from Early Sources*	149
Saint Brendan and the White Birds—*translated by Helen Waddell*	159
Brendan—*Padraic Colum*	163
Ponce de Leon Finds the Land of Flowers—*adapted from The Spanish Settlements, by Woodbury Lowery*	167
The Fountain of Youth—*Constance D'Arcy Mackay*	172

"AS THE CUSTOM IS"

Waking-Up Time—*Carol Ryrie Brink*	187
April—*Elizabeth Coatsworth*	191
Aniela's Easter—*Marguerite De Angeli*	199
A Happy Easter—*Helene Pelzel*	210
Elena's *Ciambella*—*Anna Milo Upjohn*	227
Easter Eggs—*Kate Seredy*	234
Easter—*Valenti Angelo*	244

IT HAPPENED AT EASTER

In All Things Beautiful—*Carol Ryrie Brink*	263
Easter Lambs—*Anne D. Kyle*	268
Daffodils Out of the Dark—*Carol Ryrie Brink*	285
Easter Candle—*Anne D. Kyle*	295

IN THE SPIRIT OF WORSHIP

A Child's Easter—*Annie Trumbull Slosson*	315
Ivan's Easter Service—*Amelia W. Swayne*	319
The Sacred Flame—*Selma Lagerlöf*	322
The Easter People—*Winifred Kirkland*	361
The Alleluiatic Sequence—*translated from the Latin by John Mason Neale*	375

An Easter Wish—*Author Unknown* 378

NOTES

INDEX OF AUTHORS

INDEX OF TITLES

FOREWORD

Through the centuries the Christian Church has celebrated the festival of the Resurrection with songs of joy and praise; the old Latin hymns, mediaeval carols, later lyrics. This "Day of Days" has been, in the Christian year, a period of rejoicing and exultation, as everywhere glad voices have been lifted triumphantly in hymns of victory for the Risen Christ.

In northern climes Easter-tide is also the time of reawakening life in tree and plant; "for, lo, the winter is past . . . ; the flowers appear on the earth; the time of the singing of birds is come." All nature seems to rejoice with the Christian Church and so it is that much of the imagery and symbolism of Easter is drawn from the dancing sun; the blossoming trees; the rose, the lily, the daffodil. To the poet the recurring miracle of green things growing "whispers of the life to be," the golden trumpets of the jonquil become a symbol of the Easter Victory, and the butterfly brings its winged message of hope and faith.

Long before the Christian era the rebirth of nature was celebrated with the returning springtime and some of the customs and observances of Easter today may be traced back to the pagan festival of olden times. The name itself, derived from the old Saxon feast day, may signify joy at the earlier rising of the sun and the new beginnings of the earth's life. Traditional rites and ceremonies, persisting as they did into later periods, were accepted and assimilated by the Church in its early days but with a new interpretation and frequently a spiritual significance. In the course of the centuries many varying customs have developed among the peoples in different lands—some strange and curious, some expressing deep religious faith. Even the seemingly most commonplace of Easter accompaniments,—the lively rabbit and the gaily colored eggs—point backward to a recognition of the upsurge of new life, the glory of the rosy-fingered dawn and the rising sun.

The literature of Easter comprises not only Biblical narrative, sacred song, and nature verse, but other poems, plays, legends, and stories associated with the Day. The selections for this Easter book for children and young people have been chosen out of this abundance. They represent both the old and the new; from the early "Smile Praises, O Sky" to Robert Frost's "Prayer in Spring" and Jan Struther's "Sing, All Ye Christian People!" They offer pictures of Easter celebrations in various countries. They commemorate the joyful aspects of nature. Above all, they echo the notes of the trombones which for nearly one hundred years have summoned worshipers at the sunrise services of the Moravians at Bethlehem in Pennsylvania: "The Lord is Risen Indeed."

VERY EARLY IN THE MORNING

ST. MARK XVI: 1-3. ST. MATTHEW XXVIII: 2-6.
ST. MARK XVI: 7. ST. LUKE XXIV: 8, 9, 11-12. ST. JOHN
XX: 11-18. ST. MATTHEW XXVIII: 16, 18-20.

And when the sabbath was past, Mary Magdalene, and Mary the mother of James, and Salome, had bought sweet spices that they might come, and anoint him.

And very early in the morning the first day of the week, they came unto the sepulchre at the rising of the sun.

And they said among themselves, Who shall roll us away the stone from the door of the sepulchre?

And, behold, there was a great earthquake: for the angel of the Lord descended from heaven, and came and rolled back the stone from the door, and sat upon it.

His countenance was like lightning, and his raiment white as snow:

And for fear of him the keepers did shake, and became as dead men.

And the angel answered and said unto the women, Fear not ye: for I know that ye seek Jesus, which was crucified.

He is not here: for he is risen, as he said. Come, see the place where the Lord lay.

But go your way, tell his disciples and Peter that he goeth before you into Galilee: there shall ye see him, as he said unto you.

And they remembered his words.

And returned from the sepulchre, and told all these things unto the eleven, and to all the rest.

And their words seemed to them as idle tales, and they believed them not.

Then arose Peter, and ran unto the sepulchre; and stooping down, he beheld the linen clothes laid by themselves, and departed, wondering in himself at that which was come to pass.

But Mary stood without at the sepulchre weeping: and as she wept, she stooped down, and looked into the sepulchre,

And seeth two angels in white sitting, the one at the head, and the other at the feet, where the body of Jesus had lain.

And they say unto her, Woman, why weepest thou?

She saith unto them, Because they have taken away my Lord, and I know not where they have laid him.

And when she had thus said, she turned herself back, and saw Jesus standing, and knew not that it was Jesus.

Jesus saith unto her, Woman, why weepest thou? whom seekest thou? She, supposing him to be the gardener, saith unto him, Sir, if thou hast borne him hence, tell me where thou hast laid him, and I will take him away.

Jesus saith unto her, Mary. She turned herself, and saith unto him, Rabboni, which is to say, Master.

Jesus saith unto her, Touch me not; for I am not yet ascended to my Father; but go to my brethren, and say unto them, I ascend unto my Father, and your Father; and to my God, and your God.

Mary Magdalene came and told the disciples that she had seen the Lord, and that he had spoken these things unto her.

Then the eleven disciples went away into Galilee, into a mountain where Jesus had appointed them.

And Jesus came and spake unto them, saying, All power is given unto me in heaven and in earth.

Go ye therefore, and teach all nations, baptizing them in the name of the Father, and of the Son, and of the Holy Ghost:

Teaching them to observe all things whatsoever I have commanded you; and, lo, I am with you alway, even unto the end of the world. Amen.

ARTHUR CLEVELAND COXE

TELL US, GARD'NER, DOST THOU KNOW?

MARY AND SALOME

Tell us, Gard'ner, dost thou know
Where the Rose and Lily grow,—
Sharon's Crimson Rose, and pale
Judah's Lily of the Vale?
Rude is yet the opening year;
Yet their sweetest breath is here.

####GARDENER
Daughters of Jerusalem,
Yes, 'tis here we planted them.
'Twas a Rose all red with gore;
Wondrous were the thorns it bore.
'Twas a body swathed in white;
Ne'er was Lily half so bright.

####THE WOMEN
Gentle Gard'ner, even so:
What we seek thou seem'st to know.
Bearing spices and perfume,
We are come to Joseph's tomb.
Breaks even now the rosy day:
Roll us, then, the stone away.

####GARDENER
Holy women! this the spot.
Seek Him; but it holds Him not.
This the holy mount of myrrh,
Here the hills of incense were,
Here the bed of His repose,
Till, ere dawn of day, He rose.

####MAGDALENE
Yes, my name is Magdalene:
I myself the Lord have seen.
Here I came but now, and wept
Where I deemed my Saviour slept:
But he called my name; and, lo!
Jesus lives,—'tis even so.

GARDENER

Yes, the mountains skipped like rams;
Leaped the little hills like lambs;
All was dark, when shook the ground,
Quaked the Roman soldiers round,
Streamed a glorious light, and then
Lived the Crucified again.

WOMEN

Magdalene hath seen and heard!
Gard'ner, we believe thy word;
But, oh, where is Jesus fled,
Living, and no longer dead?
Tell us, that we, too, may go
Where the Rose and Lily grow.

MAGDALENE

Come, the stone is rolled away;
See the place where Jesus lay;
See the lawn that wrapped His brow;
Here the angel sat but now.
"Seek not here the Christ," he said;
"Seek not life among the dead."

ALL

Seek we, then, the life above;
Seek we Christ, our Light and Love.
Now His words we call to mind:
If we seek Him, we shall find;
If we love Him, we shall know
Where the Rose and Lily grow.

JOHN MASON NEALE

THE WORLD ITSELF

The world itself keeps Easter Day,
  And Easter larks are singing;
And Easter flowers are blooming gay,
  And Easter buds are springing:
    Alleluya, Alleluya:
The Lord of all things lives anew,
And all his works are rising too:
    Hosanna in excelsis.

There stood three Maries by the tomb,
   On Easter morning early;
When day had scarcely chased the gloom,
   And dew was white and pearly:
     Alleluya, Alleluya:
With loving but with erring mind,
They came the Prince of life to find:

But earlier still the angel sped,
   His news of comfort giving;
And 'Why,' he said, 'among the dead
   Thus seek ye for the Living?'
     Alleluya, Alleluya:
'Go, tell them all, and make them blest;
Tell Peter first, and then the rest':

But one, and one alone remained,
   With love that could not vary;
And thus a joy past joy she gained,
   That sometime sinner, Mary,
     Alleluya, Alleluya:
The first the dear, dear form to see
Of him that hung upon the tree:

The world itself keeps Easter Day,
   Saint Joseph's star is beaming,
Saint Alice has her primrose gay,
   Saint George's bells are gleaming:
     Alleluya, Alleluya:
The Lord hath risen, as all things tell;
Good Christians, see ye rise as well!

JOHN OXENHAM

RISEN

While dawn still lingered in the shade
The women sought the guarded tomb,
Where in their sorrow they had laid
With streaming tears their much-loved dead.

Now with sweet spices they were come
To consecrate Love's martyrdom,

But all life's hope and joy had fled,—
Their Lord was dead!—Their Lord was dead!—

But with amaze they found instead—
The rolled-back stone,
Their loved one gone,
And one in gleaming white, who said,—
   Put past your fear!
   He is not here,
   But for your cheer is risen.
   Love broke the bars of Death's dark prison,
   The Lord of Love and Life is risen,
   The Lord indeed is risen!

The Lord is risen!
Now earth again
Lift up to heaven the joyful strain,
Life-out-of-Death's eternal gain—
The Lord is risen, is risen, is risen,
To wake the souls of men.
   The Lord indeed is risen
   From out His earthly prison,
   And now, all kings above,
   He reigns for evermore—
   The Lord of Life, the King of Love,
   Life's loving Conqueror.

The Lord is risen!
The heavenly choir
With all creation doth conspire
To swell the strain still higher, higher,—

The Lord is risen, is risen, is risen,
Mankind with love to inspire.
   The Lord indeed is risen
   From out His earthly prison,
   And now, all kings above,
   He reigns for evermore—
   The Lord of Life, the King of Love,
   Life's loving Conqueror.

The Lord is risen!
O Wondrous Word,
Which heaven and earth enraptured heard,
And to their heights and depths were stirred,
The Lord is risen, is risen, is risen,
Our loving, living, Lord.
   The Lord indeed is risen
   From out His earthly prison,
   And now, all kings above,
   He reigns for evermore—
   The Lord of Life, the King of Love,
   Life's loving Conqueror.

The Lord is risen!
Immortal Love,
That for mankind so greatly strove
On earth below, in heaven above,—
The Lord is risen, is risen, is risen
To show that God is Love.
   The Lord indeed is risen
   From out His earthly prison,

And now, all kings above,
He reigns for evermore—
The Lord of Life, the King of Love,
Life's loving Conqueror.

ALICE CORBIN HENDERSON

EASTER MORNING: A PLAY OF THE RESURRECTION FOR CHILDREN

... *"For I am not yet ascended to my Father: but go to my brethren, and say unto them, 'I ascend unto my Father, and your Father; and to my God, and your God.'"* ...

SCENE: *Before the tomb of Jesus, the third day after the Crucifixion, very early in the morning.*

Before the curtain, an Angel with a Sword makes announcement:

Archangel Michael, leader of God's Host,
I come, who seldom on such journeys post,
To bid you now put by all worldly thought,
And enter in where time and space are naught.
Awhile on earth, the Son of God behold,
A little while, and then the Heavenly fold
Reclaims Him, and a thousand voices rise
Upraising benedictions through the skies,
And all the myriad stars with streaming hands,
Reach down and lift Him through their silver bands,
And all the golden orders of the orbs,
From whom the earth the light of light absorbs,
Rejoice among themselves and sing to-day,
That Christ is risen whom men thought to slay!
And you, who dwell awhile upon the earth,
Ponder full well the Saviour's second birth;
That when you leave this bed and lodging bare,
You too may rise and meet your Lord in air!

(Exit.)

The scene is before the Tomb of Jesus. The background represents a hillside of gray stone, into which is cut a doorway or narrow entrance about as high as a man. A large slab of stone is fitted into this entrance and sealed with the seal of Caesar. The time is in the early dawn, about three o'clock in the morning. As the play opens, two Centurions are standing outside the Tomb. The second Centurion is an older man, with more experience than the first. When the curtain goes up, the second Centurion is standing at rest beside the Tomb, and the first Centurion is walking up and down.

FIRST CENTURION:
If I had not been sworn to fight for Caesar,
To make his cause my cause, I had not stood there!
SECOND CENTURION:
Yea, in all the wars that I have served in,
In the wars of nation fighting against nation,—
And I have fought for Caesar east and west,—
I never have seen sight so pitiful!
FIRST CENTURION:
And here he lies, who was as great a soldier
As ever led attack or took a city,—
And when he died, no sound of shouting trumpet,
No gentle warrior music, and no banners,—
But only a few women weeping, a small handful
Of men that dared not trust themselves for speech.

(Pause.)

So cowardly the deed, that now the Rulers,—
After the clamor and the wild appeal
Of men to "Crucify him!" "Crucify him!" . . .
The quietness, and the dark pall on the sun

Have made the Rulers think upon themselves,
And fear their own commandment,—was it just?
So, lest the few believers, the few followers,
Take up the body, and hide it, and make out
That what the man said was most truly so—
That after three days he would come again,
We are set here to guard the Tomb of Jesus,
And this great heavy stone before the Tomb,
Sealed over tightly with the seal of Caesar!
SECOND CENTURION:
No fear,—their coming. What so pitiful
As their downcast and sad and sorrowful faces!—
The one who was their creed, and joy, and life,
Killed, crucified, and—as a handful of dust,
Laid here to rest within the silent Tomb.
FIRST CENTURION:
What if it *were* true? If he really rose?
If he should really come to life again?
SECOND CENTURION:
I have seen men slain by the hundreds—thousands,
Men barely covered on the field of war
By a light sprinkling of earth, and never yet
Have I seen one shake off the light coverlet
And spring again to life and bodily vigor!
A spirit would have a hard time moving this
Impregnable great rock that no two men
In all their bodies' strength can even move.
FIRST CENTURION:
Well, it is very sad that even a stranger
Should feel the sorrow so, and his own people

Hard-hearted as this rock that walls him in.—
The air grows very cold. I'll try to rest.

> (*He lies down.*)

SECOND CENTURION:
I feel the air more sharp than I was wont.
> (*He sits down at right of the door of the Tomb, wrapping his cloak about him. They both go to sleep. An angel appears and stands between them.*)

ANGEL:
For three days Christ has been among the dead,
Has gone down into the shadowy realm of Hades,
While these, the ignorant, though not unkind,
Suppose Him fast shut up within the Tomb.
Now, on the third day, Christ in Paradise,
With the repentant thief on his right hand,
Remembers Him his promise to return
And walk on earth in likeness of a man,
To comfort these his heart-sick followers,
And make most true his word of prophecy.
And to confound and fool the unbelieving,
I am sent here to roll away the stone.
> (*The angel touches the stone and rolls it to one side. He stands beside it.*)

FIRST CENTURION (*waking*):
What's happened? It's so bright here!
   Had I fallen
Asleep?

> (*The second Centurion wakes.*)

FIRST CENTURION:
The stone! Good comrade, while we slept,—some one
Has stolen—
ANGEL:
Not so, comrade. It was I moved the stone.
FIRST CENTURION:
You moved it?
SECOND CENTURION:
Are you Christ, indeed, re-risen?
ANGEL:
I am Christ's servitor, and know you this!
The while you two were watching, three days ago,
Even as the great, imperial seal of Caesar
Was placed upon the rock here, Jesus passed
Between you, and descended unto Hell,
And there received the souls of lost and damned,
And blessed them and restored them to their peace;
From thence returned to Paradise.—Fear not,
But go now into all the world and tell
The Truth!—
FIRST CENTURION:
        'Twould never be believed!
SECOND CENTURION:
Yet must we try it—
Or fly!— I do believe it truly,
For light has fallen on my inmost soul!
But how confess, how show it to the world?
FIRST CENTURION:
To Pilate—and to Caiphas! The Scripture
Is, even as the prophets said, fulfilled!

(They go out, running.)
(The angel sits at one side of the Tomb. Enter Joana and Mary, weeping.)
ANGEL:
Why do you sorrow, women?
MARY:
      For Christ crucified!
ANGEL:
He is not dead! What seek you? Behold the stone.
JOANA:
Christ is risen! Christ is risen!
Come and tell the others!
  (They start to go out, but meet Peter and John. The Angel goes out the other side of stage.)
JOANA:
Christ is risen!
MARY:
      As we women came,
Bearing our spices and embalming nard,
We found the Tomb was open, and the seal
Of Caesar broken, the stone rolled away,
An angel sitting by the Tomb and asking,
"What seek you, women?" He was a young man tall
And fair and shining, and he told us Christ
Was risen!—
JOANA:
The Tomb is empty—
JOHN *(running to the door and looking in)*:
    No one's there!
PETER *(going into the Tomb and coming out)*:

The napkin that was folded round his forehead,
Lay where his head lay, neatly folded.
   The linen
That was about Him, in another place!
   *(Enter Mary Magdalene during the last of this
      speech.)*
MARY MAGDALENE:
Within the garden there, as I stood weeping,
I turned and saw one standing, and besought him
To give me the body of Jesus, not to let
It be the prey of every lawless hand,—
And as I raised my eyes, I saw Him stand—
Christ crucified, the Son of God, the Saviour!
   *(The two disciples of Emmaus have come in during
      this speech.)*
DISCIPLE:
Talking among ourselves of Jesus' death,
One walked beside us, and told us of the Scriptures,
Which we had heard before, and understood not.
And as He turned to go, we then constrained Him
To break bread with us, and He brake bread with us,
And as He blessed the bread our eyes were opened,
And we beheld Him as that night at supper,
That last night when He sat with us, all twelve.
And He, at our beholding, turned and vanished,
Yet we beheld the Christ!—
JOHN:
Might I behold Him,
All sickness ever, all poverty, all suffering,
That ever the cold world could heap upon a man,

I'd count as nothing!
>   (*The figure of Christ appears in the doorway of the Tomb.*)

CHRIST:
Peace be unto you!
>   (*The people all turn toward Christ and some fall upon their knees. John and Peter stand.*)

PETER:
It is Christ!
>   (*Kneels.*)

JOHN (*in the inspiration of vision*):
'Twas Jesus died upon the Tree,
'Twas Christ that rose in ecstasy,
Hail, Saviour!— God!
>   (*The picture is held a moment, and there is music. Then the curtain falls.*)

AGNES SLIGH TURNBULL

THE MAID OF EMMAUS

Passover week, and a long, hard day at the inn in Emmaus! From early morning Martha had run here and there, carrying water from the spring, bringing sticks, washing the wooden bowls, sweeping under the long, bench-like table around which the guests ate, grinding more wheat and barley in the mill by the back doorway, hurrying faster and faster under the sharp commands from old Sarah and the quick blows from Jonas, the husband of Sarah.

Passover week was always busy. First there came the caravans from the north and west. These found it convenient to stop at the inn for refreshment before they began the last hilly climb which led to Mount Zion itself. Even as the week wore on there were still many travellers, coming singly and in groups, on foot and on donkeys, but going, going, always going toward Jerusalem. When the Sabbath was past they would all begin to come back, and then there would be another busy time at the inn.

But this week, in spite of the hard days and the blows that seemed somehow to grow more numerous as business increased, Martha had moved as if in a happy dream. She had scarcely seen the faces of the strangers as they sat about the table or passed by on the street; she had obeyed endless harsh directions and surly shouts quickly and mechanically, but with a look that was far away; she had heard never a word of the gossip or comment in the long inn room or around the doorway; for she, too, was planning a pilgrimage.

This evening when her work was finished she slipped out to the garden and stood under the gnarled old olive tree to live over again the wonderful hour that had made life, her miserable, abused, unloved life, blossom into a holy devotion which crowded out all else. Only a bare week ago it had happened. She had been sent on a most surprising commission. Every few months Jonas used to climb upon the small donkey that lived in the shed off the inn room, and ride to Jerusalem with a basket of provisions for Sarah's old sister, old Anah, who was very poor. It seemed to Martha as if these trips used to come often, but of late they had become fewer and fewer. Jonas had stiff knees and stooped over now as he walked, and even the two-hour journey was too much for him.

So, three days before Passover, after much advice about the road and her errand and dire threats as to what would befall her when she returned if she did not fulfill all the instructions, she was started off on the donkey with the baskets of food and wine hanging from the saddle, on her first trip to Jerusalem!

The wonder and importance of it! She had wished as she rode along that the way might never end, for it meant freedom, and forgetfulness of the ills that made up her days. And then Jerusalem! Somewhere back in the hazy and beautiful past before she had mysteriously become a part of the inn, there had been a mother, she remembered, who had taught her sweet songs about it and talked of its great walls and gates and of the beauty of the holy Temple there. Now she was to see it for herself.

The narrow road was often rocky and steep, but the little donkey was sure-footed and travelled steadily. At the end of two hours she was in sight of the city on its high hills, with the soft blue-green of the Mount of Olives showing behind it, and farther to the east the Mountains of Moab, like towering fortresses of amethyst and sapphire in the late morning sun.

Her road led now up the sharp ravine on the western side, through the narrow passes, and at last through the great walls of which her mother had spoken, at the Joppa gate.

Once past the soldiers with their bright trappings and in the city, the strange scenes had become a blurred confusion of beggars and shouting merchants, of full-robed Pharisees and rabbis, and moving crowds of men and women and children.

After several frightened inquiries, she had found the Street of the Bakers, where Anah lived and had given her the food and wine. Then, after she had brought fresh water and ground some meal and told her all the news of the inn, she fed the donkey, ate the bread she had brought for herself and started off again through the narrow streets, her heart almost bursting with eagerness. She was going to see the Temple!

More timid inquiries here and there, and then at last—the great stone building with its long pillared colonnade and majestic gates came into view. She dismounted from the donkey and with a hand on its bridle made her way reverently toward the sacred spot.

Within a few rods of it a group of people blocked the way. They had been listening, evidently, to a rabbi and were waiting until He should speak again. Scarcely glancing at them, Martha tried with some impatience to skirt the crowd. Then a voice spoke, and, as though it had called her by name, she stopped wonderingly. Over the heads of the people she could hear it.

"A certain man planted a vineyard, and let it forth to husbandmen, and went into a far country."

It seemed to draw her as if a hand had reached out and caught her own. Cautiously she moved around the outer edge of the crowd, coming up at the side, quite near to the speaker. Then she saw His face. Tired, it looked, and sad, but oh, the infinite tenderness of it! Martha watched it with starving eyes.

He went on speaking to the people, while they quieted to listen. At last he had finished. The slender young man beside Him motioned the crowd away. Reluctantly they went. All but Martha. She was waiting for the voice to speak again, with her hungry eyes on the strange rabbi's face.

Suddenly He turned and saw her standing there, one arm about the small donkey's neck. His eyes read hers gravely, then He smiled and held out His hand.

"Thou art little Martha," He said.

And at the gentleness of it she found herself at His feet, sobbing out a wordless tale of the loneliness and weariness of her life with old Jonas and Sarah. Then she felt His hands on her head, and a peace and joy indescribable came over her.

"Fear not, little Martha; thou, too, shalt be my disciple."

She raised her eyes.

"Master," she breathed, "what is Thy name?"

"I am called Jesus," He said.

"*The Christ*," finished the fair young man, who still stood close beside Him.

Then she had kissed the blue and white tassels of His robe and come away, forgetting all about the Temple.

The same rocky road; the same harsh Jonas and Sarah at the end of it; the same inn with its hard duties from daylight till dark; but not the same Martha. He, the strange Master, had called her a disciple; His hands had been laid tenderly on her head in blessing.

One thought had gradually risen above all others. She longed to make Him a gift—something to show Him how much she loved Him. At first the idea brought only a sense of helplessness and despair. What had she, Martha of the inn, that she could give? She had lain awake a long time one night, watching the stars and wondering.

Then, as she sat beside the mill in the morning, grinding the wheat and barley, the idea came. She could make Him some little loaves. He had looked hungry and tired. She could take Him some bread. Oh, not the kind she made for use at the inn, but perfect loaves of the finest of the wheat. And she would go again to Jerusalem, as soon as the Passover week was over, and lay them in His hands.

Now, as she stood under the olive tree, her brows knitted in anxious thought, for there were many difficulties in the way and there were but two days left before the Sabbath. She had discovered that over the next hill there lived a man who had a wonderful kind of wheat which made flour as white as snow. But she had learned, too, that only the very rich went there to buy. She brooded hopelessly.

Then suddenly she remembered her one possession from the fair past to which the mother belonged—a gold chain, which for some reason Sarah had not taken from her. She loved to feel it and watch the shine of the gold, but it could go for the wheat if the man would accept it.

She would do the grinding after sundown on the Sabbath when Jonas and Sarah had gone to the spring to gossip. Then very, very early on the first day of the week she would rise and bake the loaves and slip away on foot before they could miss her. She would not use the donkey, she decided. That belonged to Jonas, and this was not his errand. She could easily walk. It would all mean a frightful beating when she got back, but what did it matter if she had made her gift to the Master?

The next days, strangely enough for Martha, went as she had hoped they would. She had gone, undiscovered, with the gold chain to the man who had the fine wheat. He had looked surprised, then fingered the gold links covetously, and given her what seemed a large sackful. She had returned, undiscovered, and hidden it in the garden in a broken part of the wall beneath the oleander tree.

The Sabbath came and dragged its burdensome length till sundown. Martha was trembling with eagerness and daring. Now was the time to begin the preparations. Jonas and Sarah left for the spring, where the old folks gathered in the evenings. Martha watched them out of sight, then worked feverishly. She took the sack from its hiding-place and seated herself with it at the mill, a shallow pot beside her to receive the flour.

She poured a few of the precious grains down the hole in the middle of the upper millstone, then ground slowly until the mill was thoroughly cleaned of the common flour still in it. Then, dusting the edges carefully, she poured more wheat and ground again, and then again and again, slowly, using all her strength upon the handle. The flour was as white as snow. She tested it softly between her thumb and finger. It was finer than any she had ever felt. It was almost worthy!

When it had all been placed in the pot she hid it carefully under a bushel measure in one corner of the inn room. She inspected the leaven, saved from the last week's baking. It still looked fresh and light. Then she went out for wood. She chose each piece with the greatest concern. Sometimes the smoke marred the loaves if the wood was too green. At last everything was done, even to selecting a fresh napkin in which to wrap the loaves and deciding upon the basket in which to carry them.

She went out to the garden and stood with her hands clasped on her breast, watching the Mountains of Moab, clothed in the purple and rose of the evening. Below them lay Jerusalem like a secret thing, hushed and hidden. Not a breath stirred the bright green leaves of the oleanders along the garden wall. Not a sound rose from the village. It seemed as if the whole world was still, waiting, dumbly expectant, breathlessly impatient, as she was, for the morrow.

When Jonas and Sarah returned Martha was already unrolling her pallet. Jonas drew the fastening of the door and they went on up to the roof-chamber where they slept.

A still, starry darkness crept on. Martha lay watching it through the small, open window. A strange stillness it was, soundless and yet athrob with mysterious anticipation as though angels might be hurrying past, unheard, unseen, but pressing softly, eagerly on toward Jerusalem.

Martha awoke, as she had prayed she might, very early—while it was yet dark. It was the first day of the week. It was her great day. In the twinkling of an eye she had slipped into her clothes, rolled up and put away her pallet and started her work. Into the clean baking-trough she poured the snowy flour, and mixed with it the salt and water and leaven, leaving it to rise while she built the fire in the oven. She moved softly, taking up and setting down each article with stealthy care. If Jonas or Sarah should wake? The fear was suffocating.

At the end of two hours the mists that had hung over the Mountains of Moab had broken into tiny feathers of cloud against the golden glory that had risen behind them.

The mountains gleamed with blue and amber. Over Jerusalem the light of the sunrise seemed to gather and spread as if, perchance, the hurrying angels of the night-time might now be risen to brood above the city with shining wings.

Martha bent over the small, low oven in an agony of hope and fear, then lifted out the loaves with shaking hands. If there should be one mark, one blemish!

But there was not. In the full light of the doorway she realized with a trembling joy, past belief, that they were perfect. All four of them. White as snow, and light and even.

A stirring came from overhead. She caught up the fresh napkin and spread it in the basket. Upon it she laid the little loaves with exquisite care, folded it over them, and then fled out of the inn door and along the street in the direction of the shining light.

When Emmaus was left behind and she had started up the first long hill she stopped running and drew a long, shuddering breath of relief. She was safely on her way to the Master. Jonas and Sarah could not stop her now. And here in the basket were her gifts of love.

As she walked on she became aware of a new aliveness

in the air about her. Every bird seemed to be singing. The very sky bent down like a warm, sentient thing. And over the steep hillsides, bright masses of anemones, scarlet and white and blue, breathed out the clear, living freshness of the morning as if they had all just been born into bloom. Martha's heart leaped at the beauty of it. Joy gave her strength and lightness of foot. Before she thought it possible she was entering once more the Joppa gate.

Her plan had been quite simple. She would find the Master, doubtless, near the Temple where He had been before. She would wait with the crowd and listen as long as He taught. Then when the others were all gone she would go up to Him and give Him the loaves.

When she came at last in sight of the Temple there were several groups of people in the street. She approached each and scanned it carefully before going on to the next. After a second patient searching the fearful certainty came that He was not there.

She was near the entrance of the Temple now, pausing uncertainly. One of the chief priests was walking back and forth along the corridors. She went close behind him.

"Hast thou seen Jesus, the Christ?" she asked timidly.

The great man started violently. His face was ashy grey. One arm shot threateningly toward her.

"Why askest thou *me*?" he shouted. *"Speak not that name to me! Begone!"*

Martha trembled with dismay as she ran away from the Temple and down to the next street. What could the gentle Master have done to anger the priest so?

She continued her search. Everywhere people hurrying

about their duties; here and there groups excitedly talking; but no sign of the rabbi and the young man who had stood beside Him. It was noon and Martha was hungry and tired. She must ask again or she would never find Him.

Two soldiers passed. She feared them, yet respected their power. Perhaps they could help her. She cautiously touched the arm of the one nearest her.

"Dost thou know where the rabbi Jesus is? They call Him the Christ."

The soldier looked at the other and laughed a strange, mirthless laugh. It pierced Martha's heart with a sense of impending doom.

"Hearest thou that?" he said loudly. "She asks us if we know aught of Jesus—we who helped crucify Him the other day."

From Martha's bloodless face her great dark eyes met the soldier's, agonized. He paused and spoke a little more softly:

"Thou hast the truth, child. He was crucified three days ago on Golgotha Hill. Devils they were who ordered it, but so it fell. Thou hast the truth."

They passed on. Martha leaned, sick and fainting, against the wall. *Crucified! Dead!* And in her basket were the little white loaves for Him. And He would never know. His hands would never touch them. The gentle Master, with only love and pity in His face—crucified! And the loaves were white as snow . . . perfect . . . to show her love for Him.

At last she roused herself and dragged her way wearily toward the Joppa gate.

A woman was sitting sadly in a doorway. She had a sweet, patient face, and Martha halted, her heart lifting ever so little. One more inquiry; the soldier might have been mistaken.

"Didst thou know—Jesus?" she asked softly.

For answer the woman's reddened eyes overflowed. She rocked herself to and fro.

"And I trusted," she moaned, "that He was the redeemer of Israel. Some say today that He is alive again, risen; but it is only an idle tale. For I saw Him"—her voice sank to a choking whisper—"I saw Him die."

Martha moved slowly on, the woman rocking and moaning in the doorway.

The afternoon sun was hot now, and Martha's feet were heavy. The deep dust of the road rose to choke and blind her. The sharp stones tripped her and cut her feet. The way back was endless, for now there was no hope. She thought wearily of the freshness and joy of the morning. There would never be such beauty and happiness for her again. She stumbled on—and on.

When she reached the inn, at last, it was late afternoon. She was about to enter the main door when she caught her breath. No, she *could not* surrender the basket to Jonas and Sarah. Better to crush the little loaves in her hands and allow the birds of the air to have them.

She set the basket down beside the eastern door—Sarah rarely went out that way—then went to the front of the inn. With a shout they were both upon her.

"Thou shalt be taught to run away!" old Sarah cried. "Thou shalt be taught to go to Jerusalem without leave! Thou wast seen! It was told us!"

The blows came, as she had known they would. She had

no strength to resist. She lay where she had fallen, beside the oven—the oven where only at daybreak she had laboured in ecstasy.

At last Jonas snarled: "It is there thou shouldst lie. It is there thou dost belong, under people's feet. But, hearken to this! If any shall come, thou shalt rise up and serve them. The caravans have long since passed, but if there should come a belated traveller rise up and serve him! Or thou shalt receive . . ."

He was still shaking his great fist as they went out.

Martha lay still. Soon, darkness; but not as of last night, filled with angels. Dead, despairing, empty darkness, tonight. She closed her eyes.

All at once there were footsteps along the street. Voices were talking earnestly. She recognized one of them. It was that of Cleopas, the rich vineyard owner. He always stopped at the inn on his trips to and from Jerusalem. A hand opened the door.

"Abide with us," she heard Cleopas say eagerly, "for the day is far spent."

Then they entered: Cleopas and his brother Simon, and another—a stranger, whose face was in the shadow.

Martha had risen with infinite pain and now set about placing the food upon the table. She brought the barley cakes and oil, the wine and the raisins, and the meal was ready. Then she stopped. Just outside the eastern door was the basket with its precious offering—the gift of love that could not be bestowed. Here were three men, weary from their journey and hungry.

The struggle in her breast was bitter but it was brief. She opened the door and lifted the basket. From their napkin she took the four loaves and placed them before the stranger, who sat in the shadows at the head of the table. Her eyes, dim with tears, watched the loaves as they lay there, snowy and fair. The longing love of her heart; the gold chain, her one treasure; her aching limbs; the swelling bruises on her poor beaten body; all these had helped to purchase them. She raised her eyes to the stranger's face— Then, a cry!

It was as though all the colour of the sunset and the radiance of the morning had united behind it. And out from the shining, majestic and glorified, yet yearning in its compassion and love, *The Face,* but not that of a stranger, appeared.

He was gazing steadfastly upon the little loaves. He touched them, broke them, extended them, and raised His eyes to heaven, while the blinding glory increased.

Cleopas and Simon were leaning forward, breathless, transfixed. Martha had crept closer and knelt within the circle of light.

"Master," she tried to whisper. "Master . . ."

He turned and looked upon her. No need to speak that which was upon her heart. He knew. He understood.

Gently the radiance enfolded her. Upon her shone the beneficent smile, fraught with heavenly benediction and healing for all earth's wounds.

Then, as softly as the sunset had gone, the celestial light died away. The Master's chair was empty.

Cleopas and Simon sat spellbound, gazing at the place where the splendour had been. Martha still knelt in a rapture of joy and peace.

On the table lay the little white loaves, uneaten, but received and blessed.

**FROM THE MESSIAH
BY GEORGE FREDERICK HANDEL**

HALLELUJAH

Hallelujah: for the Lord God Omnipotent reigneth.

The kingdom of this world has become the kingdom of our Lord, and of His Christ; and He shall reign for ever and ever.

King of Kings, and Lord of Lords. Hallelujah!

NANCY BYRD TURNER

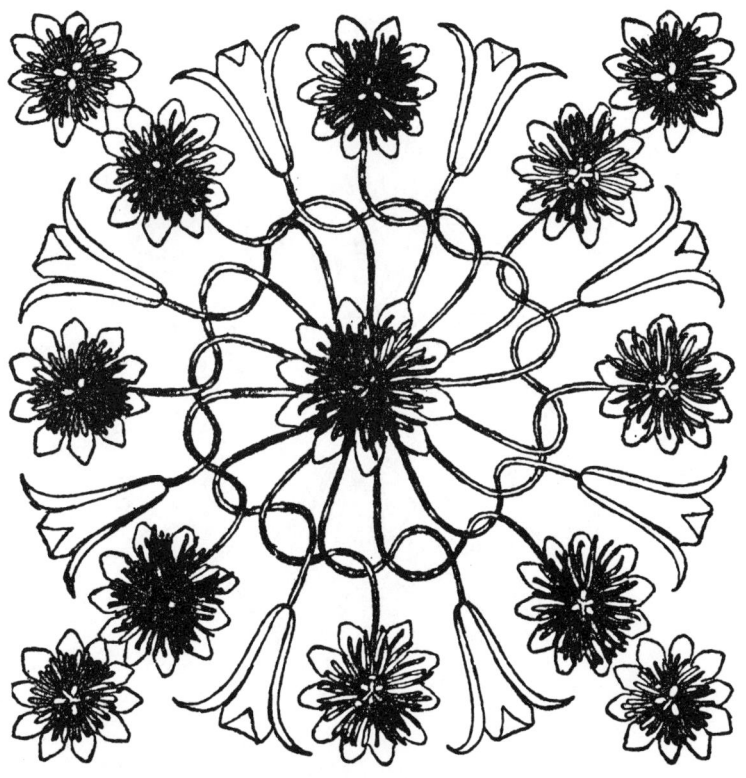

EASTER AGAIN

Again the ancient miracle,
  As new as though it had not been!
Blossom by blossom, bell by bell,
  The south winds usher Easter in.

On every hill beneath the skies,
  Where winter storms have worked their strife,
April, that shining angel, cries
  The resurrection and the life.

EMILY DICKINSON

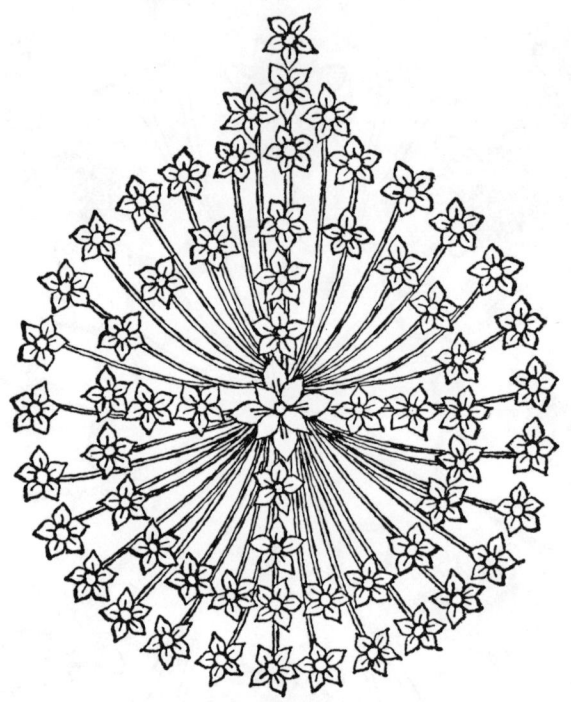

THE WAKING YEAR

A lady red upon the hill
   Her annual secret keeps;
A lady white within the field
   In placid lily sleeps!

The tidy breezes with their brooms
   Sweep vale, and hill, and tree!
Prithee, my pretty housewives!
   Who may expected be?

The neighbors do not yet suspect!
   The woods exchange a smile—
Orchard, and buttercup, and bird—
   In such a little while!

And yet how still the landscape stands,
   How nonchalant the wood,
As if the resurrection
   Were nothing very odd!

ELLA YOUNG

PASQUE

All so frail, so white,
The blossoms on the thorn,
So pale this first daylight
On Easter morn.

Hear the cry:
"Christ is risen!"

Hear the cry:
"Christ is risen!
Our Lord sets free
The souls in prison."

The sun acclaims it
Burgeoning red:
Christ! Christ is risen
From the dead.

A. E. HOUSMAN

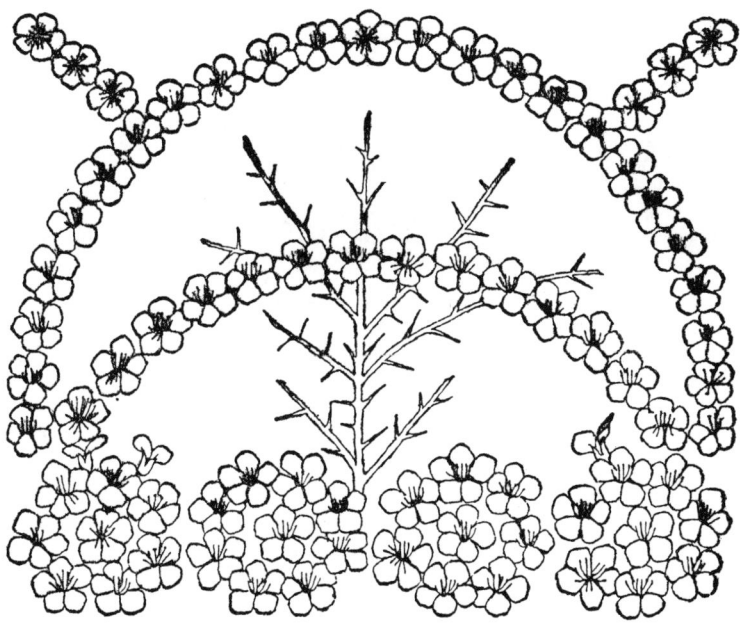

LOVELIEST OF TREES

Loveliest of trees, the cherry now
Is hung with bloom along the bough,
And stands about the woodland ride
Wearing white for Eastertide.

MARY A. LATHBURY

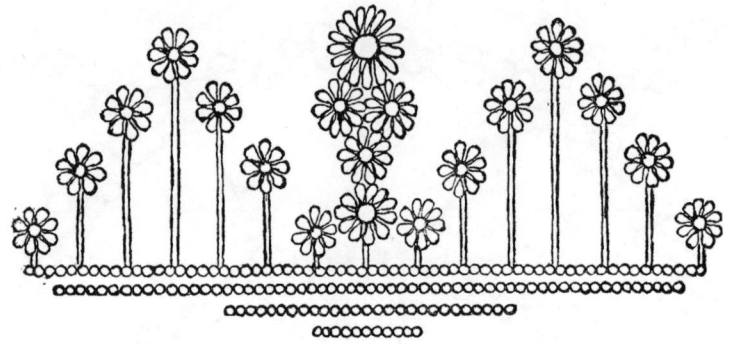

RISE, FLOWERS, RISE

Little children of the sun,
Wake and listen, every one!
Hear the raindrops as they fall,
Hear the winds that call, and call,
  "Rise, flowers, rise!"

Children, little sleepy-heads!
It is time to leave your beds,
Snowdrop and hepatica,
Pink spring-beauty, lead the way;
  "Rise, flowers, rise!"

Tell the grasses and the trees,
Tell the bluebirds and the bees,
Tell the ferns, like croziers curled,
It is Easter in the world,
  "Rise, flowers, rise!"

Waken, tardy violets;
Waken, innocent bluets;
Waken, every growing thing,
It is Easter, it is spring!
  "Rise, flowers, rise!"

Rise, for Christ the Lord arose,
Victor over all His foes;
Rise, with all the souls of men,
Into light and life again;
  "Rise, flowers, rise!"

MARGARET E. SANGSTER

EASTER FLOWERS

Blooming to garland Easter,
   White as the drifted snows,
Are the beautiful vestal lilies,
   The myriad-petaled rose,
Carnations with hearts of fire,
   And the heather's fragrant spray—
Blooming to garland Easter,
   And strew our King's highway.

Late we had gloom and sorrow,
   But the word from Heaven forth
Has scattered the clouds before it
   Like a trumpet blown from the north;

And east and west and southward
  The flowers arise to-day
To garland the blithesome Easter,
  And strew the King's highway.

Carry the flowers of Easter
  To the darkened house of woe,
With their message of strength and comfort
  Let the lilies of Easter go;
Scatter the Easter blossoms
  In the little children's way;
Let want and pain and weakness
  Be cheered on our Easter day.

For lilac, and rose, and bluebell,
  And whatever name they wear,
The spell of the flowers of Easter
  Is a spell to banish care;
And blooming to garland Easter,
  They will shine in church to-day,
The lovely things that have awakened
  To deck our King's highway.

TRANSLATED FROM THE LATIN

FLOWER CAROL

Spring has now unwrapped the flowers,
    Day is fast reviving,
Life in all her growing powers
    Towards the light is striving:
Gone the iron touch of cold,
    Winter time and frost time,
Seedlings, working through the mould,
    Now make up for lost time.

Herb and plant that, winter long,
    Slumbered at their leisure,
Now bestirring, green and strong,
    Find in growth their pleasure:
All the world with beauty fills,
    Gold the green enhancing;

Flowers make glee among the hills,
   And set the meadows dancing.

Through each wonder of fair days
   God himself expresses;
Beauty follows all his ways,
   As the world he blesses:
So, as he renews the earth,
   Artist without rival,
In his grace of glad new birth
   We must seek revival.

Earth puts on her dress of glee;
   Flowers and grasses hide her;
We go forth in charity—
   Brothers all beside her;
For, as man this glory sees
   In the awakening season,
Reason learns the heart's decrees,
   And hearts are led by reason.

Praise the Maker, all ye saints;
   He with glory girt you,
He who skies and meadows paints
   Fashioned all your virtue;
Praise him, seers, heroes, kings,
   Heralds of perfection;
Brothers, praise him, for he brings
   All to resurrection!

MARY A. NICHOLSON

EASTER FLOWERS ARE BLOOMING BRIGHT

Easter flowers are blooming bright,
Easter skies pour radiant light;
Christ our Lord is risen in might,
Glory in the highest.

Angels caroled this sweet lay
When in manger rude he lay;
Now once more cast grief away,
Glory in the highest.

He, then born to grief and pain,
Now to glory born again,
Calleth forth our gladdest strain,
Glory in the highest.

As He riseth, rise we too,
Tune we heart and voice anew,
Offering homage glad and true,
Glory in the highest.

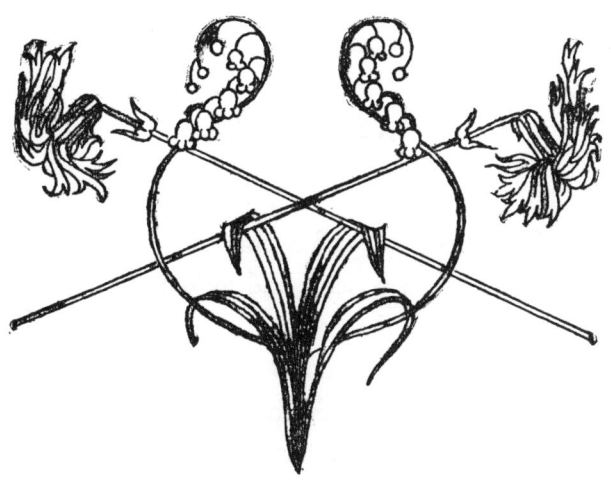

LAURA E. RICHARDS

EASTER-TIME

The little flowers came through the ground,
   At Easter-time, at Easter-time;
They raised their heads and looked around,
   At happy Easter-time.
And every pretty bud did say,
"Good people, bless this holy day;
For Christ is risen, the angels say,
   This happy Easter-time."

The scarlet lily raised its cup,
   At Easter-time, at Easter-time;
The crocus to the sky looked up,
   At happy Easter-time.
"We hear the song of heaven!" they say;
"It's glory shines on us to-day,
Oh! may it shine on us alway,
   At happy Easter-time."

'Twas long and long and long ago,
    That Easter-time, that Easter-time;
But still the scarlet lilies blow
    At happy Easter-time.
And still each little flower doth say,
"Good Christians, bless this holy day;
For Christ is risen, the angels say,
    At blessed Easter-time."

BLISS CARMAN

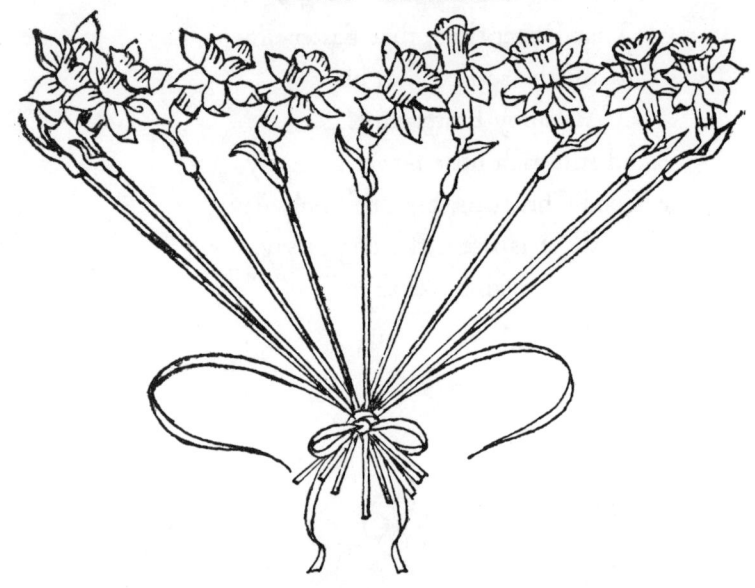

DAFFODIL'S RETURN

What matter if the sun be lost?
What matter though the sky be gray?
There's joy enough about the house,
For Daffodil comes home to-day.

There's news of swallows on the air,
There's word of April on the way,
They're calling flowers within the street,
And Daffodil comes home to-day.

O who would care what fate may bring,
Or what the years may take away!
There's life enough within the hour,
For Daffodil comes home to-day.

KATHARINE TYNAN HINKSON

DAFFODIL

Who passes down the wintry street?
  Hey, ho, daffodil!
A sudden flame of gold and sweet.

With sword of emerald girt so meet,
And golden gay from head to feet.

How are you here this wintry day?
  Hey, ho, daffodil!
Your radiant fellows yet delay.

No windflower dances scarlet gay,
Nor crocus-flame lights up the way.

What land of cloth o' gold and green,
  Hey, ho, daffodil!
Cloth o' gold with the green between,

Was that you left but yestere'en
To light a gloomy world and mean?

King trumpeter to Flora queen,
    Hey, ho, daffodil!
Blow, and the golden jousts begin.

A. E. HOUSMAN

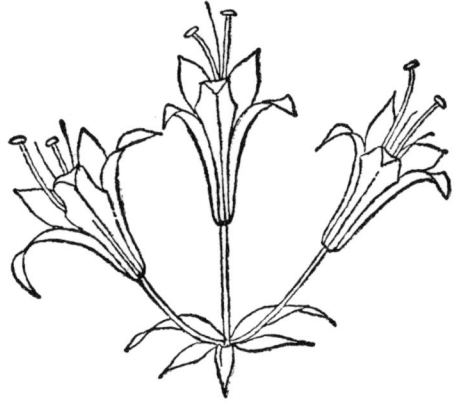

THE LENT LILY

'Tis spring; come out to ramble
  The hilly brakes around,
For under thorn and bramble
  About the hollow ground
  The primroses are found.

And there's the windflower chilly
  With all the winds at play,
And there's the Lenten lily
  That has not long to stay
  And dies on Easter day.

And since till girls go maying
  You find the primrose still,
And find the windflower playing
  With every wind at will,
  But not the daffodil,

Bring baskets now, and sally
   Upon the spring's array,
And bear from hill and valley
   The daffodil away
   That dies on Easter day.

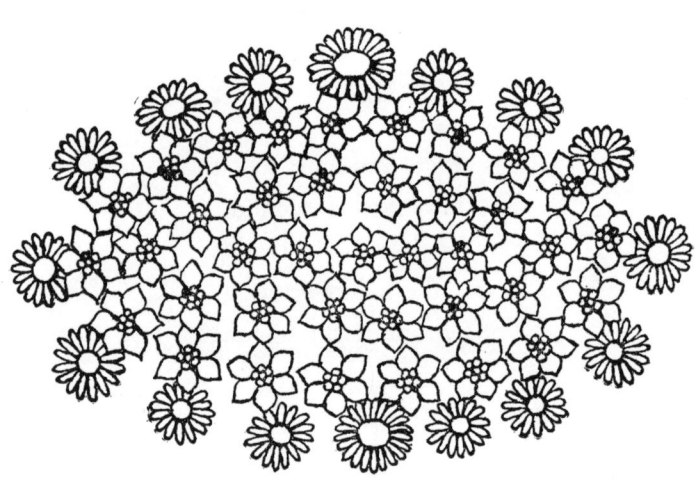

MARGARET DELAND

EASTER MUSIC
JONQUILS

Blow, golden trumpets, sweet and clear,
Blow soft upon the perfumed air;
  Bid the sad earth to join your song,
  "To Christ does victory belong!"

Oh, let the winds your message bear
To every heart of grief and care;
  Sound through the world the joyful lay
  "Our Christ has conquered Death to-day!"

On cloudy wings let glad words fly
Through the soft blue of echoing sky:
  Ring out, O trumpets, sweet and clear,
  "Through death immortal Life is here!"

AUTHOR UNKNOWN

EASTER SONG

Snowdrop, lift your timid head,
  All the earth is waking,
Field and forest, brown and dead,
  Into life are breaking;
Snowdrops, rise and tell the story
How He rose, the Lord of glory.

Lilies! lilies! Easter calls,
  Rise to meet the dawning
Of the blessed light that falls
  Thro' the Easter morning;
Ring your bells and tell the story,
How He rose, the Lord of glory.

Waken, sleeping butterflies,
   Burst your narrow prison;
Spread your golden wings and rise,
   For the Lord is risen;
Spread your wings and tell the story,
How He rose, the Lord of glory.

MARGARET WIDDEMER

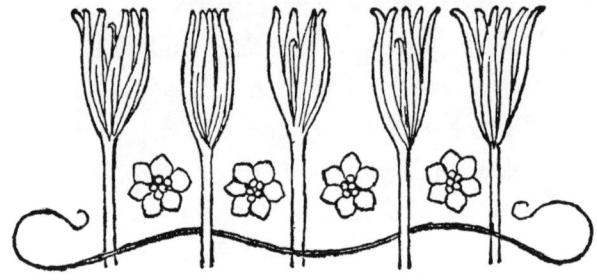

A CHILD'S EASTER SONG

The world has come awake
And will be lovely soon
With warm sunlight at noon
And ripples in the lake.

Now soon the ground will flower
And scarlet tulips grow
Down borders in a row
All opened in an hour;

For where the earth was brown
The pointed leaves of green
Reach out, and there are seen
Red flowers folded down:

The snows have gone away
And all the little birds
Sing songs that need no words,
For this is Easter Day.

TRANSLATED FROM THE LATIN BY
ELIZABETH CHARLES

SMILE PRAISES, O SKY!
(Plaudite Coeli.)

Smile praises, O sky!
　Soft breathe them, O air!
Below and on high,
　And everywhere.
The black troop of storms
　Has yielded to calm;
Tufted blossoms are peeping,
　And early palm.

Arouse thee, O spring!
　Ye flowers, come forth,
With thousand hues tinting
　The soft green earth;
Ye violets tender,
　And sweet roses bright,
Gay Lent-lilies blended
　With pure lilies white.

Sweep, tides of rich music,
  The full veins along;
And pour in full measure,
  Sweet lyres, your song.
Sing, sing, for He liveth,—
  He lives, as He said;
The Lord hath arisen
  Unharmed from the dead.

Clap, clap your hands, mountains!
  Ye valleys, resound!
Leap, leap for joy, fountains!
  Ye hills, catch the sound.
All triumph! He liveth,—
  He lives, as He said;
The Lord hath arisen
  Unharmed from the dead.

TRANSLATED FROM THE GERMAN

HILARITER

The whole bright world rejoices now,
    Hilariter, hilariter;
The birds do sing on every bough
    Alleluya, Alleluya.

Then shout beneath the racing skies,
    Hilariter, hilariter,
To him who rose that we might rise,
    Alleluya, Alleluya.

And all you living things make praise,
    Hilariter, hilariter;
He guideth you on all your ways,
    Alleluya, Alleluya.

He, Father, Son, and Holy Ghost—
    Hilariter, hilariter!—
Our God most high, our joy and boast.
    Alleluya, Alleluya.

CHRISTINA GEORGINA ROSSETTI

AN EASTER CAROL

Spring bursts to-day,
For Christ is risen and all the earth's at play.

Flash forth, thou Sun,
The rain is over and gone, its work is done.

Winter is past,
Sweet Spring is come at last, is come at last.

Bud, Fig and Vine,
Bud, Olive, fat with fruit and oil and wine.

Break forth this morn
In roses, thou but yesterday a thorn.

Uplift thy head,
O pure white Lily through the Winter dead.

Beside your dams
Leap and rejoice, you merry-making Lambs.

All Herds and Flocks
Rejoice, all Beasts of thickets and of rocks.

Sing, Creatures, sing,
Angels and Men and Birds and everything.

All notes of Doves
Fill all our world: this is the time of loves.

TRANSLATED FROM THE RUSSIAN OF MAIKOW
BY MARTHA GILBERT DICKINSON BIANCHI

AN EASTER GREETING

The lark at sunrise trills it high—
The greeting Christ is risen!
And through the wood the black-bird pipes
The greeting Christ is risen!
Beneath the eaves the swallows cry
The greeting Christ is risen!
Throughout the world man's heart proclaims
The greeting Christ is risen!
And echo answers from the grave
In truth, yes, He is risen!

AUTHOR UNKNOWN

YE HAPPY BELLS OF EASTER DAY

Ye happy bells of Easter Day!
  Ring! ring! your joy
  Thro' earth and sky;
 Ye ring a glorious word.
The notes that swell in gladness tell
  The rising of the Lord!

Ye carol-bells of Easter Day!
  The teeming earth
  That saw His birth
 When lying 'neath the sward
Upspringeth now in joy, to show
  The rising of the Lord!

Ye glory-bells of Easter Day!
   The hills that rise
    Against the skies
Reecho with the word—
The victor-breath that conquers death—
  The rising of the Lord!

Ye victor-bells of Easter Day!
   The thorny crown
    He layeth down:
Ring! ring! with strong accord—
The mighty strain of love and pain,
  The rising of the Lord!

HELEN GRAY CONE

AN EASTER PROCESSIONAL

Let us sing of bright morn breaking
   From the glorious east;
Lilies fair their sheaths forsaking;
Larks in light their music making;
Sing the song of wings and waking
   That befits our feast!

Apple boughs in white are dressing,
   And in heaven's blue arch
Little clouds, like cherubs pressing
Rank on rank with cheeks caressing,
Shed their softness like a blessing
   On our joyful march!

JOYCE KILMER

EASTER

    The air is like a butterfly
        With frail blue wings.
    The happy earth looks at the sky
        And sings.

ELIZABETH COATSWORTH

THE SUN COMES DANCING

On Easter morn,
On Easter morn,
The sun comes dancing up the sky.

His light leaps up;
It shakes and swings,
Bewildering the dazzled eye.

On Easter morn
All earth is glad;
The waves rejoice in the bright sea.

Be still and listen
To your heart,
And hear it beating merrily!

CLINTON SCOLLARD

A CANTICLE

Once more is the woodland ringing
  With buoyant mirth;
Once more are the green shoots springing
  From under-earth;
Out of the gates of glooming,—
  The depths of dole,—
Like a bud unto its blooming,
  Rise thou, my soul!

Once more there are lyrics lifted
  From all the rills;
Once more there is warm light sifted
  On God's fair hills.
Out of the slough of sadness,
  Again made whole,

Into the glow of gladness
   Rise thou, my soul!

Once more the exultant spirit
   Through nature runs;
Once more from heaven to hear it
   Lean stars and suns.
Freed from thy wintry prison,
   Seek thou the goal
Of Christ, the re-arisen,
   My soul, my soul!

KATHARINE TYNAN HINKSON

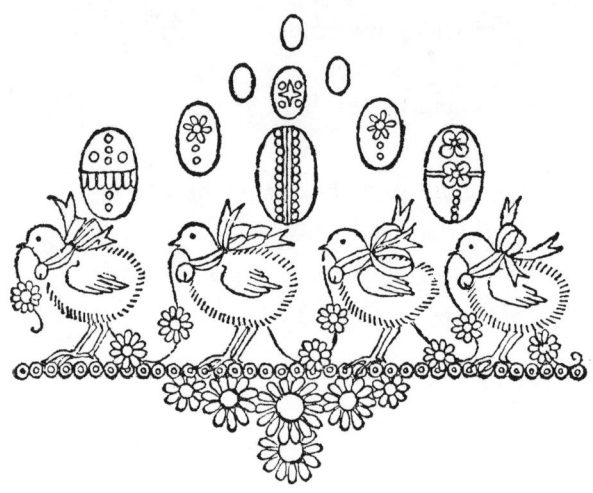

LOVE AT EASTER

Sing to the Lord a new song!
  Because the Spring comes newly,
And every slender sapling
  Has budded green and red.
Sing to the Lord a new song!
  The skylark sings it truly,
Since all in dewy April
  His love and he are wed.

Sing to the Lord a new song!
  For every bird's a lover,
And o'er the purple furrows
  The green spears nod and wave.
Sing to the Lord a new song!
  Since Lenten fasts are over,

And Easter's come in glory,
    And Christ has left the grave.

Sing to the Lord a new song!
    A song of love and wedding,
For every bird is building
    His nest in bower and tree.
Sing to the Lord a new song!
    The tufts of soft wool spreading
Where a brown wife and babies
    This Easter-tide shall be.

LOUISE ABNEY

EASTER MORNING

Pines whose whispers fill the air . . .
Birches bowed as if in prayer . . .
Benedictions everywhere
    On Easter morning.

On the mountain's azure crest,
Far above the placid breast
Of the lake, are clouds at rest
    On Easter morning.

Butterflies, and birds, and bees . . .
Altar-hills, and singing trees . . .
Faith is born of things like these,
    On Easter morning.

EMILY D. CHAPMAN

AN EASTER CAROL

Sweetly the birds are singing
   At Easter dawn,
Sweetly the bells are ringing
   On Easter morn,
And the words that they say
On Easter day
Are—"Christ the Lord is risen."

Birds! forget not your singing
   At Easter dawn;
Bells! be ye ever ringing
   On Easter morn.
In the spring of the year,
When Easter is here,
Sing—"Christ the Lord is risen."

Buds! ye will soon be flowers,
   Cherry and white;
Snow-storms are changing to showers,
   Darkness to light.

With the wak'ning of spring,
Oh, sweetly sing—
"Lo! Christ the Lord is risen."

Easter buds were growing
 Ages ago;
Easter lilies were blowing
 By water's flow.
All nature was glad,
No creature was sad,
For Christ the Lord was risen.

WORDS ADAPTED FROM AN ANCIENT CANTICLE

A SONG OF PRAISE

Come, ye children, praise the Lord,
Raise your song with sweet accord,
To His name all glory bring,
Day and night His praises sing.

Praise Him, clouds that onward sweep,
Thunders rolling loud and deep,
Flood and storm and winter snow,
Praise Him, frost and summer glow!

Praise Him, all ye pow'rs that be,
Praise Him, earth and air and sea,
Praise Him, all things near and far,
Praise Him, sun and moon and star!

EASTER

On Easter morn
   Up the faint cloudy sky
I hear the Easter bell,
   Ding dong . . . ding dong . . .
Easter morning scatters lilies
On every doorstep;
Easter morning says a glad thing
Over and over.
Poor people, beggars, old women
Are hearing the Easter bell . . .
   Ding dong . . . ding dong . . .

MARY ROOT KERN

EASTER RABBIT

Easter Rabbit, wake, O wake!
Leave your home within the brake.
Dark the forest is and lonely,
Fit for winter dreaming only.
See! the sun is shining clear;
Wake and hasten, Rabbit dear!

Easter Rabbit, sit upright;
Lift your ears, so long and white.
Easter chimes are clearly ringing,
Easter voices sweetly singing.
Bring the eggs, all red and blue;
Many children wait for you!

CHARLES HANSON TOWNE

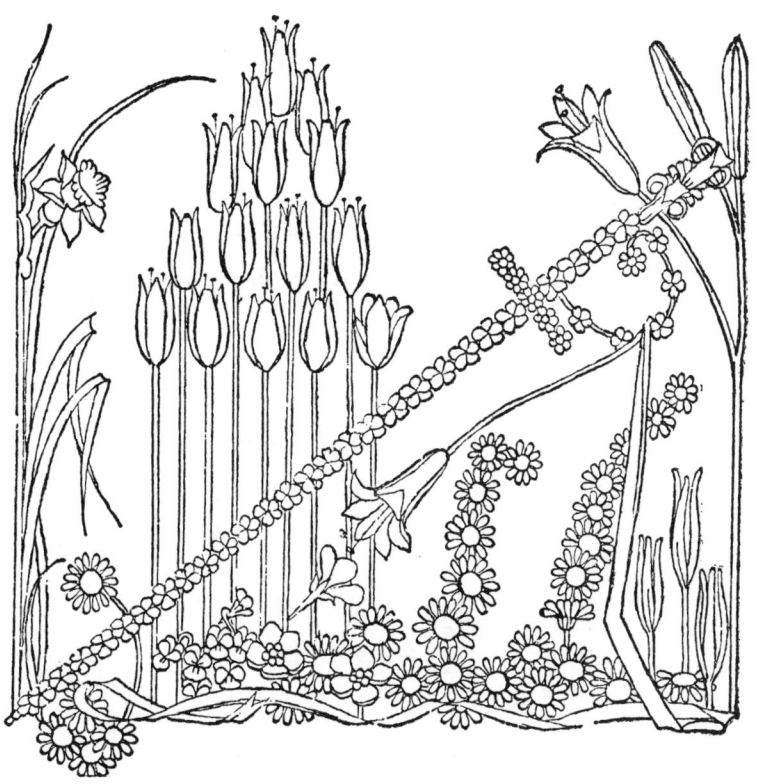

AN EASTER CANTICLE

In every trembling bud and bloom
   That cleaves the earth, a flowery sword,
I see Thee come from out the tomb,
   Thou risen Lord.

In every April wind that sings
   Down lanes that make the heart rejoice;
Yea, in the word the wood-thrush brings,
   I hear Thy voice.

Lo! every tulip is a cup
   To hold Thy morning's brimming wine;
Drink, O my soul, the wonder up—
   Is it not Thine?

The great Lord God, invisible,
   Hath roused to rapture the green grass;
Through sunlit mead and dew-drenched dell,
   I see Him pass.

His old immortal glory wakes
   The rushing streams and emerald hills;
His ancient trumpet softly shakes
   The daffodils.

Thou art not dead! Thou art the whole
   Of life that quickens in the sod;
Green April is Thy very soul,
   Thou great Lord God.

WRITTEN FOR A FRENCH CAROL TUNE

EASTER CAROL

Cheer up, friends and neighbours,
    Now it's Easter tide;
Stop from endless labours,
    Worries put aside:
Men should rise from sadness,
    Evil, folly, strife,
When God's mighty gladness
    Brings the earth to life.

Out from snowdrifts chilly,
  Roused from drowsy hours,
Bluebell wakes, and lily;
  God calls up the flowers!
Into life he raises
  All the sleeping buds;
Meadows weave his praises,
  And the spangled woods.

All his truth and beauty,
  All his righteousness,
Are our joy and duty,
  Bearing his impress:
Look! the earth waits breathless
  After winter's strife:
Easter shows man deathless,
  Spring leads death to life.

Ours the more and less is;
  But, changeless all the days,
God revives and blesses,
  Like the sunlight rays.
'All mankind is risen,'
  The Easter bells do ring,
While from out their prison
  Creep the flowers of Spring.

EMILY DICKINSON

A FUZZY FELLOW

A fuzzy fellow without feet
Yet doth exceeding run!
Of velvet is his countenance
And his complexion dun.

Sometimes he dwelleth in the grass,
Sometimes upon a bough
From which he doth descend in plush
Upon the passer-by.

All this in summer—
But when winds alarm the forest folk,

He taketh damask residence
And struts in sewing silk.

Then, finer than a lady,
Emerges in the spring,
A feather on each shoulder—
You'd scarce accredit him.

By men yclept a caterpillar—
By me—but who am I
To tell the pretty secret
Of the Butterfly!

MARGARET GATTY

A LESSON OF FAITH

"Let me hire you as a nurse for my poor children," said a Butterfly to a quiet Caterpillar, who was strolling along a cabbage-leaf in her odd lumbering way. "See these little eggs," continued the Butterfly; "I don't know how long it will be before they come to life, and I feel very sick and poorly, and if I should die, who will take care of my baby butterflies when I am gone? Will *you*, kind, mild, green Caterpillar? But you must mind what you give them to eat, Caterpillar!—they cannot, of course, live on *your* rough food. You must give them early dew, and honey from the flowers; and you must let them fly about only a little way at first; for, of course, one can't expect them to use their wings properly all at once. Dear me! it is a sad pity you cannot fly yourself. But I have no time to look for another nurse now, so you will do your best, I hope. Dear! dear! I cannot think what made me come and lay my eggs on a cabbage-leaf! What a place for young butterflies to be born upon! Still you will be kind, will you not, to the poor little ones? Here, take this gold-dust from my wings as a reward. Oh, how dizzy I am! Caterpillar! you will remember about the food—"

And with these words the Butterfly drooped her wings and died; and the green Caterpillar, who had not had the opportunity of even saying Yes or No to the request, was left standing alone by the side of the Butterfly's eggs.

"A pretty nurse she has chosen, indeed, poor lady!" exclaimed she, "and a pretty business I have in hand! Why, her senses must have left her, or she never would have asked a poor crawling creature like me to bring up her dainty little ones! Much they'll mind me, truly, when they feel the gay wings on their backs, and can fly away out of my sight whenever they choose! Ah! how silly some people are, in spite of their painted clothes and the gold-dust on their wings!"

However, the poor Butterfly was dead, and there lay the eggs on the cabbage-leaf; and the green Caterpillar had a kind heart, so she resolved to do her best. But she got no sleep that night, she was so very anxious. She made her back quite ache with walking all night long round her young charges, for fear any harm should happen to them; and in the morning says she to herself—

"Two heads are better than one. I will consult some wise animal upon the matter, and get advice. How should a poor crawling creature like me know what to do without asking my betters?"

But still there was a difficulty—whom should the Caterpillar consult? There was the shaggy Dog who sometimes came into the garden. But he was so rough!—he would most likely whisk all the eggs off the cabbage-leaf with one brush of his tail, if she called him near to talk to her, and then she should never forgive herself. There was the Tom Cat, to be sure, who would sometimes sit at the foot of the apple-tree, basking himself and warming his fur in the sunshine; but he was so selfish and indifferent!—there was no hope of his giving himself the trouble to think about butterflies' eggs. "I wonder which is the wisest of all the animals I know," sighed the Caterpillar, in great distress; and then she thought, and thought, till at last she thought of the Lark; and she fancied that because he went up so high, and nobody knew where he went to, he must be very clever, and know a great deal; for to go up very high (which *she* could never do) was the Caterpillar's idea of perfect glory.

Now, in the neighbouring corn-field there lived a Lark, and the Caterpillar sent a message to him, to beg him to come and talk to her; and when he came she told him all her difficulties, and asked him what she was to do, to feed and rear the little creatures so different from herself.

"Perhaps you will be able to inquire and hear something about it next time you go up high," observed the Caterpillar timidly.

The Lark said, "Perhaps he should;" but he did not satisfy her curiosity any further. Soon afterwards, however, he went singing upwards into the bright, blue sky. By degrees his voice died away in the distance, till the green Caterpillar could not hear a sound. It is nothing to say she could not see him; for, poor thing! she never could see far at any time, and had a difficulty in looking upwards at all, even when she reared herself up most carefully, which she did now; but it was of no use, so she dropped upon her legs again, and resumed her walk round the Butterfly's eggs, nibbling a bit of the cabbage-leaf now and then as she moved along.

"What a time the Lark has been gone!" she cried, at last. "I wonder where he is just now! I would give all my legs to know! He must have flown up higher than usual this time, I do think! How I should like to know where it is that he goes to, and what he hears in that curious blue sky! He always sings in going up and coming down, but he never lets any secret out. He is very, very close!"

And the green Caterpillar took another turn round the Butterfly's eggs.

At last the Lark's voice began to be heard again. The Caterpillar almost jumped for joy, and it was not long before she saw her friend descend with hushed note to the cabbage bed.

"News, news, glorious news, friend Caterpillar!" sang the Lark; "but the worst of it is, you won't believe me!"

"I believe everything I am told," observed the Caterpillar hastily.

"Well, then, first of all, I will tell you what these little creatures are to eat"—and the Lark nodded his beak towards the eggs. "What do you think it is to be? Guess!"

"Dew, and the honey out of flowers, I am afraid," sighed the Caterpillar.

"No such thing, old lady! Something simpler than that. Something that *you* can get at quite easily."

"I can get at nothing quite easily but cabbage-leaves," murmured the Caterpillar, in distress.

"Excellent! my good friend," cried the Lark exultingly; "you have found it out. You are to feed them with cabbage-leaves."

"*Never!*" said the Caterpillar indignantly. "It was their dying mother's last request that I should do no such thing."

"Their dying mother knew nothing about the matter," persisted the Lark; "but why do you ask me, and then disbelieve what I say? You have neither faith nor trust."

"Oh, I believe everything I am told," said the Caterpillar.

"Nay, but you do not," replied the Lark; "you won't believe me even about the food, and yet that is but a beginning of what I have to tell you. Why, Caterpillar, what do you think those little eggs will turn out to be?"

"Butterflies, to be sure," said the Caterpillar.

"*Caterpillars!*" sang the Lark; "and you'll find it out in time;" and the Lark flew away, for he did not want to stay and contest the point with his friend.

"I thought the Lark had been wise and kind," observed the mild green Caterpillar, once more beginning to walk round the eggs, but I find that he is foolish and saucy instead. Perhaps he went up *too* high this time. Ah, it's a pity when people who soar so high are silly and rude nevertheless! Dear! I still wonder whom he sees, and what he does up yonder."

"I would tell you, if you would believe me," sang the Lark, descending once more.

"I believe everything I am told," reiterated the Caterpillar, with as grave a face as if it were a fact.

"Then I'll tell you something else," cried the Lark; "for the best of my news remains behind. *You will one day be a Butterfly yourself.*"

"Wretched bird!" exclaimed the Caterpillar, "you jest with my inferiority—now you are cruel as well as foolish. Go away! I will ask your advice no more."

"I told you you would not believe me," cried the Lark, nettled in his turn.

"I believe everything that I am told," persisted the Caterpillar; "that is"—and she hesitated—"everything that it is *reasonable* to believe. But to tell me that butterflies' eggs are caterpillars, and that caterpillars leave off crawling and get wings, and become butterflies!—Lark! you are too wise to believe such nonsense yourself, for you know it is impossible."

"I know no such thing," said the Lark, warmly. "Whether I hover over the corn-fields of earth, or go up into the depths of the sky, I see so many wonderful things, I know no reason why there should not be more. Oh, Caterpillar! it is because you *crawl*, because you never get beyond your cabbage-leaf, that you call *any* thing *impossible*."

"Nonsense!" shouted the Caterpillar, "I know what's possible, and what's not possible, according to my experience and capacity, as well as you do. Look at my long green body and these endless legs, and then talk to me about having wings and a painted feathery coat! Fool!—"

"And fool you! you would-be-wise Caterpillar!" cried the indignant Lark. "Fool, to attempt to reason about what you cannot understand! Do you not hear how my song swells with rejoicing as I soar upwards to the mysterious wonder-world above? Oh, Caterpillar! what comes to you from thence, receive as *I* do upon trust."

"That is what you call—"

"*Faith,*" interrupted the Lark.

"How am I to learn Faith?" asked the Caterpillar—

At that moment she felt something at her side. She looked round—eight or ten little green caterpillars were moving about, and had already made a show of a hole in the cabbage-leaf. They had broken from the Butterfly's eggs!

Shame and amazement filled our green friend's heart, but joy soon followed; for, as the first wonder was possible, the second might be so too. "Teach me your lesson, Lark!" she would say; and the Lark sang to her of the wonders of the earth below, and of the heaven above. And the Caterpillar talked all the rest of her life to her relations of the time when she should be a Butterfly.

But none of them believed her. She nevertheless had learnt the Lark's lesson of faith, and when she was going into her chrysalis grave, she said—"I shall be a Butterfly some day!"

But her relations thought her head was wandering, and they said, "Poor thing!"

And when she was a Butterfly, and was going to die again, she said—

"I have known many wonders—I have faith—I can trust even now for what shall come next!"

ALICE FREEMAN PALMER

THE BUTTERFLY

I hold you at last in my hand,
   Exquisite child of the air.
Can I ever understand
   How you grew to be so fair?

You came to my linden tree
   To taste its delicious sweet,
I sitting here in the shadow and shine
   Playing around its feet.

Now I hold you fast in my hand,
   You marvelous butterfly,
Till you help me to understand
   The eternal mystery.

From that creeping thing in the dust
   To this shining bliss in the blue!
God give me courage to trust
   I can break my chrysalis too!

ROBERT FROST

A PRAYER IN SPRING

Oh, give us pleasure in the flowers to-day;
And give us not to think so far away
As the uncertain harvest; keep us here
All simply in the springing of the year.

Oh, give us pleasure in the orchard white,
Like nothing else by day, like ghosts by night;
And make us happy in the happy bees,
The swarm dilating round the perfect trees.

And make us happy in the darting bird
That suddenly above the bees is heard,

The meteor that thrusts in with needle bill,
And off a blossom in mid air stands still.

For this is love and nothing else is love,
The which it is reserved for God above
To sanctify to what far ends He will,
But which it only needs that we fulfil.

JAN STRUTHER

SING, ALL YE CHRISTIAN PEOPLE!

Sing, all ye Christian people!
Swing, bells, in every steeple!
  For Christ to life is risen,
  Set free from death's dark prison.
With joyfulness, with joyfulness your Alleluyas sing,
For Christ has come again to greet the spring.

Green now is on the larches;
Spring-time in triumph marches
   And every day uncloses
   A host of new primroses:
Then daffodils and Mary-buds let us in garlands bring,
For Christ has come again to greet the spring.

Skylarks, the earth forsaking,
Soar to their music-making,
   And in the roof-tree's hollow
   Now builds the trusting swallow:
So cries to Him, so flies to Him, my soul on fearless wing,
For Christ has come again to greet the spring.

CELIA THAXTER

A SONG OF EASTER

    Sing, children, sing!
    And the lily censers swing;
Sing that life and joy are waking and that Death no more
    is king.
Sing the happy, happy tumult of the slowly brightening
    Spring;
    Sing, little children, sing!

Sing, children, sing!
Winter wild has taken wing.
Fill the air with the sweet tidings till the frosty echoes ring!
Along the eaves the icicles no longer glittering cling,
And the crocus in the garden lifts its bright face to the sun,
And in the meadows softly the brooks begin to run,
And the golden catkins swing
In the warm airs of the Spring;
Sing, little children, sing!

Sing, children, sing!
The lilies white you bring
In the joyous Easter morning for hope are blossoming;
And as the earth her shroud of snow from off her breast doth fling,
So may we cast our fetters off in God's eternal Spring.
So may we find release at last from sorrow and from pain.
So may we find our childhood's calm, delicious dawn again.
Sweet are your eyes, O little ones, that look with smiling grace,
Without a shade of doubt or fear into the future's face!

Sing, sing in happy chorus, with joyful voices tell
That death is life, and God is good, and all things shall be well;
That bitter days shall cease
In warmth and light and peace,
That Winter yields to Spring,—
Sing, little children, sing!

MARGUERITE CLEMENT

YS AND HER BELLS

Do you know how quaint they are, those folk from Brittany? Now ordinary people, like you and me, enjoy reading or writing about ghosts once in a while. Dear ghosts! Barefooted, long-robed, leisurely and reserved, they are such a pleasant change from the humans we come across, in the subway! Still, when we are more than, say, nine years old, we no longer take ghosts too seriously, not as seriously as ourselves. They have their little room in our lives, close to the children's corner, and they disturb but little our busy, sensible thoughts.

Not so in Brittany. I suppose it is misty too often over there for people to make such a difference between what they see and what they fancy. Besides, they fancy very beautiful things, which have got a right to be believed in. I told you those people were quaint: they actually meet their dreams alive, walking round the corner.

Not so long ago, for instance, in a small village, by the sea, two girls came home late at night. They were breathless and excited, although not exactly scared. And this is what they said.

They were talking and laughing along that little path which runs by Thomas's field. As a matter of fact, they were talking about the boys making fun of them, for they were young, they were pretty, they thought a lot of themselves and had, as yet, no pity to waste on their humble admirers. They may have laughed a little too loud; they could not tell. Anyway, all of a sudden, an old man, a very old man with sad eyes and a bushy beard, stood there, by their side. They had not heard his footsteps, which was strange. How long had he been following them?

Yes, he had said things, oh! nothing very particular. He had asked them if they were good, if they were happy, if they loved their father, if they were not too fond of dancing. He seemed somewhat afraid of that. And then he had paid them little sad compliments about their rosy cheeks. A good little girl's rosy cheeks, he said, were the only sight which made him forget his grief. . . . No, they had not asked him what grief. Oh! dear, no! He was too sad, don't you see. Also, he was not that sort of a man one dares to ask questions of. He had left them suddenly and noiselessly, before they reached the church, and they did not know where he had gone.

Now, the girls' father did not hesitate a minute. That's the beauty of the story. He knew the ghost right away. "Poor King Gralon," he said, "it's quite a while since he was heard of in this neighborhood! We'd better recite the De Profundis, girls, for the Lord to give peace, at last, to his poor soul."

But will poor King Gralon ever get any peace, considering that he has been roaming over the small paths of Brittany for some fifteen hundred years? Would you like me to tell you his story, the terrible tale of a daughter's wickedness and a father's despair? I believe you ought to know it, though it is so tragic, because it hovers over all the land and sea, over there, strange and glittering like their golden mist. They tell it in many ways. You may even find a few details in my story that are nowhere else. Never mind that. Nobody knows for sure what happened, don't you see, although we are almost certain that some terrible thing, once, did really happen.

How long ago did King Gralon live? I could not tell. Surely very long ago, since the people of Brittany had just been converted to the Christian faith, and not all of them, yet. And so hermits and bishops were very busy working miracles every day, to make the last pagans ashamed of their senseless powerless gods. And they preached a rather austere creed, as you will see. They could not take liberties with the Gospel in those early days. When we read, "If thy hand offend thee, cut it off and cast it from thee," we say it is a metaphor, and it just means we have got to be careful; when we read, "Woe to the rich," we say it means we must not possess too much; and when we read, "Put back thy sword into its scabbard," we say it means we are allowed to make war only when we cannot help it.

But the saintly preacher whom King Gralon knew was not so clever, by far. He accepted and revered, for himself and for his people, every single word of his book. His name was Guénolé, and he had no fear of kings, and he spoke his mind very plainly to Gralon about his daughter Dahut. Several times a year, he would leave his cell, dug out of the rock by the roaring sea, to make a trip to the palace and there deliver his warning.

"Thy daughter is a curse, King. Stop her ways; have her tried by the judges of thine own court. Because it is written, 'If thy heart offend thee, cut out thy heart and cast it from thee.' The wrath of God will visit thy house, King, and thy kingdom, if thou dost not heed His word. Help thyself against thyself, man. Save thy soul."

Gralon would listen and grow pale and kneel down before the holy hermit, but he would not do anything else: Dahut was too precious to him.

He always remembered the day when little Dahut was born, the same day on which his queen died.

And Dahut was so much like her! She had the same glossy braids, the same fathomless eyes. You never could tell what was in her thoughts and, when she sang, it seemed as if the waves themselves made less noise so that they could hear. As for the beauty of her face, after eighteen years, Gralon had not got used to it, and he looked at her every morning with a fresh delight. She made him think of the sun and of the stars and of the sea and of all the joy and of all the sadness of living. Could it be possible that Dahut was wicked at heart, as Guénolé said? Gralon did not dare to think.

Certainly, her ways were strange. Had she been just a sweet coquette, as so many of them are, Gralon would not have worried. But she was not a coquette. She despised all men, except, perhaps, her own father. The idea that one of those boys might become her lord and master made her shiver with cold disdain. They say that, when she was still a little girl, she had betrothed herself to the ocean, as it was the only strong thing which she respected and admired.

Now, such being the case, she might have become a nun, in the quiet convent that Guénolé had just established in one of the wild islands, amid the foam and the fog, and the rocks and the wind. Why did she not go there, to be thrilled by the tempest, to her heart's content, and forget about life and her inhuman contempt of it?

But she did not want to go to the nuns, in the island. Because she was as cruel as she was proud. She wanted men to look at her freely, to fall desperately in love with the glittering beauty of her face, and then to throw themselves down from the cliff, into that adyss which is still called the Devil's Pit, hoping that it would be more merciful to them than those cold, fathomless eyes.

And so, one after the other, for the two past years, all

the boys in Gralon's kingdom had followed the same way. It would take some but a little time; others would resist longer. And when Dahut felt afraid that some young man might escape her power, she would then give a ball in the huge hall by the sea, and she would dance and dance and dance with the rebellious youth until he gave way in his turn and drowned himself early, at dawn, the following morning.

And Dahut would say to her father, "Why, Father, I never promised any of those men anything. Must I be responsible for the foolishness of those weaklings? Or do you want me to go with a veil over my face, like the nuns on the island? I could not, Father. I'd die if I could not look at the sun and the stars and the white waves. And I must look at the boys too, in case I see one whom I might love. I am not doing anything wrong. A girl has her free choice."

And then poor King Gralon would mutter a few indistinct words about the mad dancing in the huge hall by the sea, and Dahut would retort with anger, "Will all the girls in your kingdom be allowed to dance except me, or do you want me to dance by myself?" And then she would sigh and say, "Aren't you tired of it all, anyway, Father? Sometimes I wish that your palace and its huge hall, and your kingdom with its cowardly men, and all of us could be washed away by the strong, splendid sea. I wish I were a white wave, Father, to dance and sing with them forever."

Poor Dahut! There are moments when I feel as if I could pity her, too. She was not made for the Christian faith and the new era. She belonged with the wild things which were dying. It was right for Guénolé to be her mortal enemy.

But what about the mothers and the sweethearts of the men who had gone down? Whenever Dahut strolled along the streets, they closed their doors and put a black curtain across their windows.

And yet Gralon did nothing. And, all in vain, several times a year did Saint Guénolé come out of his cell by the roaring sea, to curse Dahut and threaten her father with the wrath of the Lord.

I have not told you yet the name of Gralon's capital. It was called Ys and lay by the ocean, just below the level of the water, so that they had built an enormous dam to protect the town from the fury of the flood. And the key of the dam was made of pure gold, and it was hidden in a secret place, as the safety of so many depended upon it. The dam was opened but seldom, once a year, perhaps, during a very low tide. Then they would clean the massive wall quickly, for fear the mud and the sand and the shells and the weeds might eat away the stone, little by little. And then they would shut the dam in a great hurry, as the flood rushed in like a galloping horse, and Gralon would hide the key until the following year.

Nobody but he knew where the key was hidden—he and the poor young man whose father had built the dam. Gralon had deemed it safer to tell just one person in case he, the king, died a sudden death, and he had told that one because he was his father's son, a devout, silent youth, and because he was a hunchback, not likely to marry, thought

Gralon, nor to attract the attention, the deadly attention of Dahut.

In fact, the hunchback had never looked at her once, having given his love to Ys, his town, to Ys and her hundred spires, where a hundred big bells sang the glory of God louder than the sea. And his name was Gavin, and he was happy all day and all night, because the safety of Ys, the beautiful, depended upon his faith.

And so, of course, it was Gavin whom, one terrible day, at springtime and just before Easter, Dahut, the sorceress, sought along the numberless little streets winding around the gorgeous churches with their dazzling white spires.

She found him alone in a narrow passage which led to the wide sea. She opened her lovely mouth, breathed the salt air, which made her frantic, and called the boy by his name:

"Gavin," she said, "why don't you ever look at me?"

And then Gavin looked at her, but he did not see the wonderful face because of the vision which was in his head: the image of Ys the beautiful, with the hundred bells of its hundred spires, stood like a veil between him and her and protected him.

"Princess Dahut," answered he, "what can I do for your service?" Dahut stood disconcerted. For the first time she had seen neither fear nor love in a man's eyes. She soon recovered though. "Give me the key," she said, "which my father has hidden with thee."

Now, Dahut knew nothing about the key. It was just a new idea which had visited her at night, while she lay wide awake, listening to the clamoring flood and mad with the devilish desire to see it engulf all things, as well as all men. But Gavin was a simple boy. He thought the king had told her, unable as he was to resist any of her demands. And so he grew as pale as Death, and he clutched his fingers over his poor shriveled chest and he said: "Never."

And then Dahut knew. She knew that the key was there, hidden against the faithful heart, and she laughed aloud, a terrible laugh which the sea echoed amid the wild rocks, and the boy crossed himself, aghast but unconquered.

She began wrestling with him. A poor cripple he was, but with all the courage of mankind. For he was a man, and he felt she was not human. She was strong as the wind, slippery as a weed, and cool like the green water. And she smiled while she fought, and her smile was like the golden joy of dawn. But, all the same, Gavin went on fighting. He could not win, of course, but he could be faithful to the end, faithful to Ys and her bells. And, as Death came nearer and nearer, he could hear them all, the hundred bells of the hundred spires, ringing through his dizzy head their great victorious song.

She pushed the dead body into the sea with her foot, and she just said, "One more."

She did not want to use the key at once, or perhaps ever. It was enough for her to know that it was there, cool and powerful, close to her wicked heart; enough to feel that *she could do it* the next time she felt tired of men, of bells and of life altogether. She also wondered what Gralon would say when he heard that his dear hunchback had gone the way of all men—not willingly, though. That one had escaped her magic—she could not enslave them all.

Guénolé, in his cell, was safe too. . . . How he hated her! . . . "If thy heart offend thee, King, cut out thy heart." . . . She laughed again. So much fuss for a few despicable fishermen whose death had been graced by the memory of her smile! . . . What about the rights of queens, then? If the likes of Guénolé had their way, some day, the world would become a dull place, indeed. . . . A good thing the key was there.

She strolled back to the palace, but her heart was heavy. The recollection of her wrestling with a hunchback was disgusting beyond words. And the look in his eyes was strange, too. What could he behold which was more beautiful than Dahut's face, and what had helped him to die?

She had now been back for a few hours and was sitting with her father in the big hall, by the sea. All of a sudden, it seemed as if the wind had put a few words to its wild tune. Yes—and the words were, "Death to Dahut! Death to Dahut! . . ."

She thought she was feverish; she went and opened the window . . . "Death to Dahut!" clamored the tempest, which shouted now with a human voice. . . . Down, at the foot of the cliff, a crowd was coming toward the palace, like a living, furious flood. The women were there, waving their black veils like a standard. And the old men were there, flourishing their crutches. And there were little girls and tiny boys who swelled their pure cheeks to try to scream, "Death to Dahut!" Dahut could see, in front, the dead body of the hunchback, dripping with water, on a bed of seaweed. And he was the only silent and serene figure among that hellish crowd.

... "Death to Dahut!" chanted the wind, which seemed to take sides with the mob and make its yelling beautiful. ... "Death to Dahut!" ... "Death to Dahut!"

King Gralon was brave. He faced the human tide which was surging against his walls, with stones and sticks and curses.

"What do you want, people?" he said. "Am I no longer your king?"

"Death to Dahut!" answered the crowd. "Deliver her up to our justice, O King! Death to Dahut!"

And Gralon could hear within his conscience, "If thy heart offend thee, cut out thy heart." But he also thought of his dead queen, who had left him nothing except Dahut's eyes. He fancied what an empty place the world would be without them, and he said, "Take me, people. I am ready to pay for her, if you can prove her guilt."

But the mob respected Gralon. They were not seeking vengeance, but justice. And an old man in the crowd exclaimed: "Have her judged, King, by thine own Court."

That was the last word Dahut heard. And then she threw a white cape on her shivering body; she ran to the secret door which led to the huge, massive dam, and she went out and looked at the sky. The watchful moon was there. But Dahut did not mind the moon—the moon which has seen so many cities rise and fall beneath her cold eyes while the joyful sea bounces and leaps, as young as ever, toward the silvery face which she tries to kiss eternally. Of course, the moon was on Dahut's side and Dahut knew it.

The night was clear, although the wind was strong, and she could now hear both the human tide—Death to Dahut!—and the coming flood, charging against the wall of the dam like a despairing army in a desperate fight. Dahut quietly smiled. She was going to give the beaten one his chance. It took very little time, just one flash upon the shining key, then the massive door glided, unconscious, like a sentry asleep, and, with a roar which disturbed the stars, the whole ocean stood erect, defying Ys, her spires, and her bells, and the vain anger of her mob. And then it thundered down, foaming, into the streets, while the people gave one last scream—a screaming appeal to the Lord.

The Lord did not answer the people of Ys. He received them in His Paradise, I suppose, as soon as they were drowned, for they had done nothing wrong, and they were not responsible for the wickedness of Dahut, and I'll tell you in a moment what the Lord did for Ys and her bells, because He loved the way they sang to His glory.

But, for the time being, the wrath of the Lord visited Gralon and his house, as Saint Guénolé had so often predicted. King Gralon wandered through his halls, sick with despair. His instinct had been to shut the big window, and so he was safe for a little time—the palace stood high and the walls were so thick! But King Gralon did not think of his safety. He knew that Dahut had done it, he knew her soul was lost forever, and he felt no desire to go to heaven where she would never be, or to remain on earth where she was no more. He had loved her better than God and His law, don't you see, better than the poor people committed to his care. But, since his sin had been a sin of love, there was no bitterness in him—nothing except a great fatigue, as if he had carried the burden of every man, ever since man had been. He wanted to sleep until doomsday and, if possible, beyond. And, instead of sleep, who was coming for him but Saint Guénolé holding the king's horse, Morvark, by the bridle! And Guénolé said, "Get up on thy horse and ride, O King! because the Lord needs thee elsewhere." And they went out through the big window, and Morvark galloped on the beach, breast deep in the water, while Guénolé, the man of God, ran on the waves ahead of them, to show the way.

And it was then that the terrible thing happened, that thing which Gralon cannot forget and which keeps him roaming, in his grief, along the paths of Brittany. All of a sudden, Gralon felt as if somebody were clinging to the horse in a desperate effort to climb up. He looked, and he saw Dahut, and at first he did not know her, for the deadly pallor on her face and the ghastly fright in her eyes. She could hardly speak and she could not breathe. She just pointed to the pit—you know—to the Devil's Pit. . . . "There," she said—"there. . . ." And the story said that what she saw there was the procession of all the young men who had died for her. Each wave brought up a new one, and the ghosts beckoned to Dahut from the depths of the sea. And Dahut felt like a woman for the first time in her life, and there was nothing left in her except a savage desire to escape, to get on Morvark's back and taste of life once more.

But Guénolé, too, had turned round; his hour had come and he was unmoved.

"Cast her away, King, where she belongs. It would have been better for all if she had never been born."

"Father," implored Dahut, "I am your only child. I want to stay with you and I am afraid, Father, I am afraid. Don't give me back to them."

And Guénolé repeated, "Cast her away."

"I am like my mother," stammered the terrified girl. "For her sweet sake, let me get up here."

But Guénolé: "Take thy choice between her and God. O King, it is written, 'Cut out thy heart, if thy heart tempt thee.'"

They say that, at this moment, Gralon, too, saw the young men whom the pit was bringing forward, one after the other, to bear witness against his only love, and Morvark, at last, all of a sudden, neighed to heaven and refused to advance farther.

And then—then—Gralon freed himself from Dahut's embrace; Morvark kicked the waves wildly, and the King fell upon the back of his horse, like a dead man, while Guénolé led the two thither, where they were called.

Don't ask me what has become of Dahut, because I am afraid the young men of Brittany are not yet freed from her charm. They hear her sing in the tempest, her glossy braids shine in every sunset, and it is her smile which, in summer, lights up the sea. Despite their mothers' prayers, despite their wives' tears, they all want to join her, amid the merry round of the wild white waves. They all go, sooner or later, and not all of them come back. Dahut is now one with the strong, splendid sea. The people call it, sometimes, by her name.

And although King Gralon became a saintly king, later on, in his new kingdom, although Saint Guénolé would willingly lead him before the throne of God the minute he wants to go, Gralon has not wanted to, yet. He prefers lingering down below, a harmless ghost among the people of Brittany. He converses at twilight with some of their fair daughters, to try to keep them pure, kind, and happy. They say that those narrow paths are so pretty, in spring, when the gorse is in bloom, that Gralon must not be pitied too much, after all.

And on Easter Day—not every year, of course—but when the day is unusually quiet and when the year is going to be a blessed one, if you sit on the rock and try to look through the blue water, as far below as you can see, the spires of Ys the beautiful will rise from the depths, before your wondering eyes.

If there is no sin in your heart, you will even hear the bells, those bells which the Lord liked so much that He has sheltered them down there in the abyss, where they keep ringing forever to Him alone, forever.

KATHARINE GIBSON

APOLLON, A GARDENER

"Praised be thou, my Lord, with all thy creatures,
Especially the honored Brother Sun,
Who makes the day and illumines us through thee.
And he is beautiful and radiant with great splendor.

> Praised be thou, my Lord, for Sister Moon and
>   the stars,
> Thou hast formed them in the heavens clear and
>   precious and beautiful."
>
> . . . .St. Francis of Assisi

Though the small French town of Petit Michel is long since gone to ruins, some six hundred years ago it stood on the king's highway, a half day's journey from the much larger town of Auxerre, with its great cathedral. Within its walls was the castle of a powerful duke. He was one of the great house of Burgundy. Guarded by the thickness of high towers and ramparts, the Duke lived with his sword out of its scabbard. For these were troubled times. There, too, lived his daughter, the Lady Jehane, she whose long hair, black as a thunder cloud, gave to the pallor of her face and the quickness of her smile, the surprising brightness of a rainbow after a storm. Though he was often away for months, listening to the words of great scholars, the Duke's young son, François, also lived within the thick walls of the castle. He was slender and his hair so blonde it gleamed like silver. Yet, for all his youth and seeming delicacy, he was quick with the broadsword and could ride a horse as though he and the animal were one single creature. But his chief delight was in books and old parchment rolls over which he spent long hours. Inside the town walls lived staid and sober folk, merchants and cobblers and weavers, all safe from marauding bands of outlaws and the fierce packs of wolves that ranged the forest hungrily in winter time.

Outside the walls, in a wooded place almost beyond sight

of the highest gate tower, lived only Apollon, a gardener, and his sister. No one ever saw her; it was rumored she went abroad only at night. And none of the townsfolk ventured far from their firesides once twilight fell. Strange stories were told of Apollon. To have lived without the walls was enough to cause much whispering, but there was more than this. Even on the dullest days, a warm glow could be seen around his hut; and on the blackest night, an unearthly whiteness shone behind the winter mists or spangled the velvet-darkness of midsummer eves; it was as though the moon were shining low among the thickets behind a veil of cloud.

Apollon was rarely seen in the town except on market days. He had a stall where he sold vegetables and fruit and flowers. The poor folk kept away from him, but soon after he had taken up his stand, word came to the cooks in the castle that his beans and cucumbers or peas were ready for picking before those of other gardeners were leafed out. His peaches and pears were smooth and showed a blush while those growing against the walls of the castle or any other wall, even the most protected, were hard and green. But the real marvel was Apollon's flowers. Violets, white, and deep still purple, bloomed in March. The grass around his hut was golden with buttercups in early April; and his roses, larger than two cupped hands, blossomed on their strong stems while November winds blew coldly.

Though the poor would have none of him, now and then Apollon would stop at the threshold of one who was old or sick and leave a new green cabbage, a basket of strawberries in early June. Those who tasted his gifts said they felt warmed and strengthened as if they had dined on sunbeams. No child ever looked at his flowers in vain. In a grubby, small fist, Apollon would place a flaming tulip or a spiced carnation that could win the heart of a princess. These offerings, far from softening the hard thoughts of his fellow townsmen, only made them the more bitter. "Such waste," they said.

When the story was told, that the night before Black Pierre was to be hanged, his jailer found a bowl heaped with greens outside his cell, the men of the town growled like angry watch dogs. Who did not know that greens were Pierre's favorite food? He'd even pause in hunting the Duke's deer if he caught sight of the smallest patch of dandelions at the edge of the wood. And everybody knew nothing except this tasty dish would ever make him stop chasing forbidden game. He'd be hanged for poaching some day. Well, now he was going to be, and on the night before, a bowl was left at his barred door. In it were heaped beet tops with coral stems, fringed parsley, borage leaves and sky-blue flowers. Nesting among them, small, white onions shone like little moons, and beside the bowl was an earthenware flagon of olive oil, yellow like thickened light, and another of wine vinegar, its sharp taste warmed by peppers and secret herbs. "Encouraging crime, that's what it is." And when the town worthies charged Apollon with the deed, he only smiled and said,

"The sun shines upon the blessed and doomed alike, as surely as the rain falls upon the just and the unjust."

The ladies of the castle, hearing of such tales from their maids and pages, donned their furred cloaks and gathered round Apollon's stall. He served them politely, but never smiled. Yet they lingered, fingering his green wares delicately. They noted his height and, beneath his rough tunic, the whiteness of his throat like a lighted candle. They remembered long the fine cutting of brow and chin and the wide, blazing amber of his eyes, deeply shaded by bronzed lashes. He always wore, both summer and winter, a tight-fitting black cap. But one morning the Lady Jehane noted that a single lock, slipping from beneath it, shone so golden she could feel its gleam upon her downcast lids.

It was she who had the strange adventure one cold, March morning. Restless, unable to sleep, she woke her sulky maid and set out to the town church for early mass. Her heart was dead within her and her youth grown grey and withered like the lichen which clings, whether it so wills or not, to some rotted tree. For all her fragrant gaiety had been given into the keeping of the Duke's rival to quiet his greed. Her husband was aged by his own cruelty and hate. Nothing could grow or thrive within the circle of his craftiness.

After the service in the church, which fell upon her ears like a blessed, yet distant sound, she came into the misted air. Urged by a weighted misery, she walked toward the town gate, and hardly knowing what she did, climbed the great tower and stood upon a little wooden platform outside a high window. Beneath her, at the foot of narrow, curving stairs, the maid drooped, heavy with sleep. Though she could see but little, Jehane knew that beyond the shifting wall of fog, a straight, wide road, the King's highway, ran up a long, wooded hill. She stood silent, cold drops of mist settling on her hair and wide sleeves. Suddenly the fog was parted, slit by bright lances of light. Then on the rise of the hill, she saw that these seemed to be gathered at some burning core, and out of the blaze came two white horses driven by a young man. He was clad only in a short, white tunic; he held the horses by long reins that cracked like harnessed lightning. His head was thrown back and such power was in him that his flying heels drove sparks from the stones and hard packed dust of the road. As he came nearer, the air became clear with dawn and clouds scurried from the sky like frightened owls. As he came nearer, the light seemed to come with him; it burned in every separate curled lock and streamed across the fields. Birds rose with strident cries and followed; frosted grass blades grew green. And as he passed beneath the window where she stood, to drive his horses into the town, an intolerable and unbelieved delight flowed in the Lady Jehane's veins. He looked up. She could not mistake the amber brilliance of the gardener's eyes or the supple tallness of his frame. He waved one arm and called out.

"Apollon no longer has a chariot, but this one day, the first of spring, he may still drive his horses out of the East. Few are those that see him, but they who do will never again move in greyness or in dark."

That morning, the story went through the town that the Duke's two Arabian steeds, lately brought from Hasa, had kicked their way out of their stalls and galloped through the main gate of the town the evening before, just as the watch was about to close it. Though half the men of town and castle were turned out to look for them, not an ear, a hoof, a mane or tail had been seen until, shortly after dawn, who should come driving them back to their stable but

Apollon, the gardener. And when the Duke offered him a whole bag of gold, that daft Apollon had shaken his black-capped head and said,

"Look at the meadows, there's gold enough!"

And as the Duke's household looked, they saw whole fields yellow with lemon day lilies. These had never been seen so early before. But that could have nothing to do with money bags. It is clearly not possible to buy bread with flower petals. Yet Apollon had not taken a single coin.

"You cannot pay the sun to shine," was what they heard him say, as he bowed his way out of the Duke's dark hall.

The story of the Duke's horses was quite forgotten by evening, overshadowed by one of much greater import. The Lady Jehane was gone; she had disappeared like dew at noon tide. None had seen her go. Yet all guessed she had fled from her husband's bitter cruelty. Her maid had been found in a deep sleep at the foot of the stairs of the massive tower that guarded the town's east gate. But what with her weeping and moaning, little could be got from her except that as she and the Lady Jehane had walked home from mass, they became mazed in the fog. How she came to be in the tower, she could not remember. She was bewitched, she thought. She recalled the cold mist, and a stab of light from a high window had awakened her. That was all she knew, quite, quite all. No one found the slightest trace of her mistress, though the Duke offered a ransom which sent men of seven duchies hunting every wood and road and even fishing in every deep pond or river.

Strange, the Lady had been lost on the very day Apollon brought back the Duke's steeds, those that had come from

Hasa, out of the East. The townsfolk could make nothing of the conjunction of these two happenings, but for lack of any better way out of their puzzlement, that night two of them cut all Apollon's choicest artichokes and threw them in his well.

The months passed and no single word was heard of the Lady Jehane. The first night of spring, a year after she had been lost, her young brother, François, had his dream of walking in the wood near Apollon's hut. It was quite dark, yet in his dream he could see his way as he came near Apollon's garden because of a strange, pale light around it, like the light seen glowing on old stumps in swampy places. At first he could not discover any one place from which the light came; it seemed to shine palely over the whole clearing. Yet, as he walked, behind the hut it seemed to grow brighter, and François felt a sharp longing to see if he could find its source. But as he went forward, the light seemed to go farther and farther away. If he hurried, it moved the more quickly. Soon he was panting and breathless, his chest heaving, his whole body wracked. Brambles tore at his clothes and branches struck him as he passed, as though, suddenly, the trees had become guards armed with long, swinging staves. He came to the edge of a wide swamp; his foot slipped and he fell, face down in thick mud. The more he struggled, the deeper he sank; the ooze covered his nose and mouth. All was a bitter, thick, suffocating blackness. He awoke, beating helplessly the soft feathers of his bed that had become heaped around his head.

The following day, one moment he froze in horror because of his memory of the swamp, and the next he was filled with a longing to find the secret of the cold, white light. That night and many after, he dreamed the same dream, only each time he went farther into the woods, and each time the light grew brighter. But he was always stopped just as he seemed about to reach it. Sometimes it was an impenetrable bramble thicket; sometimes the swamp. As the days passed, his longing fought so mightily with his fear that he knew little else. When his father, or those of his father's court, spoke to him he scarcely heard. He had had the cleverest head for Latin of any in the large town of Auxerre, but now he looked with unseeing eyes at meaningless black marks on his parchment scrolls.

The Duke, hurt by the loss of his daughter, now called together the wisest alchemists in the land and ordered them to heal his son. These only shook their heads and said François had been poisoned by some strange plant. He could only be cured if he could find that plant. And this could hardly be, because they, themselves, knew all herbs and simples and had tried them, every one; and still he was sunk in his mysterious malady. François grew paler, more wandering in his thoughts. His dark eyes burned feverishly in his thin face. Some said he would be better when summer came. For the spring days were cold as December. Hardly a blade of green showed in dull clods of earth, frosted so hard the peasant's pick could scarcely break them. Fear was in the lashing wind; and the dismal croak of half-starved crows was the voice of famine.

Lent, a bleak and bitter time, was coming to an end. Hopelessly, the Duke and his court made ready for their journey to the great cathedral of Auxerre for the Easter mass.

Young François lay helpless upon his curtained bed, and the night before the mass he dreamed his last dream of Apollon's garden. He followed the white glow as before, but this time along a path he had never seen either when hunting in the woods or in the fever of his dreams. Branches bent to let him pass; twigs snapped with welcoming chirps under his swift heels. On a flattened rise of ground he came, at last, to a clear pool which, draining into a network of small brooks, had made of low fields a treacherous swamp.

The pool was bright as a fine lady's mirror, and every tree was touched with silver and every reed become a tube of shining glass. As he watched, the brightness grew more piercing and came close. Then, suddenly, on a sandy strip by the pond's edge, he saw a figure moving. It shone brighter than all else and was, indeed, the source of all the cold brilliance; yet he could see through it as though it were made of stilled water or frozen light. The figure was that of a woman wrapped in a cloak. Her fair hair was unbound; in one strong white hand, listless now and nerveless, she carried a bow with loosened string; in the other, an arrow with a single barb at its tip, flanked by two other smaller barbs, their points curved downward toward the shaft.

As François watched, she loosened her cloak and for one breathless moment he saw her slim figure, clad only in a short, white tunic, bound with a girdle of dimmed stars. She moved toward the pond and bent above it as if about to slip into its waveless surface. Her face was half turned from him, but its deathless beauty was stamped upon the darkness of the wood, as is the moon against the night sky. In wonder, he knelt before her; it had been granted to him to see with mortal eyes the goddess Artemis who, with her torch, lights the heavens at evening until they burn like day. Dead leaves stirred and an owl cried warningly. The goddess straightened, turned toward him, and, in a final blaze of light, fitted her arrow to its bow. Though in that second François felt he would welcome death from her merciful, bright hands, yet some lingering warmth of life made him swerve aside. The arrow, winging its way, passed just above his shoulder and fell to earth near Apollon's garden. Blackness closed over François.

So deep was that darkness, that he lay in a stupor when they carried him, next morning, to the cathedral, helpless in a silken litter. The cathedral was crowded. The townsfolk, with sad faces and despairing eyes, made way for the Duke walking beside the bearers of his sick and wasted son. Though it was indeed Easter, no single ray of warmth had pierced dark clouds to tell them so. It was the seventeenth day with no sun. Fields were still bare, and gardens empty. In the cathedral, finely woven tapestries were hung along the aisles, but their colors were dimmed in the cold greyness of the morning. The many hued windows were leaden. Only the altars were bright with tapers. All eyes turned toward the tall Easter, or Paschal candle burning at the feet of the carved statue of the Virgin. It was made of whitest beeswax. For are not the worker bees like holy monks in their cells and worthy to have what they have so wisely made used in this great hour of the Church? The most learned among the people remembered that St. Jerome had said, "Candles are lighted when the gospel is read, not indeed to put darkness to flight, but ever as a sign of joy." On this

Easter day, joy seemed to have turned her face from that stricken countryside.

For all the gold of crosses, the silver of patins and winking jewels on small chests or pixes, the high altar shone somewhat coldly. There was not a single flower. True, a long bank of strong, green plants was placed at the feet of the Virgin, but no blossom was to be seen. This green, so the word was passed, had come from the garden of Apollon; but even he, folk noted spitefully, could do nothing to make it bloom.

When the long service was ended, the Bishop announced the Easter hand ball game. It had been the custom to play this each year in the cathedral of Auxerre since the grey stones of the cathedral were white with newness. Each Easter, the sun leaps three times into the sky to greet the risen Lord. Who does not know that? To acknowledge this courtesy of the sun, and for the glory of Him who is greater than all suns, the game was played.

The Bishop spoke. "This Easter let us play with a firm spirit and perchance," he smiled at his people as if he were speaking to expectant children who had been disappointed at some looked-for feast, "perchance, seeing the ball bounce right smartly and rise above our heads, the sun will take heart and shine in its appointed place."

He gave the signal; the older members of the choir began to chant and the game was started, slowly at first. Choir boys, priests began it; then, here and there, some from the crowd of worshippers joined in. Among them was Apollon. He moved more swiftly than the rest. When he struck the ball, it rose high among the topmost vaults of the cathedral roof. A few said that each time he touched it, it became a warmer hue until it gleamed golden like a whirling star. The game was played fast and faster. Children laughed; women watched, breathless. Their skirts, black and purple, swirled about the ankles of priests and deans as they leaped and jumped. The choir boys' crimson vestments shone like fleeing sparks; but none tossed the golden ball so often or moved with such lightning grace as did Apollon. Where he played, the game became a whirling maze. As though time had moved even more quickly than the ball, all too soon the chanting of the choir died away. The folk were still.

Before the carved statue of the Virgin, beside the high altar, François lay as ivory white as were Her garments. His fair hair tumbled on his brow was blonde as spun moonlight. Beside him stood a Sister from a nearby convent, her face hidden in her dark veils. At his feet was Apollon, the gardener.

Given a sign by the Bishop, all knelt, all save Apollon. He stood silent for a moment, then with both hands lifted his tight black cap from off his head. As he did so, shafts of light filled the cathedral and he seemed the very center of the splendor. The whiteness of the Virgin was patterned with scarlet, blue and gold from the newly bright glass of the windows. At Her feet, suddenly, the green plants were starred with white buds that, opening, filled the air with all the fragrance of spring. From the fields, through the opened door, came the voice of small birds rising to meet the sun with new songs as old as earth.

The dark veil worn by the Sister, touched by a warm breeze, blew from her face. An amazed whisper went from lip to ear among the crowd. Before them, protected by her black habit as she had been protected by secret convent walls, stood she who had been the Lady Jehane. In a clear voice, she spoke to Apollon as though the meeting was not their first.

"Oh, fair Apollo, god of day, where are now your horses and where your flaming chariot?"

Strange were her words and stranger still, the gardener's answer.

"Good Sister, no god can live save in the hearts of his worshippers. Gone are those who knew cloud-capped Olympus, mighty Zeus, grey-eyed Athena, her golden helmet now pale with dust. Hermes, messenger between the skies and the fair land of Greece, no longer moves swift as a shooting star. He who in his last flight plunged, a spent meteor, into the wine-dark sea, now lies forgot."

"And you, Apollon?"

"Only I have lingered because of man's love of warmth. No longer great Apollo, driver of the sun's chariot, he with far-shooting bow, but a gardener, spade in hand. And my sister, Artemis, once the fair huntress of the evening sky, the silver goddess of the moon, is now but a misted shade seen only in young dreams."

As Apollon spoke the name of Artemis, François stirred in his sleep.

"You will stay with us, gardener, and help bring greenness to our dun fields?"

"No, good Sister, now we go. The old gods must always make way for the new. But our memory will linger in the warmth of words like those your St. Francis spoke of:

'. . . . . the honored Brother Sun
Who makes the day. . . .'

Apollon bowed proudly. But his eyes were lifted to the figure of the Child Jesus held high in the Virgin's arms. The cold stone from which it had been carved, now shone in the sunlight so brightly that the flame of the Paschal candle at His feet seemed a pale icicle.

"It is the new God who lives in men's hearts, now; a God, not born on high Olympus, but in a small Syrian stable, come to earth in the guise of a man child, wrapped in swaddling clothes and lying in a manger. Though they are seen no more, in Him the old gods live transfigured. Did He not say, 'I am the light of the world; he that follows me shall not walk in darkness, but shall have the light of life?'"

As Apollon finished speaking, the crowd stirred. They went out of the stone arched cathedral to the boundless blue arch of the heavens. A faint green showed on the warmed earth. The gardener was lost in the crowd. The Sister returned to the convent where she had fled on that first day when she was lost to the sight of men. The litter bearers carried François to his bed. He slept a quiet sleep and on the third day, waking, ordered his amazed gentlemen-in-waiting to carry him to Apollon's hut.

They had to hack a way through interwoven brambles with their swords. When they reached the hut, it was covered with vines, seemingly a century old; its windows were closed with dripping moss; its door sealed with a lock of scarlet lichen. The garden was now a grove of saplings, except for one spot where grew a blade of green, straight and slender, with a single barb at its tip, flanked by two other barbs that curved downward to its shaft-like stem. From these three petals came a sharp, haunting fragrance. As it struck his nostrils, François rose on one elbow; color flowed into his cheeks. He stepped from the litter and knelt in wonder before the flower. His doubts were gone; he had, indeed, seen Artemis, chaste goddess of the skies. Here was his proof. With a glad cry, he made his way back to the castle. The alchemists could only say, the cause of the strange malady was found. They declared they were right from the first; he had been struck down by some poisoned root of the forest and was now cured by his return to the spot on which it grew.

Never again was Apollon seen, or the white light around the hut when darkness fell. His name, as gardener, and this story would have been quite forgotten were it not that each spring village children sought out the place where his hut had been. In this spot, and here alone, grew a small lily, with a sharp fragrance, which they gathered to place at the feet of the Virgin for the Easter mass. Because of its icy whiteness, it was sometimes said to be like a moonbeam, but it was the barbed petals that gave it the name by which it became known. It was called the Arrow Lily, or, by the learned, the flower of Artemis.

MARGARET J. PRESTON

THE FIRST TE DEUM

'Twas Easter night in Milan; and before
The altar in the great Basilica,
St. Ambrose stood. At the baptismal font
Kneeled a young neophyte, his brow still wet
With the symbolic water, and near by
The holy Monica, her raised eyes strained,

As with unearthly ecstasy she breathed
Her *Nunc Dimittis, Domine.* The words
Of comfort spoken— "Be sure the child for whom
Thy mother-heart hath poured so many prayers
Shall not be lost"—had full accomplishment,
And her tired heart found peace.
                              St. Ambrose raised
His hands to heaven, and on his face there shone
Such light as glorified the Prophet's, when
An angel from the altar bare a coal
And touched his lips. With solemn step and slow,
He turned to meet Augustine, as he rose
Up from the pavement; and thereon he brake
Forth in ascriptive chant:
                         "We praise Thee, God,
And we acknowledge Thee to be the Lord!"
Augustine, on the instant, caught the tone
Of answering exultation:
                        "All the earth
Doth worship Thee, the Father Everlasting!"
And from the altar-rail came back again
The antiphony:
               "To Thee all angels cry
Aloud, the heavens and all the powers therein."
And from the font,
                   "To Thee the cherubim
And seraphim continually do cry,
Oh, Holy, Holy, Holy, Thou Lord God
Of Sabaoth! Heaven and earth are full of all
The glory of Thy Majesty!"

                        And then,
With upward gaze, as if he looked upon
The infinite multitude about the throne,
St. Ambrose uttered with triumphant voice,
"The glorious company of the Apostles"—
"Praise Thee"—burst reverent from Augustine's lips;
"The goodly fellowship of all the Prophets"—
"Praise Thee:" "The noble army of the Martyrs"—
"Praise Thee!"
                Thus back and forth responsive rolled
The grand antiphonal, until the crowd
That kneeled throughout the vast Basilica,
Rose to their feet, and toward the altar pressed,
With one strong impulse drawn! The breath of God
Had to their thought inspired these mortal tongues
To which they listened, as beneath a spell
Vatic and wonderful.
                     And when the last
Response was reached, and the rapt speakers stood
With eyelids closed, as those who had seen God,
And could not brook at once a mortal face,
Awestruck, the people bowed their heads and wept,
Then uttered with acclaim, one long—*Amen!*

ADAPTED FROM EARLY SOURCES

SAINT PATRICK AT TARA

Now Patrick, son of Cualfarnus, was of the British race and born in Britain. When a lad sixteen years old he was with others carried captive into Ireland and was kept in slavery in the house of a certain chieftain, a heathen man and a harsh. After some years he forsook this man and sailed to Britain. And again, after may years, he suffered captivity, but afterward he found rest as beforetime in his own native land. And many visions were shown to him. So he set forth to learn and understand and fulfill the sacred mysteries. He crossed the southern British sea and stayed no little time with a certain very holy bishop, Germanus, ruling in the city of Auxerre. And there he learnt, loved and kept everything that is profitable to the spirit and the soul.

When he had spent there a long time it was said to him in a vision that the time had arrived for him to go that he might bring the Irish by the net of the Gospel to the harbour of Life. And it was said to him in a vision, "The boys and girls of the wood of Fochlath are calling thee."

So he set forth on the journey to the work for which he had made ready. And when he had received the episcopal rank and all things were accomplished according to custom he got on board a ship prepared for him and arrived in Britain. Then with all speed and with a favoring wind, he crossed the sea to Ireland.

Now in the days in which these things happened, there was in Ireland a certain great king named Loiguire, son of Niall, a fierce and heathen High-King of barbarians. In Tara were his residence and his royal grip.

Now he had about him wise men and magicians and augurs and enchanters and inventors of every evil art, who through their heathenish and idolatrous religion had skill to know and foresee all things before they came to pass. And of these there were two who were preferred beyond the others, whose names were Lochru and Lucetmael. And these two by their magical arts frequently foretold the coming of a certain foreign religion, in the manner of a kingdom, with a certain strange and harmful doctrine brought from a long distance across the seas, proclaimed by a few, accepted by the many, and honored by all; one that would overturn kingdoms, slay kings that resist it, lead away multitudes, destroy all their gods, and, having cast down all the resources of their art, reign for ever and ever. And then, as it was prophesied and figured, so it came to pass and was fulfilled.

Now when the high-tide of Easter drew nigh, Patrick thought there was no place fitter for the chief solemnity of the year, that is, for celebrating Easter, than in the place wherein was the chief abode of the idolatry and wizardry of Ireland, to wit, in Tara.

So they left their vessel in the estuary where they were and went along the land till they came to the place called The Graves of the Men of Fecc, near Slane, which, as the story goes, was dug by the men, that is the slaves of Feccol Ferchertni, who was one of the nine great prophets of Breg. And having pitched his tent there, Patrick with his companions paid to the most high God the due vows of the Paschal feast and the sacrifice of praise with all devotion, according to the words of the prophet.

It happened then, that that was the time at which was celebrated the high-tide of the heathen, to wit, the Feast of Tara, with many incantations and magical devices and other superstitions of idolatry. And there were also gathered together kings, satraps, leaders, princes and chief men of the people; and, moreover, magicians and enchanters and augurs and those who sought out and taught every art and every wile were called to Loiguire, as once upon a time to King Nebuchadnezzar, to Tara, their Babylon.

On that night, then, the fire of every hearth in Ireland was quenched and it was proclaimed by the King that no fire should be kindled in Ireland before the fire of Tara, and that neither gold nor silver should be taken as compensation for him who should kindle it, but that he should go to death for his crime. Patrick knew not that and even though he had known it would not have hindered him.

Accordingly Saint Patrick, in his celebration of the holy Paschal feast kindled a divine fire, very bright and blessed, which as it shone forth at night, was seen by almost all the dwellers in the plain.

Accordingly it happened that it was seen from Tara, and when it was seen, all beheld it and were amazed. And when all the nobles and elders and magicians had been gathered together, the king said to them, "What is this? Who is it that has dared to do this impiety in my kingdom? Let him die the death!"

And all the nobles and elders made answer, "We know not who has done this thing."

Then the magicians answered and said, "O king, live for ever. As for this fire which we behold, and which has been lighted up this night before one was lighted in thy house, that is, in the palace of Tara, unless it be put out on this night on which it has been lighted up, it will not be put out for ever. Moreover it will overcome all the fires of our religion. And he who kindled it, and the kingdom that will follow, from which it is kindled this night, will overcome both all of us and thee too, and it will draw away all the men of thy kingdom, and all kingdoms will yield to it, and he will fill all things, and will reign for ever and ever.

When King Loiguire had heard these things, he was, like Herod of old, sore troubled, and all the city of Tara with him.

And he answered and said, "It shall not be so; but now we will go that we may see the issue of the matter; and we shall take and slay those who do such an impiety against our kingdom."

And so, having yoked nine chariots, in accordance with the traditions of the gods, and taking with him for the conflict those two magicians who excelled all others, that is to say, Lucetmael and Lochru, Loiguire proceeded at the close of that night from Tara to the Graves of the Men of Fecc, turning the faces of the men and of the horses to the left, in accordance with their notion of what is fitting in such a case.

And as they went on their way, the magicians said to the king, "O king, thou must not go into the place in which the fire is, lest afterwards perchance thou worship him who kindled it; but thou must be outside it, near at hand; and he will be summoned to thee, that he may worship thee and thou have dominion over him. And we and he shall parley with one another in thy presence, O king; and in this way thou wilt test us."

And the king answered and said, "Ye have advised well; I will do as ye have said."

And when they arrived at the appointed place, they alighted from their chariots and horses; and they entered not into the enclosure of the place where the fire had been kindled; but took their seats close by.

And Saint Patrick was called to the king outside the place where the fire had been kindled.

And the magicians said to their people, "Let us not rise up at the approach of this fellow, for whosoever rises up at the approach of this fellow will afterwards believe in him and worship him."

At last Saint Patrick rose; and when he saw their many chariots and horses, he came to them, singing with voice and heart, very appropriately, the following verse of the Psalmist: "Some put their trust in chariots and some in horses; but we will walk in the name of the Lord our God."

They were biding before him with the rims of their shields against their chins and none of them rose up before him save one who willed not to obey the words of the magicians. And Patrick blessed him and the man believed in the everlasting God.

And when they began to parley with one another, the second magician, named Lochru, went angrily and noisily with contention and questions against Patrick. As he uttered such things, Saint Patrick looked wrathfully upon him and cried with a great voice unto God, and this he said, "O Lord who canst do all things, and in whose power all things hold together, and who has sent me hither—as for this impious man who blasphemes Thy name, let him now be taken up out of this and die speedily."

And when he had thus spoken, the magician was caught up into the air, and then let fall from above and he was dashed to pieces and the heathen folk were dismayed.

Now the king with his people, enraged with Patrick on

account of this thing, was minded to slay him and said, "Lay hands on this fellow who is destroying us."

Then Saint Patrick, seeing that the ungodly heathen folk were about to rush upon him, rose up, and with a clear voice said, "Let God arise, and let his enemies be scattered; let them also that hate him flee before him."

And straightway darkness came down, and a certain horrible commotion arose, and the ungodly men fought amongst themselves, one rising up against another, and there was a great earthquake, "and He bound the axles of their chariots, and drove them with violence," and they rushed in headlong flight—both chariots and horses—over the level ground of the great plain, till at last only a few of them escaped half alive to the mountain of Monduirn; and, at the curse of Patrick, seven times seven men were laid low by this stroke in the presence of the king and his elders, until there remained only himself and his wife and two others of his companions; and they were sore afraid.

So the queen approached Patrick and said to him, "O man, righteous and mighty, do not destroy the king; for the king will come and kneel and worship thy Lord."

And the king, compelled by fear, came and knelt before the Saint, and feigned to worship Him whom he did not wish to worship.

And when they had parted from one another the king went a little way, and called Saint Patrick with feigned words, saying, "Come after me to Tara, that I may believe in thee in the presence of the men of Ireland." And straightway he set an ambush on every path from the Graves of Fecc's men to Tara, before Patrick to slay him. But God permitted not this to him.

But Saint Patrick, knowing the thought of the villainous king, blessed his companions, eight men and a lad, in the name of Jesus Christ and came to the king. And for protection of their bodies and their souls Patrick sang this hymn:

> At Tara to-day in this fateful hour
> I place all Heaven with its power,
> And the sun with its brightness,
> And the snow with its whiteness,
> And fire with all the strength it hath,
> And lightning with its rapid wrath,
> And the winds with their swiftness along their path,
> And the sea with its deepness,
> And the rocks with their steepness,
> And the earth with its starkness:
>   All these I place,
>   By God's almighty help and grace,
> Between myself and the powers of darkness.

The king counted them as they came and straightway a cloak of darkness went over them so that not a man of them appeared. Howbeit, the heathen who were hiding in the snares saw nought but eight stags and a fawn going as it were to the wilderness. And King Loiguire, with the few that had escaped, returned at dawn to Tara, sad, cowed, and humiliated.

Now on the next day, that is, the day of the Paschal feast, the kings and princes and magicians of all Ireland were sitting at meat in Loiguire's house, for the same day was the chiefest of their festivals. And as they were eating and drinking wine in the palace of Tara, and some were talking and others thinking of the things which had come to pass, Saint Patrick came, with five men only—the doors being shut, like as we read about Christ—to contend for the holy faith, and preach the word of God in Tara before all the tribes of the Irish people there gathered together.

So when Patrick appeared, he was invited by the heathen to partake of food, that they might prove him in respect of things that should come to pass. He, however, knowing the things that should come to pass, did not refuse to eat.

Now while all were feasting, the magician Lucetmael, who had taken part in the contest at night, was eager, even when his comrade Lochru was dead, to contend with Saint Patrick.

So Patrick and Lucetmael contended in trials and miracles. And each time the magician began his trial or his magical incantations the people marvelled at the great things which he could do. But each time, also, Patrick contended with a still greater miracle which offset all that Lucetmael had done, even to the test of fire.

Then all the people marvelled even more, and shouted aloud, and gave thanks. And in the end Lucetmael, like Lochru, was judged in the sight of the Most High and was no more. And Patrick said, "In this hour is all the heathenism of Ireland burnt up."

And the king was greatly enraged against Patrick, because of the death of his magician, and he almost rushed upon him, minding to slay him; but God hindered him.

For at the prayer of Patrick and at his cry, the wrath of God fell upon the ungodly people, and many of them perished.

And Saint Patrick said to the king, "Unless thou believest now, thou shalt die speedily, because the wrath of God will fall upon thy head."

And the king feared exceedingly, "and his heart was moved," and his whole city with him.

And so when the elders and all his senate were gathered together, King Loiguire said to them, "It is better for me to believe than to die." And after taking counsel, he believed on that day, and turned to the everlasting God of Israel; and many others believed as well.

And after all these things Saint Patrick, according to the command of the Lord Jesus, to "go and teach all nations, baptizing them in the name of the Father and of the Son and of the Holy Ghost," set out from Tara and preached, "the Lord working with him, and confirming the word with signs following."

TRANSLATED FROM THE LATIN BY HELEN WADDELL

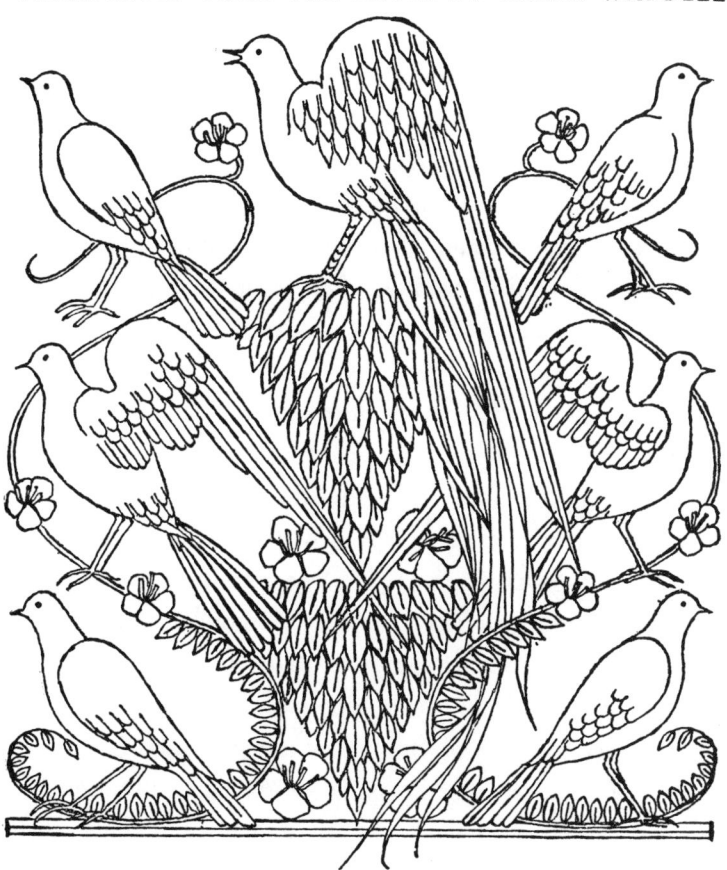

SAINT BRENDAN AND THE WHITE BIRDS

After voyaging many days, Saint Brendan and his brethren came to an island that was very fair and filled with flowers in bloom and trees in fruit. And when they sought a harbour where they might enter in, they found on the southern coast of the island a little river of sweet water running into the sea, and there they brought their ship to land. . . . Then Brendan said to his brethren, "Behold, our Lord Jesus Christ, the good, the merciful, hath given us this place wherein to abide His holy resurrection. My brothers, if we had naught else to restore our bodies, this spring alone would suffice us for meat and drink."

Now there was above the spring a tree of strange height, covered with birds of dazzling white, so crowded on the tree that scarcely could it be seen by human eyes. And looking upon it the man of God began to ponder within himself what cause had brought so great a multitude of birds together on one tree.

And so great was the bewilderment of his thoughts that he prayed with tears for the revealing of the mystery. . . . And even as the man of heavenly desires spoke within himself, behold one of the birds flew from the tree, and its wings rang against the ship, like the chiming of a bell: and perching on the highest part of the prow of the ship, it began to spread out its wings in token of inward joy, and to gaze with a placid regard upon the man of God. And straightway the man of God knew that the Lord had given heed to his prayer, and he spoke to the bird. "Inasmuch," said he, "as thou art God's servant and his messenger, then tell us whence came ye hither, and by whom was so mighty a multitude of birds gathered in one place."

And the bird spoke to him. "We are," it said, "of that great ruin of the ancient foe, who did not consent to him wholly. Yet because we consented in part to his sin, our ruin also befell. For God is just, and keepeth truth and mercy. And so by His judgment He sent us to this place, where we know no other pain than that we cannot see the presence of God, and so hath He estranged us from the fellowship of those who stood firm. On the solemn feasts and on the Sabbaths we take such bodies as ye see, and abide here, praising our Maker. And as other spirits who are sent through the divers regions of the air and the earth, so may we speed also. Now hast thou with thy brethren been one year upon thy journey: and six years yet remain. Where this day thou dost keep the Easter Feast, there shalt thou keep it throughout every year of thy pilgrimage, and thereafter shalt thou find the thing that thou hast set in thy heart, the land that was promised to the saints." And when the bird had spoken thus, it raised itself up from the prow, and took its flight to the rest.

And when the hour of evening drew on, then began all the birds that were on the tree to sing as with one voice, beating their wings and saying, *"Praise waiteth for Thee, O Lord, in Sion: and unto Thee shall the vow be performed."* And they continued repeating that verse, for the space of one hour. It seemed to the brethren that the melody and the sound of the wings was like a lament that is sweetly sung. Then said Saint Brendan to the brethren, "Do ye refresh your bodies, for this day have your souls been filled with the heavenly bread." And when the Feast was ended, the brethren began to sing the office: and thereafter they rested in quiet until the third watch of the night. Then the man of God awaking, began to rouse the brethren for the Vigils of the Holy Night. And when he had begun the verse, *"Lord open Thou my lips, and my heart shall show forth Thy praise,"* all the birds rang out with voice and wing, singing, *"Praise the Lord, all ye His angels: praise ye Him, all His hosts."* And even as at Vespers, they sang for the space of one hour. Then, when dawn brought the ending of the night, they all began to sing, *"And let the beauty of the Lord our God be upon us,"* with equal melody and length of chanting, as had been at Matins. At Tierce they sang this verse: *"Sing praises to God, sing praises: sing praises unto our King, sing praises: sing ye praises with understanding."* And at Sext they sang, *"Lord, lift up the light of Thy countenance upon us, and have mercy upon us."* At Nones they said, *"Behold how good and how pleasant it is for brethren to dwell together in unity."* And so day and night the birds sang praises to God. And through the octaves of the Feast they continued in the praises of God. . . .

Here then the brethren remained until the Whitsun Feast: for the sweet singing of the birds was their delight and their reviving. . . . But when the octave of the Feast was ended, the Saint bade his brethren to make ready the ship, and fill their vessels with water from the spring. And when all was made ready, came the aforesaid bird in swift flight, and rested on the prow of the ship, and said, as if to comfort them against the perils of the sea: "Know that where ye held the Lord's Supper, in the year that is past, there in like fashion shall ye be on that same night this year. . . . And after eight months ye shall find an island . . . whereon ye shall celebrate the Lord's Nativity." And when the bird had foretold these things, it returned to its own place.

Then the brethren began to spread their sails and go out to sea. And the birds were singing as with one voice, saying, *"Hear us, O God of our salvation, Who art the confidence of all the ends of the earth, and of them that are afar off upon the sea."* And so for three months they were borne on the breadth of ocean, and saw nothing beyond sea and sky.

PADRAIC COLUM

BRENDAN

On the third day from this (Saint Brendan said)
I will be where no wind that filled a sail
Has ever been, and it blew high or low:
For from this home-creek, from this body's close
I shall put forth: make ready, you, to go

With what remains to Cluan Hy-many,
For there my resurrection I'd have be.

But you will know how hard they'll strive to hold
This body o'me, and hold it for the place
Where I was bred, they say, and born and reared.
For they would have my resurrection here,
So that my sanctity might be matter shared
By every mother's child the tribeland polled
Who lived and died and mixed into the mould.

So you will have to use all canniness
To bring this body to its burial
When in your hands I leave what goes in clay:
The wagon that our goods are carried in—
Have it yoked up between the night and day,
And when the breath is from my body gone,
Bear body out, the wagon lay it on;

And cover it with gear that's taken hence—
"The goods of Brendan is what's here," you'll say
To those who'll halt you; they will pass you then:
Tinkers and tailors, soldiers, farmers, smiths,
You'll leave beside their doors—all those thwart men
For whom my virtue was a legacy
That they would profit in, each a degree—

As though it were indeed some chalice, staff;
Crozier, or casket, that they might come to,
And show to those who chanced upon the way,

And have, not knowing how the work was done
In scrolls and figures and in bright inlay:
Whence came the gold and silver that they prize,
The blue enamels and the turquoises!

I, Brendan, had a name came from the sea—
I was the first who sailed the outer main,
And past all forelands and all fastnesses!
I passed the voiceless anchorites, their isles,
Saw the ice-palaces upon the seas,
Mentioned Christ's name to men cut off from men,
Heard the whales snort, and saw the Kraken!

And on a wide-branched, green, and glistening tree
Beheld the birds that had been angels erst:
Between the earth and heaven 'twas theirs to wing:
Fallen from High they were, but they had still
Music of Heaven's Court: I heard them sing:
Even now that island of the unbeached coast
I see, and hear that white, resplendent host!

For this they'd have my burial in this place,
Their hillside, and my resurrection be
Out of the mould that they with me would share.
But I have chosen Cluan for my ground—
A happy place! Some grace came to me there:
And you, as you go towards it, to men say,
Should any ask you on that long highway:

"Brendan is here who had great saints for friends:
Ita, who reared him on a mother's knee,

Enda, who from his fastness blessed his sail;
Then Brighid, she who had the flaming heart,
And Colum-cille, prime of all the Gael;
Gildas of Britain, wisest child of light."
And saying this, drive through the falling night.

ADAPTED FROM THE SPANISH SETTLEMENTS, 1513-1561, BY WOODBURY LOWERY

PONCE DE LEON FINDS THE LAND OF FLOWERS

In the year 1513 came the famous expedition of Ponce de Leon. The conclusion of the Moorish wars had thrown out of employment a multitude of men, trained in arms and in the endurance of hardships, who swarmed over to the New World, prepared to conquer kingdoms for themselves and their followers. Of such was Juan Ponce de Leon, of noble blood and of one of the most ancient families of Spain.

Ponce had come over to Hispaniola in 1493 with Columbus on his second voyage. Some time later he heard from certain Indians that there was much gold in the neighboring island of Puerto Rico, and obtained leave to visit the island and to search for its wealth. In 1508 he crossed over to Puerto Rico in a small caravel and found many rich treasure rivers. Because of his discoveries he was appointed governor of the island, but he was not destined to remain long in command, for the king removed him from his office. Ponce found himself out of employment, but well provided with means, and with a still undaunted resolution to increase his possessions and extend his estate.

Ponce had heard of an island called Bimini, lying to the north of Hispaniola, in which there was reputed to be a spring of such marvellous virtue that all who drank of its waters were restored to youth and vigour. Here, then, was an opportunity for the scarred and battered warrior, fountains that would infuse young blood into his veins, gold that could be added to his already well-filled coffers, and lands peopled with willing subjects and obedient slaves. So Ponce, employing what influence he had at Court, obtained of Charles V a patent granting him the jurisdiction over the island for all his life.

On Tuesday, the 3d of March, 1513, Ponce set sail from the port of San German in Puerto Rico, taking with him Anton de Alaminos, a native of Palos, as pilot. The following night he stood away north-west by north and continued for eleven days sailing among the Lucayos, as the Bahamas were then called, until on the fourteenth of the same month he reached Guanahani, the San Salvador of Columbus's first landing, where he refitted a ship to cross the bay to the windward of the islands. From thence he steered northwest, and on Easter Sunday, the Spanish *Pasqua de Flores,* the 27th of March, he saw an island and passed it by. The three following days he held on in the same direction, when, the weather proving foul, he changed his course to west-north-west until Saturday the 2d of April, when, having reached a depth of nine fathoms at a distance of a league from land, for the water had grown shoal, he ran along the coast in search of a harbour and anchored at night in eight fathoms of water.

Beyond the shallowing green waters the waves rolled their white crests of foam up the long, hard, shell-paved beaches which formed a silver bar between the sea and the dense green verdure of the islands along which he was coasting. A thick forest of gray cypress, tulip, ash, and magnolia, with gnarled live-oak that reminded the strangers of the olive groves of their native land, clad the low sand-dunes and marches of the islands and cut the horizon with its dark canopy, above which floated the plumes of towering palm groves and the light tufts of the broom-pine. Between the islands the eye rested upon the glistening surface of sluggish lagoons, with brilliant borders of rush and sedge extending up to the very edge of the mysterious forest on the mainland.

It was the season of flowers. The perfumed breath of the white lily was wafted out to them from its humid haunts in the shady nooks of the islands; the fragrance of blooming orange groves, of sweet bays, of yellow jasmin, and of the sweet azalea filled the air. Upon the dark foliage, like flights of gaudy butterflies, lay spread masses of blue, crimson, and white, the blue flowers and coral berries of the *lycium salsum,* the andromeda and the azalea; along the inner shore, between the water's edge and the forest, the royal palmetto, crested with pyramids of silver-white blossom, thrust forth its sword-shaped leaves. Loons and Spanish curlews whirled overhead; in the woods strutted the wild turkey, saluting the dawn with noisy call from his perch on the lofty cypress or the magnolia, and many-hued humming-birds fluttered from flower to flower.

On some day between the 2d and 8th of April Ponce de Leon went ashore to get an interpreter and take possession. Impressed with its beauty and pleasant groves, and believing it to be an island, he named the land Florida, because he had discovered it at Easter-tide,—the Easter of Flowers.

Of the attendant ceremony there is no record. Perhaps, on landing, clad in his battered armour, Ponce offered the simple prayer said to have been used by Columbus, and from whose lips he may have learned it. And then, grasping in his left hand the unfurled banner of Castile and Leon, and with drawn sword in his right, he planted the royal standard upon the soil and proclaimed in a loud voice to the unheeding oaks and palms and to the attendant crews of his caravels the seizure of the land in the name of his king, while he called upon all present to bear witness to his act.

At last they resolved to return to Hispaniola and Puerto Rico. On his way back, Ponce evidently retraced part of his former course through the Florida Keys. Ranging back and forth until the 23d of September, Ponce refitted his ships, and sent one of them under the command of Ortubia, with Anton de Alaminos as pilot, in search of the island of Bimini, while he himself returned to Puerto Rico where he was subsequently joined by Ortubia with the caravel, who had discovered the island in search of which he had been sent, but not the wonderful rejuvenating spring reputed to be in it.

Thus ended the first attempt of the Spaniards to reconnoitre and possess the coasts of North America.

CONSTANCE D'ARCY MACKAY

THE FOUNTAIN OF YOUTH

A FANTASY

CHARACTERS:

The Guardian of the Fountain   Ponce de Leon
A Daughter of the Dawn   Silva
Other Daughters of the Dawn   Cordoba } His followers

PLACE—*Florida.*
TIME—*The spring of 1513.*

SCENE—*A clearing in a forest wrought by nature, not by man. Trees right, left, and background, with deep ferns and forest tangle amidst the tree-trunks. Moss and vines swing from the branches of the trees.*

Enter from the right, to the strains of Mendelssohn's "Spring Song," the DAUGHTERS OF THE DAWN, *clad in Neo-Grecian robes of pale and deep pink, the varying shades of dawn color. They are shod with pink sandals. Their hair falls about their shoulders. Their dance resembles a dance of the hours. As it ends they turn toward right with gestures of obeisance, and presently from right enters* THE GUARDIAN OF THE FOUNTAIN, *robed in white, with silver sandals, and the Morning Star caught in her hair. She holds aloft, as one would hold a grail, a crystal cup in which sparkles water from the Fountain of Youth. Instantly she becomes the center of a dance of worship, to the strains of Lack's "Idyllo." Throughout the dance she holds the mystic cup within her hands, and toward the end of the dance turns again to right, and exits, followed by the* DAUGHTERS OF THE DAWN.

As they exeunt, from left appear PONCE DE LEON, SILVA, *and* CORDOBA. *Their clothing, once splendid, is now worn and stained with travel.* PONCE DE LEON, *in dull crimson, is a man of middle age, with noble bearing and a questing look.* SILVA, *with rusty cuirass and dark-green cloak, is younger, and discouraged-looking.* CORDOBA *is old and rugged, with white hair and the look of a mariner.*

His costume is midnight blue. There are huge gold rings in his ears.

PONCE DE LEON: *
I thought that I heard music! 'Twas a dream.
CORDOBA:
A dream wrought of fatigue and endless search:
I pray thee let us rest us here a little.
I followed thee from Spain to Porto Rico,
Across strange seas, guided by unknown stars,
But never on such bitter quest as this.
PONCE DE LEON:
To find the Fountain of immortal Youth—
Ye call *that* bitter? All our nights and days
Of weariness shall be a story told
When once we taste of it.
CORDOBA:
                  Oh, Ponce de Leon,
I would that we were back in sunny Spain!
    [CORDOBA *and* SILVA *sit on fallen tree-trunk, left foreground.* CORDOBA *drinks from a leather flask and passes it to* SILVA. *As these two talk* PONCE DE LEON *looks raptly before him.*]
SILVA:
And half a league behind us there lie men
Outwearied in a search for what has proved
A hope like fool's fire, leading on and on.
PONCE DE LEON:
So said ye when I sought the Western Ind,

  * The English pronunciation of the name is used.

But this— Ah, this! Dost thou remember it,
The golden day when first we heard of it?
And an old mariner with sea-bright eyes
And bronzèd face all scarred with ocean storms
Whispered that in the new Americas
Bubbled a fountain crystal clear, whose taste
Was nectar of the gods: and, like the gods,
Whoso should taste of it should ne'er grow old.
And is it strange that this, the youngest land,
Should hold Youth's Fountain? Count us fortunate
That we are bound on such a mighty quest.
CORDOBA [*with utter weariness*]:
Fortunate!
PONCE DE LEON:
    Have not all things smiled on us?
Did we not find this land on Easter day?
A blessed omen! And I christened it
Florida. Flower of Easter!
SILVA [*darkly*]:
      What of thorns?
Hunger, fatigue, stark thirst, and aching limbs?
PONCE DE LEON:
Why, look ye, if I find that fountain-head
There'll be no age, nor any grief, nor pain;
Only immortal Youth for all the world.
Others have sought for riches or for lands,
Or honor for their sovereigns, rank, and fame.
But I seek Youth, the lodestar of mankind—
Yea, what are all discoveries to this:—
To keep the thrill and rapture of life's dawn,

Feet that outrun the winds, adventurous hearts
All unencompassed by the chill of age;
To know this flesh will ne'er be witherèd,
Nor this strong arm weakened by passing years.
Go back to where the camp-fire shines for ye,
For this is my adventure. Leave me here.
I will rejoin ye later in the day.
Farewell.
CORDOBA [*to* SILVA, *who is half reluctant*]:
Come, Silva, let us leave him here.
> [PONCE DE LEON *stands with his back to them, searching with eagle glance the country before him.* CORDOBA *and* SILVA, *with a backward glance or two, exeunt, left. As soon as* PONCE DE LEON *feels that they are gone he strides abruptly forward. As he nears the spot where the fountain is concealed the* DAUGHTERS OF THE DAWN, *led by one of their number, suddenly appear, to bar his passage. For an instant, as he were dreaming,* PONCE DE LEON *brushes his hand across his eyes.*]

A DAUGHTER OF THE DAWN:
Beware, rash mortal. Do not touch this spot.
PONCE DE LEON:
Who are ye, maidens?
A DAUGHTER OF THE DAWN:
    Daughters of the Dawn.
PONCE DE LEON [*gladly*]:
Then by your presence I have found the place
That holds the Fountain of immortal Youth.

[*As he speaks* THE GUARDIAN OF THE FOUN-
TAIN, *this time without the crystal cup, appears be-
fore him, beautiful and imperious.*]
And who art thou?
THE GUARDIAN OF THE FOUNTAIN:
    The guard perpetual,
The spirit of the Fountain callèd Youth.
PONCE DE LEON:
Thine eyes hold glory that doth dazzle me!
Give me to drink.
  [*As he speaks the* DAUGHTERS OF THE DAWN
withdraw a little, so that what ensues lies between
PONCE DE LEON *and* THE GUARDIAN OF
THE FOUNTAIN.]
THE GUARDIAN OF THE FOUNTAIN:
    Wilt thou snatch Youth from me?
For if this spring is touched by mortal lips
It vanisheth. No more, for all the world,
Shall there be Youth.
PONCE DE LEON:
    And I?
THE GUARDIAN OF THE FOUNTAIN:
    Adventurer,
Thou shalt have Youth. But think at what a cost
Thou, out of all the world, shalt Youth possess!
PONCE DE LEON [*unheeding*]:
Youth everlasting! Now at last I win!
I, Ponce de Leon, whom men called a fool
For following lost hopes! I win! I win!

Yea, in a moment I shall hold the cup
Within these hands and quaff supernal fire!
Guard of the Fountain—
THE GUARDIAN OF THE FOUNTAIN:
     Wilt thou rob the world?
The sweetness and the promise of the earth?
I pray thee wait. Shall all the world lose youth
Because one man would be for ever young?
Adventurer, bethink thee what thou dost!
PONCE DE LEON:
Have I crossed unknown seas, and have I borne
Despair and thirst and weariness for this—
To hear the Guardian of the Fount itself
Cry, "Wait a little!"
      [*With greatening passion.*]
   Saints! Have I not waited
And heard the tread of the invincible years
Like armies passing me? I *will* be young,
Cost what it may! Bring thou the cup to me.
I am the conqueror! I alone had faith!
And for my faith the cup is my reward!
Give me to drink, or else by this my sword
I wrest it from thee. Wilt thou serve me here,
Or must I snatch it from the fount itself?

  [*As* PONCE DE LEON *has been speaking he has taken a step or two forward. His words have drawn the* DAUGHTERS OF THE DAWN *forward from sheer terror. They stand lined at each side of* THE GUARDIAN OF THE FOUNTAIN, *who still bars* PONCE DE LEON'S *way. At his last words the*

DAUGHTERS OF THE DAWN *shrink as from a blow.*]
THE DAUGHTERS OF THE DAWN [*with a cry, poignantly*]:
Ai!
THE GUARDIAN OF THE FOUNTAIN:
Inexorably my fate compels
That I must serve. I bid thee wait.
> [*Exeunt* THE GUARDIAN OF THE FOUNTAIN *and the* DAUGHTERS OF THE DAWN, *right. The first part of the "Idyllo" is played very faintly and very slowly, as if all the rapture had gone from it.* PONCE DE LEON, *left alone, speaks triumphantly.*]

PONCE DE LEON:
A moment, and I am forever young!
A Queen of Egypt melted pearls in wine.
That was a drink for slaves compared to this!
> [*Re-enter* THE GUARDIAN OF THE FOUNTAIN *and the* DAUGHTERS OF THE DAWN. *The music ceases. The* DAUGHTERS OF THE DAWN *stand at the edge of the forest.* THE GUARDIAN OF THE FOUNTAIN *approaches* PONCE DE LEON, *the crystal cup held straight before her. She speaks with icy scorn.*]

THE GUARDIAN OF THE FOUNTAIN:
Look, thou, adventurer! Behold the cup!
Drink to the doom of youth! To glory dead!
Drink to the ending of all loveliness!
Drink to the quenching of that sacred fire
By which the world has warmed its dying hopes

And quickened them to life again. *Drink deep!*
> [*She gives him the cup. He takes it exultantly, holding it upward to the light as one who can scarcely gaze his fill.* THE GUARDIAN OF THE FOUNTAIN *watches him, statue-like, but the* DAUGHTERS OF THE DAWN *are a frieze of alternating hope and despair.* PONCE DE LEON *starts to put the cup to his lips, then hesitates.*]

PONCE DE LEON [*to himself*]:
Something . . . I know not what . . . would stay my hand.
> [*Once more he raises the cup sunward, then brings it toward his lips with an ecstatic gesture.*]

This, to my triumph!
> [*He is about to drink when very faintly, like a magic whisper, the notes of the "Spring Song" steal on the air. He lowers his hand as if an echo haunted him.*]

"Wilt thou rob the world,
The sweetness and the promise of the earth?"
> [*The music ceases.*]

Lo! How it sparkles! Mingled flame and dew!
One draught! One taste!
> [*He puts it resolutely to his lips.* THE GUARDIAN OF THE FOUNTAIN *and the* DAUGHTERS OF THE DAWN *veil their faces, standing like a Greek frieze. Once more the "Spring Song" echoes, a mere thread of sound.*]

"No more for all the world
shall there be—"
> [*He stops. The music dies.*]

Pah!

[*He turns savagely to* THE GUARDIAN OF THE FOUNTAIN.]
    Thy words have poisoned it!
Made it a thing unclean for me to touch—
How shall I drink, knowing I rob the world?
How shall I quench the only spark of hope
The gray earth keeps?
  [*Half-unbelieving joy flashes across the faces of the* DAUGHTERS OF THE DAWN *and* THE GUARDIAN OF THE FOUNTAIN.]
    Spirit, take back the cup!
[THE GUARDIAN OF THE FOUNTAIN *starts forward.*]
No! No! I spoke in jest. Oh, bitter Youth,
 [*To himself, deeply.*]
It is so short, and stays so short a time.
THE GUARDIAN OF THE FOUNTAIN [*with grave gentleness*]:
And therefore is immortal.
PONCE DE LEON [*torn*]:
    Ah, must I
Give up what I have searched for?
THE GUARDIAN OF THE FOUNTAIN [*immovable, but with her eyes on his*]:
    'Tis with thee
The matter rests. Wilt thou condemn the world?
 [*She stretches out her arms in pleading; there is a moment's silence.*]
PONCE DE LEON [*as if the words were torn from him*]:
No!

THE GUARDIAN OF THE FOUNTAIN [*with passion*]:
    By this Fountain, spoken like a man!
This land shall ever be a land of youth
To all the nations! Thou hast purchased it,
Oh, great adventurer! Knight of Ocean-Sea,
Courageous captain!
    [*She takes the cup from him.*]
PONCE DE LEON [*miserably*]:
            Ah, what shall I say
When men taunt: "Did ye find the goal ye sought,
Proud Ponce de Leon? For Americus,
Cabato, and Magellan did succeed,
Yes, and Columbus, against heavy odds.
So, Ponce de Leon, why have ye come back
With empty hands?" How shall I answer them
In verity?
THE GUARDIAN OF THE FOUNTAIN:
            Say, *I have dreamed a dream.*
Not now, but later, shall my dream come true.
So long, so long as dreamers build their dreams
Without a thought of gain shall Youth endure
Here in this land. Oh, brave adventurer,
Face thou men's scorn as thou hast faced the waves,
And for a greater reason. Now, farewell!
PONCE DE LEON [*his eyes on her*]:
But it goes hard to part with thee at last!
Oh, Youth! Lost Youth! Fountain of dreams, farewell!
    [*He bows his head.* THE GUARDIAN OF THE
    FOUNTAIN *with a last look returns to the dim forest,* the DAUGHTERS OF THE DAWN *fading*

after her, a dim glimmer through the trees. Just as they vanish SILVA *and* CORDOBA *appear at edge of woods, left.* SILVA *holds a string of fish.*]

CORDOBA:
We have come back. Good news! We found a lake.

SILVA:
A lake with fish in it. A mighty catch!
   [*He holds up the fish.*]

CORDOBA [*rubbing his hands delightedly*]:
Strength to renew the search!

PONCE DE LEON:
                    Nay, search no more.
It was a dream that led me, and the dream ends here.
   [*They are about to question him, but something in his demeanor stops them. He walks on gravely, toward left. They follow.*]

CORDOBA:
       No Fountain, Silva!

SILVA:
              And no Youth!

CORDOBA:
Eh! Eh! Said I not so?

SILVA:
              And yet he looks
Uplift, as he had found the Fount itself!
   [*To the first bars of Grieg's "Death of Ase"* THE GUARDIAN OF THE FOUNTAIN *and the* DAUGHTERS OF THE DAWN *look out in pity, then they silently withdraw.* PONCE DE LEON *and his followers exit, and the stage is left vacant.*

CAROL RYRIE BRINK

WAKING-UP TIME

Sally had never been up so early before. She shivered into her clothes in the grey light and hurried to brush her hair, for Avis was ready and waiting for her. Avis had attended the Easter sunrise service many times, but Sally had never gone before, and she was excited. Just as she finished brushing her hair the church bell began to ring. It sounded deep and solemn. How queer and grey the things outside looked without the sun's bright face! She took Avis' hand and walked sedately, feeling grown-up in her new white gloves.

"The earth is still asleep," said Avis.

"But the birds know it will soon be bright. Listen to them!" whispered Sally. In the shadowy trees the birds were twittering.

The church was all lighted by candles and full of the smell of spring flowers. But it, too, seemed strange and mysterious before sunrise. Sally sat very still listening to the familiar story of the three women who came so early in the morning to Jesus' tomb. How sad it must have been for them to think of Jesus sleeping there! And how surprised they must have been to see the angel sitting by the empty tomb!

"He is risen!" cried the angel's happy voice. "He is risen!" And then, thought Sally, the sun must have begun to shine, just as it was shining now in little golden ruffles on the tree-tops outside. And the birds, which had been only twittering before, must have burst into happy song, just as the great organ now burst into happy music.

The church bells began to ring again, and now they sounded full of joy. They said: "Come! Awake! Jesus is risen! Springtime is here again. Awake, sleepy world, awake!"

As soon as Sally got home, she took off her new white gloves, and went to the chicken yard to see if there were eggs for breakfast. Perhaps it was because she had taken off her gloves, but now she no longer wanted to walk sedately. She felt so wide-awake and happy that she wanted to skip and hop and run. Out in the chicken yard there was a great clucking and chattering.

"What is the matter out here?" asked Sally. "Don't you know that this is Easter morning?"

"Oh, yes indeed!" crowed the big red rooster. "That's why we are rejoicing! Spring is here! Winter is past and the waking-up time has come again."

"See!" clucked the brown hen. "My babies have come out of their shells to-day, and I am happy!"

"Peep! peep! peep!" cried the baby chicks. "For a long time we slept in little dark, prison-houses. But now we have broken their walls and come into the sunshine, and we are happy, too!"

"Do you have any eggs for my breakfast?" asked Sally.

"Follow me," clucked the little white hen with the bright, black eyes. So Sally followed her into the chicken house and peeped into the nests. Every nest had a round white egg in it, and soon Sally's apron was full.

"Thank you! thank you!" cried Sally gaily, "and happy Easter to you all!"

Sally had to walk very carefully with an apron full of eggs. But, when she had put them all in a bowl without cracking one, she was ready to skip outdoors again and pick some flowers for the breakfast table. The rhubarb plant in the corner of the garden seemed to have sprung up by magic since the day before.

"I am awake! I am awake! Take me!" he cried, spreading his wide leaves to the sun.

"You aren't a bouquet," laughed Sally. "Just you wait, sometime when you have grown a little more I'll pick you for a pie."

As she crossed the lawn to the tulip bed, Sally suddenly

paused and held her breath. There at the edge of the lawn sat a wild brown rabbit. He looked at Sally with round, gentle eyes.

"Oh," said Sally softly, "I thought you would be afraid." The rabbit made no noisy sounds of joy such as the chickens did, but Sally knew by the way he twitched his whiskers and cocked his ears that he was happy, too. He looked at her as much as to say: "It is waking-up time, and there are pleasant green things to eat, and I am very happy, and not afraid of anything!" With a frisk of his white tail, he turned and hopped away.

"Good-bye, brown bunny. Happy Easter to you!" called Sally.

The tulips stood in pleasant rows lifting their crimson cups toward the blue sky.

"We are giving thanks, Sally," they seemed to say. "Lift your eyes to the blue sky and give thanks, too. It is waking-up time and we are glad. Last autumn we were round, brown bulbs. We lay in the ground and slept. Snow covered us and frost chilled us. We thought we should never wake up again. But now the spring sun and rain have given us new life. We have put on our brightest colors to show our joy."

Sally picked three of the brightest tulips for the breakfast table. The sun poured in across the white table cloth and shone on Sally's blue egg cup with the round, white egg in it. Sally looked up at the blue sky and saw a happy bird fly across it singing.

She folded her hands, and bowed her head, and said: "Dear Lord, we thank thee for waking-up time. Amen."

ELIZABETH COATSWORTH

APRIL

Jean, Lydia and Mark, with Father and Cousin Mary, make up a happy family living near Boston. Each month of the twelve brings some delightful experience to them. This story tells what happened in April.

It was dark still when Father woke them. The electric lights were on, and the windows showed a dull gray.

"What's the matter?" asked Lydia.

"The house is on fire!" Jean shrilled dramatically, leaping out of her bed. "Don't be silly, Lydia. It's only Easter."

"And we're going down to Nantasket to see the sun rise," Lydia murmured, yawning. "Oh, dear, bed feels so good! Why does the sun have to rise so early?"

Mark kept falling asleep every time they woke him. Finally his sisters dressed him pretty much as they would dress a rag doll.

"Do you want to be left behind?" Jean asked, and Mark woke up a little to stare at her owlishly.

"Me too," he muttered before his head fell sideways once more against her shoulder.

But some milk and bread and jam in the kitchen roused him. He was fond of eating. It was very exciting to be awake and getting up in the dark this way. Even Cousin Mary was gayer than usual as they bundled into their coats. From the barn came the sound of Father backing out the Dragon, and a soft toot of the horn to tell them that he was ready.

They drove along a deserted highway with the wind stirring in the new leaves of the trees. The light was paling now and one could scarcely see the stars.

"We're a little late," said Father. "It will be a race between us and the sun to see which will get to Nantasket first."

The road was clear and the Dragon fairly flew along. Once they passed a truck drawn to the side of the road, with the dim figure of the driver asleep on the front seat. Once a cat, out hunting, slipped across the road ahead of

them. A sea gull drifted overhead through the dim light.
"Oh, hurry! Oh, hurry!" breathed Jean, the impatient.
"It's like the ride from Ghent to Aix," said Lydia.

> *"Not a word to each other; we kept the great pace*
> *Neck by neck, stride by stride, never changing*
> *our place."*

Mark, in the back seat with the other children, caught the spirit and brought both hands down on his father's shoulders with a sudden bang.

"If you do that again, I'm likely to gallop right into the ditch!" Father protested.

The sky was getting *very* light now. Father switched off the headlights and pressed his foot down on the throttle. The Dragon sprang ahead faster still. Cousin Mary gave a little gasp to herself, and the children sucked in their breaths with excitement. They had never driven so fast in their lives. They were charging east to meet the sun. They had an appointment with it at the edge of the ocean.

They were in time. The roller-coaster tracks looped visibly against the sky—they could see the shapes of the empty shuttered pavilions which would come alive with the summer—but the sun itself had not appeared over the horizon.

Father drove right to the sea wall and brought the Dragon to a halt; and they all jumped out and hurried down to the sand, which was gray and lifeless in this light. The air smelled of the waves which broke and seethed along the shore, and now, just as they stopped at the edge of the wet sand, something narrow and bright appeared on the horizon. The lights at Boston Light and Minot's, which had been revolving in their towers, went out and, instead, the sun shed its beams across the waters.

It rose very fast. Now they could see half its orb, and now three-quarters.

"The sun should dance on Easter morning," Cousin Mary remarked suddenly. "It's a very old belief."

Dance? Lydia expected to see the sun bound about in the sky, and dance a formal dance like a minuet. It certainly didn't do that, but, as she watched hard, the sun seemed to change—now its rays spread out, now they contracted again, and the waves that just touched its rim seemed to be dancing, too.

"It *is* dancing!" she cried. "It *is* dancing!" and a queer wild joy filled her at the sight of the sun dancing over the sea.

"That's only the mist. It's like the heat waves on a road," said Jean.

But Lydia was not disturbed. The sun could be doing what it wanted to for Jean. It was dancing for Lydia, and the ocean was its floor, and all over the country people were singing as they first saw its light. Now people along the coast who had gathered on the hills would be holding services, and then, as the earth rolled slowly eastward, the people on the Great Lakes would take up the song, and then those along the Mississippi, and then on the Rockies, and then by the shores of the Pacific they would all be singing. She set up a soft murmuring of her own, not very appropriate— "Onward, Christian soldiers"—and the sun sparkled and shone and danced in time to her singing.

And then suddenly it was just daylight and they were

all hungry, and the Dragon drove them soberly home again —past houses where people were beginning to open their kitchen doors to take in the morning milk bottles.

Mark had gone to sleep in a nice kitteny ball, and Jean yawned.

"That was fine," she said.

But Lydia said nothing. She thought that when you saw the sun dancing on Easter morning you should keep still and think about it.

The whole day was wonderful. They ate two breakfasts, which was exciting in itself, and they had spring hats to wear to church. At dinner Father disappeared mysteriously in the direction of the icebox, and returned with a platter on which sat an Easter bunny of chocolate ice cream among green pistachio grass.

Then Jean brought out a large bag of jellybean candies, shaped like eggs of every color. She had saved her allowance to buy them and had kept her secret. The egg hunt was her treat, but it was very hard to decide whether she wanted to hide eggs or to help hunt for them.

Finally she chose to have Father hide them because he was sure to find hard places. It was so warm outdoors that he hid the little eggs all over the lawn and garden, up in the crotches of the apple trees, and in and out of the paling fence. Cousin Mary and Mark hunted together and put their eggs into one basket; but, even with their four eyes, Jean was quicker and found more eggs than anyone else, and Cousin Mary gave her for a prize a little rosebush in a pot which she was bringing up on the kitchen window sill.

"It's got a bud! It's got a bud!" cried Jean, who loved

flowers. "Oh, that's a very Eastery present, Cousin Mary!"

Lydia looked at the rose admiringly, but she preferred dancing suns and ponies. She hadn't tried for a prize very hard. Some of the eggs she had found she had left where they were.

"I'll leave a few for the squirrels," she thought. "They have very few surprises."

But she was a child who was fond of sweets, and a little later, when she had eaten all the candies in her basket, she collected a few more which she knew about.

"There are still some left to surprise the squirrels," she explained to herself. "But if I stay here there won't be," she added.

It was she who suggested that they should all go for a little walk.

"Not far, Cousin Mary," she said. "You've *got* to come, too. It's so warm, and all the gold things are out to do the sun honor—the daffodils and the forsythia and everything. We won't walk fast."

Out on the sidewalk they found that it was a more golden day even than they had expected. It was very warm for the middle of April and there were no clouds between them and the radiant sun. The pollen from the elm blossoms here and there had fallen on the sidewalks in yellow carpets, and there were whole hedges of forsythia and banks of daffodils and a few leftover crocuses.

They took the road which led over the hill and down again, because the children wanted to visit the little pond under its willows beside the road, hoping to hear the spring peepers.

"Some people say," said Jean, "that the pond hasn't any bottom."

"It *has* to have a bottom, doesn't it, Father?" argued Lydia, though she liked the idea of a pond without a bottom.

"Anyway, they've tried and tried and let down weighted ropes as far as they could and never found bottom."

Lydia this afternoon took the practical side.

"How long were the ropes?" she asked.

"How should I know?" cried Jean. "It was a long time ago."

Mark was kicking a loose stone ahead of him while he walked, and had to be stopped because they were passing another group of people. He refused to leave his stone, however, and stood ready to scream if he were dragged on without it, so they all waited until the others had gone by.

"Do you remember that the Andersons put their goldfish in the pond when they went away last summer?" Cousin Mary asked.

"Lots of people do," said Jean, "and Jim Carson let out one of those little Japanese turtles here."

They had come to the dark mirror of the pond, with lawn on one side and old trees on the other three, a little piece of wild New England which had scarcely noticed that a town had grown up about it. First it had known deer coming to drink, and Indians stopping by its side to fill their hands with its water. Then cows had begun to use the deer trails, and farm children skated on its ice in winter and built bonfires by its little shore. Now only the dogs and the birds came here to drink, and it heard the hum of the passing cars like the distant waves on the beach. But the pond was not disturbed. Small and wild and quiet, it lived as it had—reflecting the sky and keeping its own secrets.

Perhaps it was because this was Easter day and the first really warm day of the spring that the pond was willing to show one of its loveliest secrets for once.

"Why, look at the leaves!" exclaimed Cousin Mary. "But they're so yellow! They look like autumn."

"Where?" asked Father.

"All through the water," explained Cousin Mary. "Willow leaves, they must be."

Jean was climbing up the fence which guarded the sidewalk from the pond's steep bank.

"They're moving!" she cried. "They *aren't* leaves, Cousin Mary! They're goldfish."

It seemed scarcely believable, but goldfish they were. As long as Father's hand, or no longer than Mark's finger, they lay in groups close to the surface, enjoying the sun. They did look like willow leaves drifting together, now three or four in a group, now twenty or more. The children had passed the pond several times a week, and had always paused to look down into it; but they had never before seen anything like this, nor would they again. Later they might make out a few fish, dulled by brown water, but never again these bright myriads, close to the very roof of the water with the Easter sun shining along their golden scales.

It was as she stood gazing down at the pond that Lydia felt sure that the sun on Easter day was really magic. At dawn it could rise and dance on the horizon, and in the afternoon it could turn even their little pond to golden life at its touch.

MARGUERITE DE ANGELI

ANIELA'S EASTER

Aniela, a little Polish girl, lives "up the hill" in a Pennsylvania mining town. Tadck, her brother, works in the mine; but he loves to draw pictures and his great ambition is to become an artist. The painter who has come to decorate a wall in the church and Uncle Stan, who is studying to be a doctor and who always has exciting things to tell about his life in the city, also have a part in the story. Then there is

Mamusia and there is Father—Aniela calls him Tatuś—who gives music lessons and who plays the organ for the Easter service.

February finally blew itself out and March came in, warm and sunny. Buds began to swell, the willows put on a yellow mist, and down in the meadow, where the creek flowed free again, spring flowers bloomed. Tadek took pencil and paper with him on a Sunday afternoon walk and sketched the tumbledown sheds that stood beside the creek. Aniela wanted to take off her long winter underwear, but Mama wouldn't let her, and a good thing it was, for cold, wintry days came again, and the warm stove felt good, especially after Mama kept the windows open while she cleaned the house.

Aniela carried water from the pump until her arms ached. She scrubbed with the brush until it was worn down almost to the wood, but still Mama found more to do. The windowpanes were so bright and clear it looked almost as if they weren't there, and the sash curtains were clean and so stiff with starch that they stood out like Aniela's petticoats. The woodwork was scrubbed until the paint was gone around the doorknobs and on the window sills. The stoves were blackened and polished and the bright trim rubbed until it glittered.

Mama's house plants stood on the floor away from the cold, but where the sun could reach them, so they would be blooming for Easter.

Every night Aniela and Mama quickly cleared the table, so that Tad could have it for his work. Father often sat at the other end to write the parts he had arranged for the Easter music. Sometimes he got out the cello and tried over the parts. When Father played, the music made Tad's pencil fly and Aniela's needle go in and out faster than ever on the new embroidery she was doing.

Sometimes Mama stopped to look at her work, and once she said:

"Be careful, child, you are going over the line there! Go slowly. Now, you had better take out that last bit."

Aniela heaved a great sigh. Take out all those tiny stitches?

"Oh Mama, must I?" she begged. "I will *never* get it done!"

"You know the old saying," Mama said firmly. "Whatever is done in a hurry, is done in the Evil One's fashion!"

Aniela began to rip out the stitches. She looked at Tad, who never seemed to tire of his drawing but patiently worked and rubbed it out when it did not please him, then drew it again. It was not perfect, of course, but when he had finished, it was the best he could do.

Already he was doing better work. When he wanted to draw one of the miners he looked at Father as the painter had told him to do to see how a man should look. Sometimes he talked out what he was thinking to Aniela.

"See how much broader Tatuś is across the shoulders than Mamusia," he would say. "See how much bigger his hands are, and how much stronger his features." Aniela didn't understand all he said, but it sounded as if he knew a great deal.

Once he had made a sketch of Babcia feeding her geese. He showed her round, plump face with the kerchief tied under her chin. He drew it in pencil but in his mind he painted it in color. The painter liked that one especially.

Mama was making a new dress for Aniela so she would be gay and bright for Easter.

"All the world puts on a new spring dress for that happy day," said Mama. "And it is right that we should be bright and gay, too, if we are able." When Aniela tried the dress on, she didn't want to take it off.

On the way from school the next day she told the girls about how pretty it was. Cecilia said she would have a new dress for Easter too, and Sue said, "Oh, so have *I* got a new dress."

"I'm going to have a new hat," Cecilia said. "A big wide one with roses on it."

They stopped to look in the milliner's window and choose which hats they liked best. Straw hats seemed a little out of place when it was so cold, but when Aniela was telling Mama about the ones they had seen, she said, "Easter is early this year, and if it is this cold, straw hats will look silly, but I guess women's pride will keep them warm. I suppose since the other girls are having new hats, you want one, too, is that it?"

"Could I have one, *could* I, Mamusia? Could it be a straw-colored one with blue flowers to match my dress? Please, Mamusia!" Aniela put her arms coaxingly around Mamusia's broad waist. Mama gave her a spank and said, as she changed her cold iron for a hot one: "Go on with your dear mamusias. Am I only your 'dear mamusia' when you want something, then?"

"Oh, no, Mamusia, oh, no, you are always my dear mamusia. But—*could* I have a new hat?"

"We shall see, my Anielcia; perhaps, but these spring hats cost so much. Right now iron these last curtains for me." She went on with her other work while Aniela ironed.

When Father came he brought a letter from Stan. It was easier for Papa to read, so he opened it, and something fell out of the envelope.

"Money," said Papa. "It is a money order! Since when has Stan had money to send home to you?"

"Read! Read!" said Mama. "Read and find out!"

Papa read the letter. In it Stan told how hard he was working to get through by June. How he had been appointed to stay at the University hospital as interne, and how he had earned some extra money, teaching.

"So," he wrote, "I am sending a little present for you, my sister, for Easter, since I cannot come home. Use the money any way you like."

Papa handed the money order to Mama, who looked at it in wonder.

It had seemed so long to look ahead when Stan began his course at the University! Mama could scarcely believe that it was nearly over, the years had passed so quickly.

"Now," said Papa, "you can soon stop going to the factory. Stan will be a real doctor and will not need your help."

Aniela was disappointed that Stan was not coming home. He always came home for Easter. "But," she thought, "since he has sent Mama money, maybe she will take some of it to buy me a hat!" She went on thinking of those she had seen in the milliner's window and of which one she liked best. Then she remembered how long Mama had worn her old one, and how hard she had worked to help Stan through. She remembered how Tad wanted money for paints and how little she had saved in the pig bank. There were only thirty-six pennies! Tad had told her that one tube of oil paint was worth more than that!

She was ashamed, but she did want the new hat for Easter.

Mama and Papa bent over the money order.

"It says 'ten dollars,'" said Papa. "That's a lot of money for Easter." When Mama folded the little piece of green paper and put it away in her sewing box without saying anything, Aniela was sure there would be no new hat for her.

The days grew longer and the sun warmer. Mama's flowers began to open. The house was sweet with their odor. Every week Aniela had more eggs to sell. Sometimes Dziadek brought them. Sometimes Aniela went for them.

Father had given Tad a whole list of orders for the eggs he was decorating. He worked at them every evening. When they were finished it was Holy Week and he took a pound of butter to carve a lamb for Easter. He followed a picture Mama had of the lamb with the cross. Mama put it in the cold where it would keep till the day before Easter when it would be put on the table with the other food to be blessed: the eggs, the salt, the bread, the sausage and the ham studded with cloves.

Every moment he could spare, Tad spent with the painter. Whenever he had an afternoon free, he was at the church, and once he came home so full of excitement that he took

Mamusia by the arms and waltzed her around until she was dizzy.

"What do you think!" he exclaimed. "I really helped to paint the picture on the church wall! And what else do you think? The painter gave me some of his own paints! And wait till you see! Just wait! There is another surprise! You are to come early on Holy Thursday afternoon, and the painter will take the covering off and let you see the picture because it is something special. You'll see!" He let go of Mama suddenly and she almost fell into the chair, she was so dizzy. But he wouldn't tell what the surprise was.

When Thursday arrived, Mama came home from the mill at noon. Tad was home from his work, and he and Aniela were ready and waiting. Father had gone.

The painter was waiting for them and had moved the great cloth covering from the wall. In the picture at one side were the miners in their blackened clothes, their faces tired and dirty, looking toward a shining light.

At the other side was a field of waving grain with flowers growing at the edge, and standing knee deep in blossoms were happy people, men, women, and children, in the dress of the different countries from which they had come. They, too, were looking toward the light. There were Bohemians, Slovaks, Poles, and Russians. There were Welsh and English, Scotch and Germans; all the many nationalities that go to make up America.

Tad turned toward Aniela. Just then Father tiptoed from the chancel to stand beside her.

Tad looked at Mama to see what she would say.

But Mamusia said nothing.

She only stood still and looked at the picture. For there, right in front, standing among the daisies, was her *own Aniela* in the striped Polish dress!

When they reached home Father said:

"This painting—I guess you are right, Mamusia. The boy should not be wasting his time in the mine. Stan is almost through. We can go on now to help Tad. The painter says he can get him into a school in Philadelphia if we can give him his living. I had hoped you could stop going to the factory soon, but—"

Mama's eyes grew brighter and brighter. She put her hand on Father's arm.

"The factory is nothing! What are a few years more? I won't mind. You will see!"

Tad looked at Mama, as Mama had looked at the painting.

Not one of them could say a single word! Papa wiped his nose and went to chop wood. Tad ran to help him. Mama bustled about getting supper, and Aniela ran upstairs to get the pennies she had saved.

Maybe there are more than I think, she hoped, but when she counted there were just as many as when she had counted them before. There were sixty. She thought of the hat in the milliner's window. How she wanted it! Before she had time to think of it again, she ran downstairs and emptied the pennies onto the table. Mama was surprised. She didn't know that Aniela was saving her egg money.

"You will not be sorry, my little one," she said. "This that you give to help your brother will come back to you many times over. Always we are happy when we do something for another."

All through the solemn three days before Easter Aniela remembered with quiet joy what she had seen in the painting. Beside the picture of herself there were the flowers in the field that Tad had painted. It didn't matter that Stan couldn't come home, it didn't matter that she hadn't a new hat. Even her new dress didn't matter so much now.

When she went to bed, she stood for a moment before the Queen of Heaven. In place of the faded paper flowers she put before her the blossoming star of Bethlehem she had found near the fence corner, to say she was thankful for all the good things that had happened.

Everything in the house was clean and ready for the Easter morning that dawned warm and beautiful. Before Aniela was quite dressed she looked out of the open window and saw Mrs. Bartoszek coming up the walk. She heard her open the door and call:

"The Lord is risen!" then heard Mama call back:

"He is risen indeed! Isn't this a beautiful Easter morning?"

"Beautiful indeed," said Mrs. Bartoszek. "More beautiful than you know! My son has come home! I just wanted to tell you." Aniela heard Mrs. Bartoszek go out and shut the door. All at once every bell in the little town began to ring. They pealed from the church around the corner where Father was already playing the organ. They rang from the steeple away up the other hill. They swelled in music from the spires down in the town, and from the little stone church farther on. They chimed from the little white church on Main Street and from the red brick church across the valley. Even the bells seemed to know that it was Easter morn!

Aniela was so stirred by the din of bells she could hardly fasten her starched petticoat. The new cashmere dress was ready over a chair and beside her brushed and polished old shoes lay a pair of new black stockings. Aniela wished she didn't have to tuck so much underwear into them, so they would look smooth and neat, but Mamusia was firm about it. She *had* to wear it.

The cool, smooth feeling of the cashmere and the soft ruching around her neck made her feel better, and when she peered into the cracked mirror, she looked so nice, it didn't matter that she must wear her old cap and coat.

"Come, Aniela," called Mama. "Tadek has gone, and Tatuś has been at the church for a long time!" Aniela skipped down the stairs where Mama was waiting. As she reached the bottom, Mama looked her over well. She lifted the edge of Aniela's dress and petticoat to see if she was properly dressed, and said before she let her come through the doorway:

"Are you as clean all the way through as you are on top?"

Aniela bobbed her head and said: "Yes, Mamusia, do I look all right?" Mama still held her there, so Aniela knew there was something she wasn't telling. Aniela looked up. There it was! There on the bust of Kościuszko, making him look very funny, was Aniela's spring hat! It was straw color, just as she wanted it, and on top were blue cornflowers.

Mamusia had a new hat, too. Hers was black and was trimmed with pink roses.

"Hurry! Hurry! Let's put them on!" cried Aniela. "Is mine on straight?" Aniela's hair was almost the color of the straw, and her eyes just matched the cornflowers. Mamusia's cheeks were pink like the roses on her hat.

Just as the bells stopped ringing two Easter bonnets went bobbing together through the church door.

HELENE PELZEL

A HAPPY EASTER

Marketa settled herself among the parcels and leaned back against the cushioned seat of the car with a relieved sigh as the train pulled out of the Wilson Station. It had seemed as though this moment would never come, so eager had she been to go to Aunt Josefina's to spend the Easter season.

Marketa lived with her mother and father in Prague, the

capital city of Czechoslovakia. Since they lived in an apartment building, Marketa's only playground was in the courtyard of the building or in the public parks. But at Aunt Josefina's little farm there was a yard, a garden, a few animals, and best of all, of course, her cousins. She had never visited the farm at the joyous Easter-tide and now as the train gathered speed and entered the countryside, her thoughts turned to the joy of seeing Aunt Josefina, Uncle Jan and the cousins.

Cousin Marie was really a young lady now and probably wouldn't pay very much attention to Marketa but doubtless Ignace would tease her as he had done on the last visit some time ago. Anerka, who was just Marketa's age, would greet her with warmth and affection and plans to make her short visit most enjoyable.

Marketa shifted impatiently among the parcels and her mother smiled understandingly.

"It seems a long time on the train?" she queried with a twinkle in her blue eyes, knowing well Marketa's answer.

Marketa smiled. "Yes, I am so eager to get there. This is the first Easter we have ever spent there, isn't it?"

"We were there once, long ago, when you were only a tiny baby. The Easter customs in the country and small villages are often different from those in the city."

It was evening when Marketa and her mother arrived at the little village and by the time supper was over it was bedtime.

Marketa and Anerka snuggled down under the fat featherbed while Anerka whispered plans for the morrow into Marketa's sleepy ears.

In no time at all the spring sunshine was on Marketa's pillow and she awakened to find Anerka had already arisen. Sleepily, Marketa gazed about the room. She had shared Anerka's bed, but across the room Marie's bed was also empty. The white plastered walls looked freshly painted; the panes in the small, double windows shone, and the large oak chest, holding the family linens, was free from the least speck of dust.

The door opened quietly and Anerka's merry face appeared. Her brown eyes were dancing; her brown braids, smooth and thick, hung over her shoulders. When she saw Marketa was awake, she bounced into the room eagerly.

"Come, you must dress quickly; it is almost breakfast time, and there is much to do today."

Marketa jumped out of her warm feathered nest and began dressing.

"What must we do today, Anerka, tell me?" she asked happily.

"Today is Maundy Thursday," said Anerka, "you know, Green Thursday, and so many preparations must be made for the joyous Easter Day."

"Oh, I'm so glad I'm here in time to help," exclaimed Marketa. "In the city, Easter is not celebrated as in the country, Mother says. You must tell me what to do, Anerka."

"Just now, you must come to breakfast—and quickly," laughed Anerka.

At the breakfast table Marketa ate the delicious spiral rolls spread with honey just as she did in the city on the morning of Green Thursday. She knew the bread was called

Judas bread, but she thought that baked by Aunt Josefina was much better than the Judas bread bought in the city.

As soon as breakfast was over Anerka and Marketa bustled about importantly. There was much to be done in preparation for the Easter and the next day would be Good Friday, which was a solemn day of fasting and worship. So the two girls helped with the dishes, the dusting, and shaking the feather-beds into fluffy, soft masses of comfort and warmth.

That afternoon as they went past the open barn door they saw Ignace with a bunch of smooth, freshly-cut willow branches.

"What will you do with those, Cousin Ignace?" asked Marketa, noting the long, pliable switches.

Ignace laughed but Anerka made a wry face and gave a little shudder.

"These are for Pomlazka," answered Ignace, laughing harder as he noted Anerka's rueful look.

"And what is Pomlazka?" queried Marketa.

"You'll find out soon enough," Ignace answered with a friendly grin. "I made Anerka promise not to tell you so it would be a surprise. You'll have to wait until Monday to see it—and feel it," he ended with a chuckle.

"Pomlazka," Marketa mused. That was new to her. She was sure there was no Pomlazka in Prague and since she had never spent Easter in a country village, she knew nothing about it. But in the rush of other preparations she soon forgot Ignace's willow switches.

There was much baking going on in the big kitchen and the fragrance of raisins, honey and spices filled the house.

By evening Marketa was tired and sleepy. She and

Anerka had rubbed and polished the heavy old furniture although Marketa could see no dust anywhere when they began. The fuel box, emptied during the day's baking, was full again; the eggs had been gathered and on the high kitchen shelf, under clean towels, was the Easter bread.

"Tomorrow," explained Anerka, "we can rest. We do not have big meals tomorrow because, as you know, Good Friday is a fast day in memory of our Lord's Crucifixion."

"Yes, I know that," replied Marketa soberly. "In the city we fast too, and attend church."

Anerka nodded. "We will go to early church, Mother said; then we will spend the day quietly. Mother doesn't cook much on Good Friday, that is why there was much to be done today."

"I am tired," confessed Marketa as she brushed and braided her flaxen hair for the night. Her wide gray eyes were solemn and thoughtful as she arose from the bedside where she had knelt for her prayers.

"Good Friday is a sad day, isn't it?" she said to Anerka, turning back the fluffy feather-bed covering.

"Yes," replied Anerka soberly. "But I always think of the joyous Easter Day that comes after. If there had been no Good Friday, there would be no Happy Easter."

It seemed to Marketa that Friday was twice as long as any other day. First there was the service at the church, a long, solemn service which seemed to carry Marketa back to that sorrowful day hundreds of years ago. Then there was a quietness over the household, the meals were very light and there was not the usual gaiety and laughter she was accustomed to around Uncle Jan's table.

The only really pleasant happening of the day was when Aunt Josefina sent Anerka and Marketa to the far end of the garden to gather some pussy-willow branches. As they walked down the path past the freshly turned earth Marketa felt the new life of the springtime. The smell of the fresh earth, the warm sunshine, the light breeze—all spoke of the joy of life and growth after the long, cold winter. When the girls reached the willow bush they discovered that the tight brown buds were bursting into the soft gray of the "pussies."

Anerka had a heavy, sharp knife and as she cut the branches she gave them to Marketa to hold.

"Aren't they lovely?" Marketa exclaimed, touching the "pussies" lightly with one finger. "Why are we cutting them, Anerka?"

"You'll see tomorrow," Anerka teased.

"Oh, you and Ignace are full of secrets," protested Marketa. "Is it for the Pomlazka, as Ignace's willows are?"

"No, no!" laughed Anerka, "I would not cut them for Pomlazka—not I!"

"Well, I suppose I shall just have to wait. When will I know about Pomlazka and these pussy-willows?"

"You'll not learn about Pomlazka until Monday but these, the 'pussies', you'll know tomorrow."

"And this is only Friday," mused Marketa. "Well, each day has some surprise; so I can surely wait," she sighed.

That evening as she drank a mug of warm goat's milk and munched a dry roll she was glad the quiet day was ended.

"Marie," she asked, as her older cousin prepared to put out the light, "do you feel that winter is like Good Friday—everything quiet and still and then spring comes—like

Easter—to wake everything into life? Does it seem like that to you?"

"Why, yes, Marketa; the Risen Lord is the new life, just as spring is."

Marketa nodded. "That's what I think, too," she answered, as the little room became dark and still.

When Marketa came to the breakfast table the next morning there on each of the table's four corners stood a vase of the pussy-willows! Under the white tablecloth straw was lightly spread and in the center of the table was a round loaf of Easter bread. On the top of the loaf, sugary white, was a cross.

Anerka watched Marketa's look of pleased surprise at the sight of the "pussies." Then as Marketa looked up, smiling, Anerka explained, "We always fix the table so for this day—it's an old custom with us."

"I think the surprise was nicer than knowing," Marketa said. "I can even wait for Pomlazka now."

Ignace's eyes were dancing mischievously. "Pomlazka is quite different," he teased. "Perhaps you won't like it."

Marketa only laughed and reached for another piece of the Easter bread. Made with sweet dough, light with eggs, full of raisins and almonds, it was the most delicious bread Marketa had eaten at Uncle Jan's table. There seemed to be quantities of it, for when one round loaf disappeared Aunt Josefina went to the shelf and got another down.

After the morning work was done Marie, Anerka, and Marketa began the exciting fun of coloring eggs. Marie put most of the eggs into a big kettle to boil, but some of the larger, whiter ones she laid aside to "blow." Making a small hole in each end, she blew out the center of the eggs into a bowl.

"Those will make noodles," she laughed.

"What will you do with the shells, Marie?" asked Marketa.

"Those we will color and hang for decorations for tomorrow," Marie answered.

"Except some that Marie will save for Pomlazka," teased Anerka.

"Pomlazka again," cried Marketa. "Can I ever wait for Monday? But what will Marie and the eggs have to do with Pomlazka? It is Ignace who talks about Pomlazka!"

"Oh," laughed Anerka, "Marie will decorate some of the blown eggs to have them ready for Pomlazka—and Rudolf!"

Marie blushed. "Anerka talks foolishly," she said quietly.

Marketa watched closely as Marie dipped a blown egg into hot paraffin. The egg cooled quickly and then with a needle Marie drew a design on the egg. Where the needle passed, the wax came off.

"When I have finished with the designs we will dip the eggs into the dyes. Only where the needle has taken off the wax will the eggs be colored," explained Marie. "Would you like to try one?" she asked, handing the delicate shell and a needle to Marketa.

"Oh, yes, but what shall I draw? I know—some flowers—some little bleeding hearts." She set to work carefully and when she finished and Marie looked it over approvingly, Marketa beamed.

At last the eggs were finished. There were two large

bowls of hard-boiled eggs in all the colors of the rainbow and a smaller bowl of blown eggs with delicate designs traced by needles. Marketa's egg with the dainty bleeding hearts was almost the prettiest of all, she thought.

"What will we do with so many eggs?" she asked, looking at the large bowls heaped high with the lovely reds, blues, yellows and greens, in all their beautiful tints.

"Monday we will take some to the sick and shut-in," explained Anerka. "Poor little Eduard, in the cottage on the hillside, will be happy to have some. All day he sits in his chair by the window and watches the roadside. He cannot walk much and his old grandfather must leave him alone much of the time in order to make a living for them both."

"Oh, may I choose the very prettiest egg for Eduard?" begged Marketa, her gray eyes shining.

"Yes, indeed," Marie answered quickly. "Choose several for him."

Marketa finally decided upon three eggs, a pink, a yellow and a rich purple. She laid them aside till Monday.

"But there are still so many," she said, looking at the heaped up bowls.

"Some we will eat," answered Anerka, "some we will take to Grandma Novak and some we will need for Pomlazka."

"Oh, Pomlazka, Pomlazka again!" cried Marketa. "Will the mystery ever be explained?"

Anerka and Marie laughed. "On Monday"—they promised, their eyes dancing with untold secrets.

"But now we must finish with the eggs," warned Marie.

"See, we will string these blown ones and hang them in the windows for the Easter Day. You may help, Marketa."

Carefully, in fear of crushing the delicate shells, Marketa and Anerka strung the bright egg-shells on the strings and when they were hung in the windows the girls stood back to admire their handiwork.

Marketa called to her mother and Aunt Josefina to come and see the decorations. Leaving their cooking and baking, they came and admired the girls' work until Anerka and Marketa beamed with pride.

At last everything was in readiness for the Easter Day. There were little cakes in the shape of lambs, covered with white frosting; there was the meat of a very young goat fried, there were loaves of special bread, and potatoes, cabbage and onions ready to cook.

The house looked very festive with the great bowls of eggs on the table, the strings of blown eggs hanging in the windows and a jar of the soft "pussies" on the shelf.

The girls were awakened Easter morn by Uncle Jan's deep voice saying, "Christ is Risen."

"He is Risen, indeed," the girls responded happily, springing out of bed. The greeting echoed all through the house as each one greeted or replied to the greetings of the other members of the family.

There was an air of joy and hope throughout the house. As they walked down the road to the church in the early light of Easter morn the glad tidings passed back and forth from neighbor to neighbor.

"Christ is Risen!" "He is Risen, indeed!"

It seemed to Marketa that not even the glad Christmas

tidings had echoed with such deep joy and hope as these simple country folk put into their oft-repeated greeting.

The whole day was full of a quiet gladness. It was a "family day" and the warm glow of affection seemed to fill Uncle Jan's house.

"Aunt Josefina, this was such a good dinner," sighed Marketa, when she couldn't eat another bite of the colored eggs nor the little lamb cakes.

"Mother, may we come again next year?"

"Wait until after Pomlazka to ask her that," laughed Ignace.

Mother only smiled and said, "I hope so."

"You shan't frighten me with Pomlazka any more," cried Marketa. "I know that on the morrow we go to take the colored eggs to the little crippled Eduard and old Grandma Novak—and that will be fun."

Monday morning Anerka and Marketa divided the eggs left in the larger bowl, putting an equal number into each of two baskets.

"Put the eggs for Eduard in the bottom of your basket," cautioned Anerka.

"All of these we take to Eduard and Grandma Novak?" asked Marketa in surprise.

"No, not all," answered Anerka.

"To whom, then, do we give the rest?" questioned Marketa.

"I do not know," answered Anerka. Anerka's face was turned from Marketa, but she thought her cousin's shoulders shook as though from laughter.

"You do not know, then why do we put them into the baskets?"

But before Anerka could answer, Ignace, who had been out at the barn, burst into the old kitchen, breathless and laughing.

"Pomlazka!" he cried, waving a long switch woven of four willow branches into which he had braided a long piece of red ribbon.

Rushing to Anerka he began to switch her on the legs. The switch whacked down sharply as Anerka dodged about the table.

"Wait, wait!" she cried breathlessly. "Here, take it," and she handed Ignace an egg out of her basket.

Marketa, who had been watching the game wide-eyed, now jumped to feel the switch stinging her legs.

"Oh, Ignace, stop!" she cried. "I'll give you an egg, too."

Running to her basket she handed him a pretty yellow egg.

Mother and Aunt Josefina had been watching the fun but Marie had been in the bedroom. Just as she opened the door into the kitchen Ignace turned and wielded his willow switch on Marie. Her longer skirts gave her some protection but she, too, cried for mercy which she received only when she surrendered an egg to Ignace.

Ignace turned to Marketa.

"Now do you see why Anerka wasn't very happy about Pomlazka?" he laughed.

"Oh, yes, I see now. It is fun only for the boys!" she answered, making a little face at her cousin.

"I didn't really hurt you, did I?" he teased, patting her shoulder.

"No, not really, but I don't like giving up the eggs," she protested with a little sigh.

"If a girl receives a switching on Easter Monday, she will be healthy all the next year," explained Ignace merrily. "And so, to be sure that no girl is missed, we must switch them all!"

"And the girls must repay your kindness with an egg," scoffed Marketa. "That is a very clever plan—for the boys!"

"And will you give Rudolf the pretty decorated eggs for Pomlazka?" she asked, turning to Marie.

Ignace and Anerka laughed but Marie turned away to hide her blushing face and answered, "Maybe."

"You had better take the eggs to Eduard now," reminded Aunt Josefina.

Tying on their shawls the girls picked up their baskets and started down the path. When they reached the road Anerka looked up and down it. There was no one in sight.

"Let's hurry," she said softly.

"Why?" asked Marketa. "It's such a lovely morning."

Just then Hans, a neighbor boy, came rushing out at them, brandishing a willow switch such as Ignace had used. Anerka started to run but the startled Marketa stood still in surprise until she felt the sting of the switch. Then she tried to run but Hans danced about her, shouting and laughing and bringing the switch down upon her whenever he had a chance.

"Oh, wait, I'll give you an egg," cried Marketa, suddenly remembering how to buy her way out of the swinging, stinging switch.

Hans stopped and held out his hand. Marketa gave him an egg and then looked about for Anerka. Her cousin was some distance down the road but not too far for Hans to catch up with her, so Anerka also went on with a lightened basket.

"I understand now why we have the extra eggs in our baskets," Marketa exclaimed.

"And why I didn't know to whom we'd give them?" laughed Anerka, shifting her basket to the other arm.

"Yes, I understand that, too," Marketa replied, looking at her lessened supply.

By the time the girls had gone through the village Marketa had only three eggs left, the ones she was taking to Eduard. Surely, thought the girls, all the village boys had taken their toll from the egg baskets by now.

But Anerka had forgotten Karl, the big, blustering bully who lived off the road a little ways. Karl, however, had not forgotten Easter Monday and Pomlazka. Jumping out from behind a low stone wall he ran at them, his woven switch upheld threateningly. Having no ribbon to braid into it he had used a strip of paper.

Anerka, knowing Karl, gave him one of her last few eggs almost before the switch touched her, but Marketa, thinking of little Eduard, decided she would not surrender so easily. Jumping to one side, she started to run but Karl swung about quickly and gave chase.

Marketa, light and swift of foot, might have escaped had it not been for a stone in the road. Stumbling over it, she fell. As she did so two of the precious eggs bounced from the basket and when Marketa scrambled up and looked about, the beautiful purple egg, the most prized of them all, lay crushed in the dust of the roadway.

Marketa began to cry and Karl dropped his switch, standing by awkwardly.

"I wanted to take it to Eduard," she explained between sobs. "He can't get them—the way you do," she cried accusingly.

Karl shifted about uneasily while Anerka brushed the dust and twigs off of Marketa's clothes.

"I'm—I'm sorry," blurted Karl in embarrassment. "It's only a game, I didn't mean to hurt anybody."

Anerka felt almost sorry for the hulking lad, ill at ease and knowing the girls disliked him for the damage he had caused.

Marketa picked up her basket. The pink egg was cracked, the yellow egg alone had remained intact. Looking down at it her tears began to fall again.

Karl stared at her. It was slowly dawning upon him that Marketa was not crying for her own hurt but because she could not take a bit of pleasure to Eduard. Poor Karl had known so little of generosity in his own life, he was slow to recognize it in others or to feel it within himself. He glanced at his own basket, full of the booty he had claimed from his squealing, protesting victims along the roadside.

Something stirred in his slow mind.

"Here," he said hesitantly, "take any eggs you want—for Eduard. I don't need them, I only took them for fun," he added lamely.

"Oh, may I?" cried Marketa, forgetting her tears. "May I have two for this cracked pink one?"

Karl nodded, a pleased smile on his dull face as Marketa looked critically over his basket.

"Here's another purple one, just as pretty as mine was, don't you think?" she cried, turning to Anerka. Her cousin nodded, surprised at Karl's generous act.

"And this bright crimson one is really prettier than the pink one," Marketa exclaimed, lifting it from Karl's basket.

"Thank you, thank you," she smiled at Karl as she placed the eggs in her own basket.

"Take this one, too," Karl said timidly, holding out an egg with a little design traced all over it. "A present to Eduard—from me," he went on, brightening a bit under his own generous impulse.

"And I'll walk the rest of the way with you; so no one else will get the eggs," he offered apologetically.

"Oh, that is so kind," Marketa accepted the egg and the offer of protection in the same breath.

Anerka, a bit surprised at the turn events had taken, picked up her basket and they walked on.

Karl had never paid any attention to his unfortunate little neighbor. Eduard had often watched Karl from the window and wished he would come in for a little visit but he had never voiced the wish to anyone. Eduard had admired from afar Karl's sturdy body and his skill in boyish activities and had wished vainly that the older boy were his friend.

Eduard saw the trio coming up the path and his thin face lighted with pleasure when they opened the door in response to his "Come in."

Anerka and Marketa placed the eggs in a bowl on the window sill beside Eduard's chair.

"I shall save the purple one and the decorated one till the very last, they are so pretty," he said shyly. "And Grandfather and I will have a good supper tonight with the blue and green ones," he said, turning to Anerka.

When the girls left, Karl was showing Eduard how to make a whistle from the willow branch and both boys were so engrossed in the process they hardly knew the girls had gone.

"Mother," announced Marketa at the supper table that evening, "this has been the very nicest Easter-tide I've ever had and I do hope we can come back next year."

"And stay for Pomlazka?" Ignace asked, his eyes twinkling.

"Yes, and stay for Pomlazka," Marketa answered happily. "In some ways Pomlazka was the best of all, because it gave Eduard and Karl each a friend and what Easter gift could be nicer?"

ANNA MILO UPJOHN

ELENA'S "CIAMBELLA"

As Elena scampered over the road, the town clock struck a quarter to four. Elena had an important engagement. Her mother had sent her to draw a jar of water from the public well outside the town; and on the way back she was to stop at the bakery to get her *ciambella,* which was to come out of the oven at four.

Now a *ciambella* is an Easter cake, but it is different from any other cake in the world. It is made of flour and sugar and olive oil, and tastes like a crisp cooky. If you are a girl yours will be in the form of a dove; if a boy, in the form of a galloping horse, with a handle of twisted dough from mane to tail to carry it by. Whichever it may be, an Easter egg will be baked inside the *ciambella*, and the cake will be stuck full of downy feathers, which wave and look festive.

Elena's cake was an unusually large one, in the shape of a dove, of course, with wings and tail feathers and an open beak. It had been brought to the bakery on a tray by Elena's mother, and left to be baked.

As Elena panted up the hill she saw Giuseppa outside the *cabane* or hut, helping her mother with the washing. The baby stood in a high, narrow box where he could look on and yet was out of mischief, and there he waved his arms and shouted with excitement as the suds flew.

"Where are you going?" called Giuseppa as Elena passed.

"To get my *ciambella*," cried Elena. "Have you got yours?"

Giuseppa shook her head. "I'm not going to have any," she said.

"Not this year," added her mother, looking up, "perhaps next. But we are going to make the *cabane* clean for Easter."

Giuseppa and Elena looked at each other sympathetically.

"Too bad!" exclaimed Elena. "Well, I must hurry. *Ciao*, Giuseppa."

"*Ciao,* Elena." (A parting that is pronounced "chow" and means good-bye.)

When Elena reached the bakery she found a great crowd there. The four o'clock cakes were coming out of the oven. Far back in the glow Elena could see her own *ciambella* on the stone floor of the oven, larger than all the rest, its feathers waving tantalizingly in the heat.

In the midst of the women and children stood the cook, with smooth black hair and huge earrings of gold and pearls, which reached to her shoulders, and with a clean flowered kerchief tucked into her corset. She was bare-armed and brown, and held what looked like a great pancake-turner with a very long handle. With this she could reach into the depths of the oven, which was as big as a pantry, and scoop out the cakes, even those quite at the back. There were all sorts of cakes, large and small; some were cookies, and some were big loaves made with almonds and honey and eggs. The whole place smelt delicious, and everyone stood on tiptoe to see his own cake pulled out of the oven. Finally Elena's *ciambella* was put into her hands, still hot and fragrant, though she had waited for it to cool somewhat on a tray.

Just then a little girl named Letitia came in to ask for coals with which to light the fire at home. The cook raked a few from the oven and put them into the pot of ashes that Letitia carried. Covering them with her apron, Letitia went out with Elena.

"Just look at my *ciambella,*" said Elena proudly, as she carried it carefully on both hands. "Isn't it a beauty?"

"Yes," said Letitia, "I am going to have one, too. It will be baked to-morrow. Of course," she added, "it won't be quite as big as yours, because Maria will have one and Gino will have a horse. But they'll all taste the same."

"Just think!" said Elena, "Giuseppa isn't going to have any at all."

"Not any?" cried Letitia. "How dreadful! I never heard of a house without a *ciambella!* They must be very poor."

"Yes, but at school Giuseppa always has a clean apron and clean hands. She helps her mother a lot, too. Well, chow, Letitia."

"Chow, Elena."

The girls parted, and Elena walked proudly through the streets, carrying the cake as though in a procession.

She climbed the outside stair, which led to her house, built over the donkey stable. Her mother had gone out to the fountain to polish her pots. The big dim room, with its brown rafters and the dark furniture ranged along the walls, was very quiet. A patch of sunshine made a bright spot on the stone floor, and in it a white pigeon drowsed. It did not move, even when Elena stepped over it. The little girl looked down and laughed at the comical resemblance between the pigeon and her *ciambella;* but her own pigeon sat up very straight and stiff, because it had an Easter egg baked inside it.

Elena set the cake carefully on a big chest while she struggled to open the bottom drawer of the bureau. There she laid the cake in a nest of clean aprons and handkerchiefs, to rest until Saturday afternoon, when it would be taken out to be blessed. Not until Sunday morning would its fine feathers be plucked and its crisp wings bitten off.

The *ciambella* safely lodged in a drawer, Elena climbed on a chair and got a piece of bread and some sheep's cheese from the cupboard; then she ran to find her mother.

The next days were very busy. Everyone in Sezze was cleaning house frantically before Easter. Washing hung over every balcony, the yellow and flowered handkerchiefs and aprons making the whole street gay. Every bit of furniture was polished, windows were cleaned, curtains washed and floors scrubbed. Above all, the copper water jars and basins were taken out to the fountains and scoured with lemon and sand until they shone like red gold. There was the warmth of spring in the air after a cold winter. On the slopes below the town the almond trees were in blossom and the snow had disappeared from the mountains, the tops of which were drifted with clouds.

Far below the town a fertile plain—the Pontine Marshes—stretched out to the sea. Often the plain was covered with mists, for it was full of swamps that bred mosquitoes and malaria. People who lived there did so at a risk. Often they came up to the town sick with fever, and sometimes they died; but the gardens and fields produced such fine vegetables and brought so much money from the markets in Rome that men kept on. There were no houses down there, so far as the eye could see, only *cabanes* or huts thatched with reeds from the marshes and in the distance looking like haystacks. Giuseppa's father worked on the flats, and the family lived in a *cabane,* but it was high up on the mountain, just below the town, where land was cheap.

It was true that Giuseppa's father was very poor, but he was also saving his money to build a little stone house to take the place of the *cabane*. He told the children that when they had the house they should also have a *ciambella* every year. In the meantime Giuseppa helped her mother to make the *cabane* as neat as possible for Easter. It was a poor place indeed; round, with a thatched roof, which came to a peak at the top. Inside there was only one room, and that had an earthen floor and no windows. There was no opening except the doors, and no chimney.

When the fire was built on the floor in the middle of the room the smoke struggled up through holes in the roof; but the family lived out in the sun most of the time, and went into the *cabane* only when it rained or was very cold. As Elena went back and forth for water those busy days she sometimes looked over the wall and saw Giuseppa hanging clothes on the bushes or beating a mattress; and there was smoke coming through the roof as if water was being heated. Elena felt very sorry for Giuseppa, and every night prayed God to send her a *ciambella*.

Giuseppa, not knowing this, felt bitter toward Elena and jealous of her great, feathered cake. Also she herself prayed earnestly for a *ciambella*. On Easter morning she made herself as fine as she could, and went to church. She combed back her short hair and laid a white embroidered handkerchief over it. She had small gold earrings and a coral necklace, and she put on a light blue cotton apron and her corn-colored handkerchief with roses, over her shoulders.

On her way home Elena came running after her. "Oh, Giuseppa," she asked earnestly, "did you get a *ciambella*?"

"No, I didn't," said Giuseppa, and passed on.

Elena was much disappointed. She had prayed hard, and felt that a cake should have been sent to Giuseppa. Then suddenly she stopped short in the street. "Why," she said, "perhaps God hasn't got a *ciambella,* and I have!"

She went home thoughtfully and opened the drawer and looked a long time at her *ciambella*. Then she ate her dinner of boiled chicken, and artichokes fried in batter. After dinner Elena took the cake lovingly in her arms and carried it into the street. It was the last time it would be on parade. She passed the groups of children, all munching *ciambella,* and made her way to Giuseppa's hut. Giuseppa was outside, feeding the baby from a bowl of bread and milk.

"Happy Easter!" cried Elena.

"Happy Easter!" replied Giuseppa, her eyes fixed on the cake.

"I brought my *ciambella* to eat with you," said Elena cautiously, "and you may hold it, and, oh, Giuseppa, you may have the egg!"

Giuseppa grew scarlet. "I never saw such a beauty," she said, "and what feathers!"

"I stuck them into the dough myself;" said Elena, "that is why there are so many."

"Do you know," said Giuseppa shyly, "I *prayed* for a *ciambella.*"

"And you got it!" cried Elena triumphantly.

KATE SEREDY

EASTER EGGS

JANCSI'S *home was a ranch on the great Hungarian plain. It was miles and miles from the village and he had no brother or sister; so he was filled with excitement when* COUSIN KATE, *a real city girl from Budapest, came to stay at the ranch. She was no golden-haired princess as* JANCSI *had fancied, but a most lively companion; and ere long he decided she was "almost as good as a real boy." This is the story of their Easter week.*

"Let's see, it's a whole week until Easter. Wish it wasn't so long. I don't like Easter anyway, you have to be all dressed up and nothing to do," said Kate.

"Oh, but Easter is wonderful!" cried Jancsi. "We make Easter eggs, and everybody goes visiting, there are millions of good things to eat and . . . !" Jancsi gasped for words to describe the wonders of Easter.

Kate interrupted: "Make Easter eggs? How can you make an egg?"

"Mother just dyes them, silly, and we write all kinds of flowers and patterns on them."

This was something new for Kate. She contemplated it in silence for a while. "What else do you do?" she asked.

"Go to church and sprinkle the girls an' everything. Wait and see—it's fun!"

"Sprinkle—what—sprinkle the girls!!?"

"'Course. All the boys and young men go to all their friends who have girls to sprinkle them with water. The girls and mothers give them meat and cakes to eat and Easter eggs to take home."

"Oh! but that's silly. Slosh water on girls for no reason at all and get cakes and everything. What do the girls get for getting wet?"

"Wait a minute, Kate," laughed Father. "It does sound silly if you put it that way, but there is a beautiful reason for it. Do you want me to tell you?"

"A story?" asked Jancsi eagerly.

"No, Jancsi, the truth," said Father. "Come on, let's sit under the apple tree and I'll tell you." He spoke seriously, almost as though he were thinking aloud.

"Easter is a holiday of joy and love and giving. We welcome our friends and offer them the best we have. For us, who live on the land, Easter means the real beginning of spring—and spring for us is new hope, new life, after the long bleak winter. Spring brings warm sunshine, life-giving soft rain. Every living thing depends on sunshine and water. So we celebrate Easter by giving each other the sunshine of hospitality, and we sprinkle each other with fresh, pure water. How does your Easter greeting go, Jancsi? Say it for Kate!"

Jancsi recited:

"My song is the song of hope,
The voice of spring is my voice,
All my dear friends, let us rejoice;
God gave us sunshine, God gave us rain,
Our prayers have not been in vain.
Gone is the cold, cheerless winter,
Here is glorious Easter again!"

Kate nodded. "I like it, Uncle Márton—only—I—well—I can't understand why only the girls get sprinkled."

"You can sprinkle us on Tuesday after Easter. That's when girls have a good time," laughed Jancsi, jumping up. "Come on, the horses are waiting for a rub."

The last days before Easter were busy and exciting ones. Father and Jancsi whitewashed the house inside and out. They painted the window boxes and shutters a bright blue. Jancsi and Kate selected the largest, most perfect eggs, and they were laid aside for decorating. Mother made piles and piles of nutcakes and poppyseed cakes, baking them in different shapes. Some of them looked like birds or lambs, some were crescent-shaped, some looked like stars and crosses. The cousins were always sniffing around the kitchen, waiting for "tastes."

Evenings Mother got out her dyepots and the fascinating work of making dozens and dozens of fancy Easter eggs kept the family busy. There were two ways to decorate them. The plainer ones were dyed first. When they dried, Father and Jancsi scratched patterns on them with penknives. The fancy ones were lots of work. Mother had a tiny funnel, with melted beeswax in it. With this she drew intricate patterns on the white eggs. After the wax hardened, she dipped them in the dye. Then she scratched off the wax and there was the beautiful design left in white on the colored egg. In this way she could make the most beautifully shaded designs by covering up parts of the pattern again with wax before each dipping. The finished ones were placed in baskets and put on a shelf until Easter morning.

"I'll make some extra fancy ones for Kate. She can give them to the boys she likes best," Mother said, smiling.

"Could I try to make one or two myself?" begged Kate. "*All* by myself. I don't want anybody to see them."

"Look out, Kate, you'll get all messed up, and this dye doesn't wash off. You have to scrub it off with sand," warned Jancsi.

Kate went to a corner with her dyepots and labored for a long time in silence. When she finally put her eggs away and came back to the table, she was a sight!

"Oh, Kate, you clumsy," cried Jancsi. "Now you look like an Easter egg. Oh, you look funny." She was red paint from head to toe. Her fingers were dripping, her nose looked like a red cherry.

Jancsi's hands were wet with the dye, too, but he carefully kept his face and clothes clean.

Kate looked at him seriously.

"Jancsi, dear, there's just a little smudge of black on your nose," she said, pointing a red finger at an imaginary spot.

"Don't touch me! I'll wipe it off," cried Jancsi and, forgetting his wet hands, rubbed his nose vigorously.

"M—m—m. That's off, but your forehead is smudged, too. The smoke from the candle, I imagine," said a very sweet and solicitous Kate.

Jancsi rubbed his forehead.

"Your chin, too. My, my, these old-fashioned candles."

Jancsi rubbed his chin. Father and Mother were laughing hard, but he didn't know why.

"It's perfect now, Jancsi," smiled Kate. "Now you look like an Easter egg yourself."

"Oh, my boy," laughed Father, "won't you ever learn the ways of our sweet pussy? You are decorated for Easter all right."

Jancsi ran to the mirror. He couldn't help laughing.

"I should have known better," he admitted. "She had her angel face on. I'll tell the boys to scrub your face for you, sprinkling isn't enough."

Saturday, Mother packed all the meats, bread, and cakes in big baskets lined with snow-white napkins. They would take them to the church Sunday to be blessed by the priest.

She put the finishing touches on the family's Sunday clothes. Kate didn't pay any attention to her own dress Mother had promised for Easter; she was satisfied with her boy's clothes.

On Sunday they started to dress after a very early breakfast. Kate's clothes were laid out on her bed. Suddenly a wail came from her room. "Oh, Auntie, which skirt shall I wear?"

"Which skirt? All of them, of course, it's a holiday!"

"But there are eighteen on my bed!"

"That's because you're only a little girl. I'm wearing thirty-six, but I'm a married woman," said Mother, appearing in the doorway. She completely filled it. Her pleated and starched skirts were all the colors of the rainbow, standing away from her body like a huge umbrella. She wore a white shirtwaist with puffed sleeves, a tight black vest, laced in front over red buttons. Her head was covered with a fringed, embroidered shawl, tied under her chin. She wore tight black boots with high heels. Kate gazed at her with awe.

"I'm really very young," she said meekly. "Couldn't I wear just one or two skirts?"

"All nice girls wear at least ten," was Mother's firm answer.

When Kate finally emerged from her room, she looked like a small replica of Mother. Her dress was even more colorful, with a scarlet red vest. Her sparkling, shimmering bonnet had long red and green ribbons on it, cascading almost to her knees. But Kate's face was sad. "My old boots," she said, "they look awful with this pretty dress."

"Oh, you poor lamb!" cried Mother. "We clean forgot your boots! Father! Jancsi! We forgot Kate's boots."

Father came in, solemnly shaking his head. "Hm-hm. Think of it! Our pussy hasn't any boots. What can we do? She will have to wear mine!"

He went to the cupboard. When he turned around, he held the prettiest, trimmest pair of little red boots in his hand.

"Oh," said everybody. Kate flew to him, crying: "Uncle Márton! You are the sweetest, best, dearest uncle!" She was trying to hug him and put her boots on at the same time.

Father left them to get the wagon while Kate was still dancing around happily. She was kissing Mother and she even attempted to kiss Jancsi. But he balked at that. "Only girls kiss," he declared and stalked out after Father.

They drove to church in great state. The wagon had been freshly painted, the horses were brushed until their coats shone like black satin. They overtook and passed more and more wagons as they approached the village. "Our wagon is best of all!" said Kate proudly.

The streets around the village church were lined with vehicles. The church square was packed with people. They were dressed in brilliant colors, the women in immense skirts, swaying, their hair-ribbons floating in the breeze. The men all had bunches of flowers in their hats, and wore snow-white pleated shirts and pants, and black, blue, or green sleeveless jackets. It made the prettiest picture Kate had ever seen. "Like a big flower garden," she whispered.

Slowly the church filled and the service began. After the last prayer and hymn, the priest blessed the food in the church square. Groups of friends stood around for a while, talking. Kate was introduced to many people. . . . She was the subject of open admiration from the village boys and girls. Here was a city girl who . . . wasn't afraid of anything!

"We'll come to your house tomorrow!" promised the boys.

When Kate woke up Monday morning, Father and Jancsi had already left for the village. Mother and Kate spread the best white tablecloth on the big kitchen table and placed huge platters of meat, bread, and cakes on it. "What a beautiful tablecloth," exclaimed Kate. "I never saw anything like it in the stores."

"I made it myself, Kate, when I was your age," said Mother. "I planted the flax, reaped it, prepared it, spun the thread, and wove it into this cloth. It's more than twenty-five years old now, but it's as good as new." Kate wanted to know more about spinning and weaving, but Mother was too busy. She promised Kate to teach her all about it in the winter.

They were still arranging the baskets of eggs when the first wagon drove in. The men and boys walked in, and one of them spoke a piece:

"Glory be to the Holy Father
Who gave us food and pure water.
As we water the rose to make it bloom,
We sprinkle the rosebud in this room.
May you live long,
Old and young.
Peace be with you on this holy day of Easter."

They all repeated the last line. Kate saw the flasks of water in their hands. "It won't be so bad, the bottles are very small," she thought. Just the same she squealed and ran when the boys stepped forward and began to throw water on her. There was great shouting and laughing in the kitchen. "We want eggs! Give us some eggs, Kate, we'll stop sprinkling if you do," cried the boys. She ran to the baskets and gave them handfuls of eggs. Mother invited them to eat anything they liked. Another wagon drove in. Young men came on horseback. It was great fun for Kate! She was pretty wet by now, but didn't mind it. Visitors came and left; the kitchen was always full of people and laughter. She liked the verses they spoke, she liked the boundless hospitality, she liked ever so much to be there and enjoy it all!

The food supply was almost exhausted when the last wagon drove off. There weren't any more eggs. She slumped in a chair, tired but happy.

Jancsi and Father came home in the afternoon, loaded with eggs. "Well, Kate," asked Father, "did you give everything away? Not one egg left for us?"

"I saved one for you and one for Jancsi," said Kate, walking to the small basket where she had hidden the eggs she had made all by herself.

"You said I had to give the best ones to people I like best." She smiled, holding out her hands to Father and Jancsi.

"Mine has a nice flower on it and—oooh—little ducks! Aren't they, Kate?"

"Yes, I drew them for you because we had such a good time with the duckies."

Father took the egg offered to him. It wasn't a very good Easter egg, being a tiny bit smeary, but to Father it was the most beautiful gift in the world. This is what Kate had written on it: "I like you best of all, Uncle Márton!"

VALENTI ANGELO

EASTER

There was much excitement at Casa Checchi as Easter Sunday drew near. The courtyard was swept clean and the house scrubbed from ceiling to floor. Everything had to be in perfect order for the many guests who were expected. They would eat at a long table in the courtyard. In preparation for the occasion, the oven had been kept hot for several days.

Allinda had made huge piles of small cakes sprinkled with red, yellow, and pale blue sugar crystals; also there was panettone, a large cake filled with pine nuts, raisins, and chopped angelica. For the children she had baked little soldiers and roosters of cake dough glazed with a mixture of beaten eggs and sugar. Raisins were used for the buttons and eyes. They came from the oven slick and shining. Long lines of chocolate cookies lay on the table. Some were shaped like stars; others like half-moons and crescents; and still others took the form of balls. Next to the cookies lay the huge round sweet bread generously sprinkled through with aniseed and looking like a giant doughnut. Last of all, Allinda made the sweet green squash tarts sprinkled with cinnamon and sugar. These were immense and looked like cart wheels before they were cut into small pieces.

Nino seldom left his mother's side these days.

"Oh, let me braid the fancy loaves!" he would beg, or: "May I beat the eggs?" or: "I want to sprinkle the colored sugar, Mother. You know how I like doing that."

Allinda worked tirelessly, calling on her son from time to time. "Nino, bring me the big wooden spoon. Nino, wash this bowl," and more often: "Nino, get out from under my feet!"

Nino knew what fun Easter could be, with all the guests and the big table set out in the open air of the courtyard.

"Easter doesn't last long enough. It's like Christmas—it comes and goes too quickly," he said to himself.

At last Easter Sunday came, and Nino, looking out of his open window, saw a cloudless sky deep emerald in color. The song of the birds sounded sweeter than usual, and, in the distance, he could hear the voices of peasants singing in the clear morning air. He jumped from his bed and dressed quickly in the clean clothes his mother had laid out for him. Today would be too full to waste any part of it. While he was washing, he could hear Grandfather and one of the neighbors in the courtyard. They were busy setting up the long table which soon would groan with the weight of the holiday meal.

The morning sun climbed higher into the sky while Nino and Grandfather walked to church to attend Easter mass. As they walked along, Nino heard the bells ringing. Allinda, who had gone to the early mass, stayed at home to get ready for the guests, who would appear directly after the second mass was over.

Nino and Grandfather entered the church. They touched their fingers to the holy water at the font and made the sign of the cross. The mass had just started and the organ was playing in deep melodious tones. Today the altar decorations were even finer than usual. There were more lighted candles and many more flowers. There were more altar boys today, too, and the choir sounded louder than it did on other days.

"I would like to be an altar boy," Nino whispered to his grandfather, kneeling beside him on the small bench.

"Perhaps some day you may be," replied the old man quietly.

There was more kneeling than on other days, thought Nino, as he shifted his weight from one knee to the other. Glancing about, he noticed that some people knelt on only one knee. He tried this position too, but found it made little difference. His knees ached just the same.

"Be still, Nino," cautioned Grandfather.

The priest had just finished drinking from the sacred chalice and setting it down covered it with a spotless white napkin. He chanted the service in low sonorous tones. Two small altar boys held up the train of his sumptuous robe, which was covered with gold embroidery. It had a blue cross on the front and one on the back. Nino craned his neck to see him better. A boy kept changing the huge missal, a large book, from one side of the altar to the other. Another rang a little bell between the chants. The priest turned, bowed, and turned again with his back to the congregation. He bowed again. The smallest of all the altar boys ran back and forth with two small bottles of water and wine. He poured a little of each into the large silver and gold chalice that the priest held firmly in both hands. The priest blessed the congregation, blessed himself, and then with both hands lifted the large chalice to his mouth and drained it to the last drop. The organ played a triumphant strain, and the voices of the choir rang out, almost drowning the priest's words.

Nino held a silver coin tight in one hand. When the collection box, which was fastened on a long handle, came round to him, he put his coin in it, noticing at the same time that the box was almost full. He was glad when the kneeling was over, and he sat back in the seat and thought of God and Easter.

Easter mass was over. The peasants, all dressed in their

best clothes, streamed out into the sunshine which flooded the square facing the church. They stood around, greeting and saluting one another. Color filled the square. The blue, red, yellow, and green dresses of the village women mixed with the sober gray and black of the men. The rich colors blended harmoniously with the somber gray walls of the church.

The priest, who had changed from his altar robes to a long black cassock with a row of buttons running all the way down the front, walked through the crowd and chatted with the village folks. Nino watched him talking with Signor Patri, the fat and jovial Mayor of the village. The priest was bareheaded; he fingered a long string of beads that hung almost to the ground and wore a silver cross that glittered in the morning sun.

"Good morning, Father Bellarosa," said Nino as the priest turned from Signor Patri and walked towards the little group made up of Signor Ditto, the Signora, Julio, Jacobo the artist, the butcher, the cobbler, and Nino's best friend the pastrycook. These and many more had been asked to come up to Casa Checchi for the feast.

"How are you, Nino?" said the priest. "How are you this fine Easter Day?" And he patted Nino's curly head.

"Oh, I'm so excited!" said Nino. "I'm so glad that you are coming to dinner today. I want to show you the rooster you gave me. It's still as good as new."

"All right, Nino. I'll be there. I would not miss your mother's cooking for anything, especially her baking," he said to Nino, as he walked over to talk with another group of villagers.

Nino was very fond of kind Father Bellarosa. He seldom scolded him at catechism and, besides, hadn't he given him the best toy he had?

Pigeons flew in and out of the belfry. Nino watched them circle the campanile and disappear in the rafters of the tower. Nino had been up in the tower once. He remembered how dizzy it made him feel when he looked down. He wondered if the pigeons didn't sometimes feel dizzy, too. Nino didn't like the way they stood around on the peaks of the roof and the eaves. Just then a pigeon alighted safely on the cross on top of the tower, and Nino knew why God had made wings.

Julio came up to where Nino stood, still looking upwards.

"What are you looking at?" asked Julio. "Haven't you ever seen the campanile before?"

"Yes, I have," said Nino. "I was just noticing how well the pigeons take care of themselves. See that one perched up on the cross?" he said pointing. "He's not at all frightened."

"They have wings, haven't they? I don't see why you worry about such things," said Julio, shrugging his shoulders.

A shy girl about Nino's age stood beside Julio. She was dressed in red, and a white embroidered apron fitted tightly high above her waist.

"Nino, this is my cousin, Gloria. She came all the way from Florence to spend a month with us," said Julio. "Won't we have fun now!" he said, jumping up and down like a marionette.

"I like the apron you're wearing, Gloria," said Nino. "Did your mother make it?"

"No, Nino," said Gloria in a shy voice. "It was bought for me in Florence."

Nino knew that Florence was a large city. He hoped that some day his mother would take him there. He had heard of all the fine things one could see in that "City of the Arts," which was what Grandfather often called Florence.

"Grandfather," said Nino, "may I go to Julio's house with him? He wants to stop for his new mandolin."

"Wait," said Signor Ditto. "There's something I want too."

"All right, Nino. Don't be long, though. Your mother is probably waiting for us all to come now," said the old man.

The four hurried off to the Dittos'. Julio found his mandolin, and his father went into the cellar and came out with an armful of bottles.

"*Viva il vino!* Hurray for wine!" he shouted, the bottles clinking against one another.

The four were panting with haste when they entered the courtyard. The long table stood under the wide grape arbor, covered with a coarse linen tablecloth which Nino's mother had woven on her loom.

There was already a large gathering of villagers in the courtyard. They talked and gesticulated, moving their arms, shrugging their shoulders, and occasionally glancing in the direction of the oven and the table. Allinda was bringing out huge bowls of thick soup and Signora Ditto followed with platters of bread cut in thick slices.

Julio went around poking his nose into this and that while Nino and Gloria walked over to the oven. The door was shut.

"Can't guess what's in there," Nino said to Gloria.

"Let's peek," she said.

Nino, with a finger to his mouth, said: "Sh!"

He opened the door of the oven just a little and they both peeked in.

"Um, um, that smells good!" said Gloria.

Nino's mother arrived just in time to give Nino a gentle box on the ear.

"Poky nose," she said.

"Mother, this is Gloria. She is Julio's cousin from Florence."

Allinda made a bow to the little girl and said: "We are happy to have you with us."

"I wonder why the pastrycook is so late," said Nino. "And the cobbler, he is late too," he added.

Julio said: "I'm hungry."

"Oh, they'll be here any minute," said Allinda as she walked toward the priest, who was shaking hands with the fat Signora Ditto for the second time that day.

"I didn't see you at mass today," said the good priest, pointing an accusing finger at Allinda. "Too busy with all this?" he said, waving a hand about the courtyard.

"No, Father," said Allinda. "I was at the early mass."

The old priest gave Allinda a gentle pat on the cheek and

said: "My eyes are getting bad. I'm getting old, I guess."

Finally both the pastrycook and the cobbler arrived and everyone sat down to eat. Grandfather sat at one end of the huge table and the priest at the other. The jovial Mayor was placed in the middle with his dark-eyed wife by his side. Corrina and Pietro, their children, sat one on each side of them. Signor and Signora Ditto were across the table from the Mayor. Julio sat between Gloria and Nino, next to Grandfather. Friends of Grandfather and Allinda filled the rest of the table.

Father Bellarosa stood up. The kind priest raised one hand heavenward and while those seated about the long table bowed their heads he said: "O Lord in heaven, bless this food, and give strength to those who partake of it. Amen." Little shafts of sunlight streamed through the leaves from the arbor above.

Immediately after the priest had finished saying grace, Julio announced in a loud voice: "The soup smells good!"

Gloria giggled, and Nino said: "Hush!"

The priest sat down, smiling, and helped himself to the soup. The two huge bowls were soon emptied.

Signor Ditto said: "Don't put all the grated cheese in your soup, Julio."

Julio handed the cheese to Gloria, who in turn handed it to Nino.

"I like my soup plain," she said.

"A little cheese makes the soup taste better," Nino replied.

Grandfather rose and, holding his glass, said: *"Salute!* A

happy Easter to all, and *salute* to Signor Ditto," he added, "who brought us this good old vintage."

Everyone except the children drank the wine.

Nino said to Gloria: "When I grow up, I'll drink wine too."

Julio told Gloria that he knew what wine tasted like.

Ravioli were served next. The little shells of dough filled with minced vegetables and chicken meat, and covered with brown mushroom sauce, were heaped high on huge terra-cotta platters.

"Oh!" said Julio. "That smells even better than the soup!"

Grandfather gave Julio a good plateful of ravioli, which disappeared fast. Everyone ate and enjoyed each other's company. The food was good, and all the guests praised Allinda's cooking.

Julio said: "Mother, why don't you make ravioli like these?"

Signora Ditto blushed a deep red and Signor Ditto looked daggers at his son.

The rack of lamb came out of the oven steaming hot and roasted to a juicy brown. Allinda cut the rack into chops. Heaps of fried squash, fried quail, and chicken followed.

"Isn't it a grand meal!" said Nino to Gloria, as he picked out a nice fat drum stick and put it on Gloria's plate.

Gloria smiled and said: "Thank you, Nino. I like the drum stick best of all the chicken."

Nino was pleased.

"Pass me a gizzard," Julio said to Nino, and Nino looked about the platter for a gizzard, found one, stuck it with his fork, and put it on Julio's plate. "Don't you like gizzards?" Julio asked Gloria. "It's the chicken's stomach, you know. My mother found a penny in one once. The chicken had swallowed it."

In spite of his many threats, Grandfather after all had not had the heart to sacrifice his pet rooster for the Easter feast. The bird, with his flock of hens beside him, strutted about the courtyard now, occasionally sidling near the table to pick up a stray fallen crumb. Once in a while he crowed triumphantly, as though he had known all along that Grandfather would never put him in the oven, and the old man, picking on a chicken wing, thought how good it was to hear his voice still.

Caesar prowled round impatiently. He had to wait until the table was cleared before he would get his share.

The bones were removed from the plates before each person, and a big bowl of curly lettuce with chopped onions and garlic was passed around. Each guest stirred the oil and red vinegar at the bottom of the bowl before helping himself. But the children had eaten so much already that they shook their heads at the salad.

Julio leaned toward Gloria and said: "Now comes the part *I* like best!"

The table was covered with cakes and tarts and sliced panettone. The men dipped the slices in wine and ate them that way. The children fell upon the roosters and soldiers first, then went after the smaller cookies.

Julio, saying: "I begin to feel not so good," took a large piece of the squash tart.

Signora Ditto said: "Julio, you'll be sick. Don't make such a glutton of yourself."

Julio replied: "Oh, Ma!" his mouth so full it was all but running over.

Gloria, too, thought that Julio was overeating.

"Don't you think so?" she asked Nino.

"I don't know," said Nino. "Julio can eat an awful lot without feeling it. I remember the time when we ate green grapes together. I was sick, but he didn't even get a tummy ache."

Black coffee came next, along with cheese, nuts, and candy which the pastrycook had brought from his shop. The food was beginning to tell on some of the guests. They stretched their legs, belched politely, and loosened their sashes. The meal had lasted two hours. The children were the first to leave the table. Their elders still lingered over their coffee cups. The bottle of cognac went up and down the table. Almost everyone took a little in the black coffee.

Signor Ditto drank a toast to the house of Checchi, and Nino felt very proud indeed.

The afternoon sun hung bright over Casa Checchi and the shadow cast by the house crept slowly over the courtyard towards the arbor.

Nino and Gloria stood on the stone terrace overlooking the village and the lowland below.

"Massarosa is a beautiful village," said Gloria. "What is that shining in the distance?" she asked Nino, pointing to the west.

"Don't you know?" said Nino. "That's the Mediterranean and right near it is Viareggio. There's Pietrasanta over there to the right and there," said Nino, pointing to the east, "is Ponte Vecchio; and there's 'le Cappane.' Look right at the end of that long canal. See the two tall poplars, one on each side?"

Gloria said: "My, what a lot of things you can see from here!"

The towns in the lowlands were dotted here and there. They looked like minute toy villages in the distance.

"You see those big gashes in the hillside?" said Nino. "Those are the Carrara marble quarries. Michelangelo and Donatello once quarried their marble there. They were the two greatest sculptors of the Renaissance. My mother told me so. I'm going to be an artist like Jacobo when I grow up," he told Gloria confidently.

Unheeded, the two gazed over the landscape. Gloria shaded her eyes from the slanting rays of the sun. Nino thought she looked beautiful standing there with the sun lighting her hair to a rich golden color.

Terraces stretched out below them, terraces that had been built by the peasants piling stone on stone to wall up the land. Onions, garlic, peppers, turnips, lettuce, and little patches of herbs were grown there.

Allinda's garden lay just below them. It went around the back of the tall stone house. Olive trees hooded the hillside between the village and the house. They could see Signor Ditto's vineyard from here too, and his house that stood at the edge of it. The little village lay below them bathed in sunshine. Its narrow streets and square stone stuccoed houses and shops were mellowed with age, gray and somber in tone. Only the red tile roofs looked new.

The tuning of instruments brought the two to attention. Music filled the air. Gloria and Nino turned to see the courtyard in shadow. The villagers were singing. Some still sat at the table. Julio was nowhere to be seen.

"Where's Julio?" Nino asked his mother, looking towards the children who had gathered in a group playing a game.

"Julio is in bed," said Allinda. "He ate too much and became so ill that we had to give him some medicine. He'll be all right in a little while."

Nino scratched his head; Gloria began to giggle, and put her hand over her mouth.

"It's no wonder," she said. "He ate an awful lot for anyone of his size."

The musicians were all neighboring friends. Jacobo played the violin, Signor Ditto the piccolo, the cobbler a clarinet, and the pastrycook the accordion. They all played well. Nino had heard them before. Signor Ditto's piccolo with its high-pitched notes could be heard much above the other instruments. They were playing a mazurka, gay and fast. The Mayor had coaxed his dark-eyed young wife to dance, and others followed. The dancers whirled and spun in circles, bouncing up and down and keeping time with the music. Clapping of hands, singing voices, and shouts filled the air, and the courtyard echoed with merriment. The children joined hands in a large circle. Around and around they went, with Nino holding tightly to Gloria. Even Grandfather's rooster joined in the excitement, flapping his wings and crowing loudly.

Julio could be seen up at the window, his face the picture of misery.

Calling to his mother, he said in a loud voice: "The medicine's working!"

His mother shouted back: "Serves you right for making a pig of yourself!" and went on dancing with one of the younger men.

The musicians played many pieces, among them a tarantella in which the peasants dance singly at first, holding one hand on the hip and tapping first one foot and then the other.

Nino saw Signor Ditto drop his piccolo and take Allinda by the hand. They joined the dancing couples. Nino knew his mother was a good dancer, lighter on her feet than any of the others.

With the setting of the sun, the music subsided and the tolling of the church bells told Nino that Father Bellarosa had left the party to perform the evening vesper service. The villagers knelt in the courtyard and with bowed heads said a long prayer, while the soft mellow tones of the bells rang out in the dusk.

A large fire built of fagots was started in the courtyard, and the group sat around it and talked. The children huddled against their parents. Nino, who was sitting next to Gloria, gazed into the flames.

"What do you see in the flames, Nino?" said Gloria.

"Oh, there are lots of things to be seen in the flames if you use your imagination," said Nino. "Right now I see two red giants fighting, and then over on that side, where the smaller flames are, I see a flock of roosters pecking at one another. See, see?" he said pointing.

Gloria peered into the fire.

"I don't see any roosters, Nino. I see people dancing and they are all dressed in gorgeous red robes," she said excitedly.

"You see the devil dancing in there," said Signor Ditto, who had been listening to the conversation.

"Oh, Signor Ditto! I can't see what you see at all," said Nino laughing.

"Oh, yes, you can if you look hard enough. Look, look. There he is now, right at the top. That big flame. There, see? Isn't that the demon? See his tail whipping about the air?" said Signor Ditto again.

"Don't believe a word he says to you," said Signora Ditto. "He's always poking fun."

The Signor laughed, gave a whistle, and hugged his fat wife.

"Ditto, Ditto," said the fat Signora, "stop being a boy and grow up."

The children laughed and clapped their hands at the two.

Strains of a tinkling mandolin came from the direction of the house.

Allinda said: "Julio must be feeling better."

Julio joined the group around the fire. The villagers teased him, till he hung his head in shame. But he soon recovered his usual spirits, and played them a piece on his mandolin by way of atonement.

The pale moon looked down on the group around the fire from a crest of the dark hills above. The children roasted chestnuts in the hot coals. Now and then there was a loud pop. One had exploded. The children went: "Boom, boom, boom!" after each report. Tales were told by the villagers as they sat smoking their pipes. As the fire burned low, the children huddled closer to their parents. A candlelight threw a faint beam from a window in Casa Checchi. The voices of the people around the fire became almost like whispers. The stars hung in the heavens like flickering candles. Jacobo played his violin. Deep sad tones stole away into the night, making tears come into Nino's eyes. He wiped them away with the back of his hand.

As Nino and his mother went indoors, Allinda said: "Why, Nino, you've been crying! What's wrong? Tell me."

"Oh, Mother," said Nino with tears streaming down his cheeks, "I—I love Jacobo's violin music so much that it makes me cry!"

"There, there, you old silly," said his mother affectionately.

But she understood. The festivities, meeting Gloria—the whole day had been too much for him.

As Nino lay in his bed that night, he heard Signor Ditto's voice ringing in the night. It came from somewhere below Casa Checchi. It echoed in the glens of the hillside; fainter and fainter it sounded and finally was lost in the night. Silence filled the room.

CAROL RYRIE BRINK

IN ALL THINGS BEAUTIFUL

Thérèse and Grand'mère were going to church in the great cathedral of Notre Dame, in Paris. They had traveled many miles from their little home village to hear the Easter service. Grand'mère had told Thérèse how beautiful it would be.

But it was even more beautiful than Thérèse had imagined.

All in their best black dresses, they came through the sunny spring morning to the open square where the great church stood. Then Thérèse clutched Grand'mère's hand tightly and looked a long time, for she had never seen so large a church nor one so old. Above the three great doors were statues of the saints, and the two great towers seemed almost to touch the clouds.

Inside the cathedral it was cool and dark except where the sunshine came through the stained-glass windows in rays of red and blue and yellow and purple. The stone pillars went up and up, and finally branched like trees far, far above their heads. But most beautiful of all was the big rose window which shone with a thousand lovely colors. Side by side Grand'mère and Thérèse knelt to pray and to take part in the Easter service. Thérèse's knees grew stiff from kneeling so long in the chilly air, but she was very happy. The cathedral had been decorated with flowers and lighted candles, and everywhere was sweetness and beauty. Then came the most wonderful thing of all—better even than the great rose window! A beautiful music began to fill the great church. Thérèse clutched Grand'mère's sleeve.

"Grand'mère," she whispered, "is it God's voice?"

"Hush, my little one," answered Grand'mère. "It is only the great organ of which I have told you." Thérèse clasped her hands and listened. The deep notes seemed to make the whole church tremble. The high notes were like the singing of birds. Then many happy voices joined the music of the organ. Thérèse had never heard anything so lovely.

At last the service was over and the people began to leave.

Thérèse and Grand'mère stayed a long time, looking at the beautiful church. When they could stay no longer they dropped money in the box for the poor beside the great door and went outside. The square in front of the great church seemed very bright and warm. Thérèse turned for another look at the great doors and high towers which had been built so long ago.

"Are you not hungry, my rabbit?" said Grand'mère. "Let us cross the river and get lunch before we start for home."

"Oh, Grand'mère, how sparkling the river is! How nice the sunshine feels! Tell me truly, Grand'mère, was that not God's voice we heard in the church?" Grand'mère's black eyes were very bright in her brown, wrinkled face. She smiled and nodded her head softly, so that her little white cap strings bobbed up and down in the spring breeze.

"God's voice is in everything beautiful, my little one," she said wisely.

As they crossed the river they heard a great singing and twittering of birds.

"Listen, Grand'mère!" cried Thérèse. "It sounds like the country, only sweeter. Oh, listen!" In an open square beside the river was the flower and bird market. Little stalls about the edge of the square were full of gayly colored flowers, and in the center were hundreds of cages of birds. Each merchant had his cages set out on a table before him. There were parrots and love birds, pigeons and cockatoos. But dearest of all were the canaries. They almost burst their little throats singing springtime gladness. Thérèse went among them, walking softly so as not to frighten them. Her heart was so happy she wanted to sing, too. Lunch was forgotten as she and Grand'mère went from cage to cage, listening and admiring.

"Come, *petite*," said Grand'mère at last. "Surely we have seen them all."

"But no! Here is one more," cried Thérèse. Sure enough, there was one more cage. A little boy in a ragged black apron was holding it upon his knees, and it was the yellowest and happiest canary of all.

"Where are the rest of your birds?" asked Thérèse.

"I have only one," answered the boy.

"You have only one, and you wish to sell it?" cried Thérèse, surprised. "But why?"

"It is because my mother is sick and we must have money to buy her medicine. Besides, we can no longer feed the little bird, because we must have all the crumbs for ourselves."

"Oh, Grand'mère," cried Thérèse, "is it not sad?" Grand'mère's wrinkled fingers began to fumble in her little black purse. The canary looked at Thérèse with his bright black eyes. Then he swelled out his yellow throat and began to sing. Thérèse closed her eyes and clasped her hands. His song made her remember the high, trembling notes of the organ. Grand'mère was looking at the price marked on the cage. It was almost as many francs as she had in her purse. She couldn't quite decide what to do.

"Thérèse," said Grand'mère. "I have some bread in my bag, left from our breakfast. Will that do for our lunch?"

"Oh, yes, Grand'mère," cried Thérèse, guessing what Grand'mère meant. "Oh, please do let us buy the bird from the poor boy." Grand'mère counted the money into the boy's eager palm. When it was all counted she slipped in an extra franc for himself. Then Thérèse took the little cage in her own hands. Now the bird belonged to Grand'-mère and her!

"Oh, Grand'mère," said Thérèse, "think how wonderful it will be to hear it sing every day—not just this once, but every day." Grand'mère nodded her head and smiled wisely.

"When the little bird sings, Thérèse," said Grand'mère, "we must listen well, for we shall hear it sing of happiness and beauty. It is one way God tells us of them."

ANNE D. KYLE

EASTER LAMBS

They found the twins that day when Daphne and her father walked up the Waddy Kelt. They had left Jericho in the cool of early morning and were presently following a little path made long ago by pattering flocks, up the ever narrowing line of the "Waddy" that was more an overgrown ravine than a valley.

"It looks as if somebody'd cut it with a knife," commented Daphne, peering up at the precipitate heights which forever seemed to be meeting just beyond the next sharp corner, blocking their progress. This was her first real outing since she had come to Palestine a month ago and she was enjoying herself hugely. She gave a little skip of pure joy, skidded on a loose pebble and bumped gleefully into her father's back, which filled the path in front of her.

"Take care!" Professor Pollack swung an arm back and held her. "Look where you're going, Daffy, or you'll be landing down there the first thing you know." He pointed to the valley bottom, where beneath the deceptive beauty of ferns and wild azaleas a mountain creek seethed and foamed menacingly.

"Oh!" Daphne had started to step back, when her quick ears caught a plaintive "baa-a."

"Where is it?" she cried, listening, alert, on tiptoe.

Another "baa-a" came up the steep banks and set them both to peering downward. There below, midway between safety and swift death, on a broad rock half in sun, half in shadow, were two little fat-tailed lambs! One of them lay stretched within the protecting shade, its tiny sides heaving spasmodically, too young and too weak to fight for existence. But the other had no intention of giving up its right to live without protest. It swayed on four wabbly sticks of legs until they refused to hold up their small burden longer. Then it collapsed in a woolly heap only to struggle up again and attempt small, uncertain steps along the rock. As it wabbled it bleated, pathetically, hopefully, and turned agonized baby eyes upward along the hillside that echoed no answering mother "baa-a."

"Oh, dad, how did they get down there?" Daphne, forgetful of caution, teetered on the outer edge of the path till her father pulled her back.

"Take care, young lady!"

"They're starving." Daphne retreated an obedient inch or two and craned her neck. "Look, their sides are all caved in. I'll bet the little one's dead. Oh, no, it isn't! I just saw it sigh."

"Very young lambs are all like that." Her father spoke to reassure her, but Daphne saw that he was frowning as he did when something troubled him. He looked up at the desolate hillside. No sign of flock nor shepherd there. He looked down again at the forlorn babies on their rock shelf, and below them at the treacherous swirl of waters. His suspicion must have shown in his face, for Daphne whispered, her eyes wide with horror:

"Oh, do you think the poor mother sheep—?"

"I'm afraid so, Daffy, but perhaps not. She may have deserted them, sheep do that sometimes, or maybe she got hurt and couldn't come back. She must have been astray, for I don't see any signs of a flock having been around here lately. Wonder how she ever got herself and family down there? But probably she slipped and they followed, but were lucky enough to land on rock instead of the water. Poor lambs." He pushed back his hat and scratched his ear. "I don't see what we can do about it," he objected helplessly.

"Daddy, I can go get them." Daphne tugged eagerly at his sleeves. "I'll just hang on to the rocks and slide down slow and . . ."

"Indeed you won't!" Her father squashed that idea peremptorily. "You stay right where you are. *I'll* go down if any one does."

The lamb, hearing a noise above it, bleated and tried to scramble up the steep slope. It slid back with a bump, tried again, fell. . . .

"You're a plucky rascal." Professor Pollack began to crawl down, fly-wise, clinging to the steep earth. Daphne in excitement sat down and slid a little way, using her feet as brakes.

It was weary work, hoisting those lambs up to safe ground, warm work, too, for the sun, by now directly overhead, was in no humane mood. Its rays quivered and rebounded from the glaring rocks. But at last with pushing and hauling and much slipping of loose pebbles they were up on the path, with Daphne hovering pitifully over them and the professor mopping his brow.

"Now we've got them, what are we going to do with them?" he inquired through his handkerchief.

Daphne looked blank. She had been so intent on getting the lambs out of their precarious position that she had not considered the future. Now, as her father had done, she scanned the ravine anxiously. Still no sign of man nor sheep. Only a lizard slithered across a rock, stared at her with filmed eyes, and melted into the dusty background of the earth. Only a hawk, high against the sky, soared and wheeled and hung motionless. Daphne remembered a picture that had hung in their parlor at home: a flock of sheep lost in the snow and the dark birds that hung over them, waiting.

"I can carry this one." She stooped and lifted the prostrate lamb in her arms. "Oh, daddy, please!" Her gray-green eyes deepened. "Let's take them home! I'll take care of them myself, and it'll be such fun to play with them. Please!"

Professor Pollack hesitated. "We-ell, if you think you can manage it. You ought to have something to amuse you, I have to be away so much, and Frau Weiss isn't much good as a playmate, is she? All right, Daffy." He lifted his kinky burden, laying it across his neck as he had seen the shepherds do. "Do you want to carry yours this way?"

They trudged on, a strange-looking pair, had there been any passers-by to appreciate it. There was the tall, lean form of the professor, bent a little to the passive weight of his burden, and Daphne at his heels, a small facsimile of him save for her skirts, warm and desiring to pant, but stubbornly determined not to give in to weariness until she had her lamb safely in the ancient Ford that had been ordered to wait for them at the upper end of the "Waddy." And she was very happy! Had she not needed to conserve her strength she would have started to sing. Daphne's tunefulness had always been a gauge of her high spirits and for more than four weeks now she had gone silently about the cold little house where she and her father lived in the suburbs of Jerusalem. She had not said much about loneliness and homesickness. Daphne was like that, but when she had opened her mouth to sing a lump had risen in her throat and choked her. If her father had only been able to stay with her! But Professor Pollack had to be off every day, searching through musty documents in old convent libraries, poking around mustier ruins, deciphering strange-looking inscriptions. That was the way with archaeologists! But after all that was why they were in Jerusalem!

When at last they were settled in the shabby Ford, Daphne pondered, "What'll we call them?"

"Gemini," suggested her father, who had also been pondering, his thoughts as usual taking a classical bend. "That's the Latin for twins, you know. I must start you in Latin this year, Daphne."

"But I can't call them both that," she protested, frowning.

"One might be Geminus and the other Gemina," offered the professor, "since they're brother and sister."

"I know," cried Daphne. "Let's have their real name Gemini, and call them Jemmy and Minnie for short."

So Jemmy and Minnie had their playground in the neglected front yard, where Daphne, her knees propped up to her chin, might sit on the old stone steps and watch their antics. She never wearied of fussing over them, laughing at the greedy way they drank, nearly butting the bottle out of her hands; washing them until even their queer fat little tails, that looked like great woolly pouches, shone pinkly through their fleece; tying big bows of ribbon, which they detested, on their soft necks. And the lambs thrived—especially Minnie. The professor often declared that had she been born with two legs instead of four she would have been addressing mass meetings and running for governor by the time she was grown! Certainly she was an energetic lambkin. Jemmy was less active.

"Henpecked," Professor Pollack declared. Probably the

long exposure on that merciless rock had brought him so near to the borderland that he had been a little bewildered with life ever since. If there was any trouble to be fallen into, Jemmy fell; any mischief waiting for luckless lamb, it pounced on him. Perversely, of course, Daphne loved Jemmy best.

Easter week came that year toward the end of April, came with a climax of flowers that covered the bare hills with happy color—all the flowers, cried Daphne, that she had ever seen in gardens—grew wild here. Look! and look! and look! What a place for Easter! They planned to sightsee during Easter Week. Daphne ticked off the places she wanted to see on her fingers.

"We'll go to Bethany on Palm Sunday and to the Mosque of Omar on Monday or Tuesday, Thursday to the Mount of Olives, of course, and on Friday to the Church of the Holy Sepulchre, I suppose, though I've been once," she sighed. "It's so dark and—and cluttered up, it doesn't seem appropriate somehow. I wish there were some place else."

"On Friday," interrupted her father, "the Jewish Passover begins. Maybe we can get ourselves invited to somebody's feast. That's why every one has a sheep now." He pointed to a near-by house in front of which was tied a disconsolate animal.

"Poor thing!" Daphne regarded the broad back with its gala daubs of red paint mournfully.

"They all do it," went on the professor, "Jews and Gentiles alike. Easter dinner without lamb would be like Thanksgiving without turkey. Jemmy and Minnie were lucky to fall into our hands instead of some Hebrew's or

Armenian's, or Moslem's, either, for that matter, since 'Ramadan' begins so soon." He smiled. "I'm afraid our orthodox neighbors will think us extravagant with two lambs for Easter."

"They're not for Easter!" Daphne was indignant. "The idea! Jemmy and Minnie!"

On Wednesday Yusef came around with a load of olive wood. He was a chuckly old man from the Lebanons. Laughter made a hundred wrinkles under his gray whiskers and he wore his little black fez cocked at a youthful angle. He was an incorrigible beggar, always hinting for "baksheesh" but so delightfully naïve about it that it was difficult to resist him. He and Daphne always carried on a friendly conversation made up of scraps of Arabic on her part and tag-ends of English on his. Now he salaamed, touching forehead and breast and lip respectfully, and beamed at her. He began to loosen the load of wood from his donkey's back. When the last stick of it had been stowed away under Frau Weiss's supervision, Yusef lingered to inspect the lambs. He always paid them a weekly visit, talking to them softly in his own tongue, going off into ripples of chuckles when Daphne "baa-ed"—her favorite way of calling them. Daphne had loved him for his interest in her pets, but today his attentions took on a new significance. He felt their woolly sides appreciatively.

"A-ah," he grinned. "Ni-ice." He rubbed his broad belt.

"La!" Daphne's Arabic negative was emphatically short. "They're not for Easter, they're mine!"

Yusef persisted. He held up two fingers and pointed them at himself. "Two," he grinned. "Me, poor man, have not none." He spread pathetic hands and shrugged. Then he indicated the lambs.

"You give me one. Baksheesh, eh?"

Daphne's eyes flashed. As she groped for a phrase indignant enough, she heard the gate creak and then her father came across the yard toward her. Daphne was surprised. He usually spent his afternoons browsing among old manuscripts in the French monastery. Yusef was forgotten as she jumped to meet him.

"Dad! How fine! Are you going to stay or did you just forget something?"

"No—oh, hullo, Yusef!" He greeted the old man absently. Yusef salaamed, a pleased smile wrinkling his childish features. Then he scrambled aboard his donkey's stern, dug his heels into its scanty stomach, and cantered off, looking, as Daphne often said, as if he would tip the boat!

"I've bad news for you, Daffy." Her father drew her arm through his as they went indoors. "You'll be disappointed, I'm afraid. I can't be here for Easter."

Daphne's eyes widened, but she waited for explanations.

"I just met Sir Arthur Kilgenny over at the library. He wants me to ride down with him to Askelon to-morrow and give my opinion on some inscriptions they've just found there. It's rather an honor, Daphne. Sir Arthur's eccentric, and if I said no, I might never get another chance. I feel I owe it to my work. Don't you see, dear?"

Yes, she saw! That was one thing about Daphne, she always saw, and she faced things head up, level-eyed, no matter how much the vision hurt.

"I'm glad I've got the lambs to amuse me," she said at last.

"Yes, and if I were you I'd stay pretty close at home and play with them. The three feasts coming so close together this year, there may be some trouble. And anyway you must never go out alone, Daffy; it isn't really safe. But you won't run out of entertainment with the lambs around, I guess."

"That reminds me," Daphne lifted an indignant face. "That awful old Yusef wanted one of my lambs for baksheesh!"

Professor Pollack laughed. "Yusef would ask for the moon if he couldn't think of anything else. Better keep an eye on Jemmy," he teased her. "He might be missing Sunday morning. I can trust Minnie to look out for herself, but a mere male. Never mind, Daffy, daughter," he hugged her brown bobbed head, "when I get back we'll make up for this, we'll see the Via Dolorosa and the Holy Sepulchre and anything else you say. And I'm going to take you to see some place else; you'll love it so much better than that stuffy church. It's a garden, but there, I'm not going to tell you! Wait till you see it."

On Saturday Daphne scrubbed the lambs until their skin showed sweetly pink beneath their snowy wool, and tied new ribbons on them. Minnie did not like her bow. She butted Daphne over backwards when that young lady sat on her heels and ordered the lambs to keep still while she dressed them up. Jemmy was more docile and in the end Daphne sat back and admired them both. The big pink and blue rosettes looked so pretty against their soft wool. There was still some ribbon left. It trailed on the grass and wound itself about their frisky legs. Just here Frau Weiss called her to supper and Daphne secured the lambs for the time being by tying the ribbons to a fig tree in the garden corner.

Halfway through her meal, Daphne paused, ears pricked.

"Is that Jemmy bleating?" she called to Frau Weiss in the kitchen.

"Nein, nein," the woman assured her. "That is a big sheep. A flock goes by to market, perhaps."

Daphne shivered. Market had an unpleasant sound. She remembered Yusef and the way he rubbed his stomach. But she forgot it again in the delights of a new book that had just come from home. Frau Weiss waddled off to her own room presently, there to fall asleep as she always did over her German Bible, and Daphne read on and on in the shadowy living room. She came out of her book at last with a start. She had left her lambs tied to the fig tree! It was a wonder they hadn't called her to come and put them to bed in the side of the woodshed that had been turned into a fold. She opened the door and stepped out. The yard was dark and silent. She "baa-ed" softly. No answering "baa-a" came across the stillness. She stumbled over to the fig tree. It was deserted! She ran to the woodshed. The twins were not there! She rushed to the gate. It was open and swinging a little creakily. Daphne leaned against it. A sob shook her. She knew! That old Yusef! He'd stolen them both! It *had* been Jemmy she'd heard during supper. What was she to do? She stiffened as an idea struck her—a desperate idea. Determination narrowed her eyes. *She would go after her lambs!*

Daphne knew where old Yusef lived, just within the Damascus Gate of the City. It would not take her long to get there. But her father said it was not safe to go out alone. She listened intently. The night was at peace. Not a sound stirred the secluded garden. After all it was not late, barely nine-thirty. Shutting her mind to all the little fears that tried to creep in, she slipped through the swinging gate. The house was at one end of a blind alley. Yusef could have gone only one way. Turning to the left, she was soon on the main road. She skirted the edge of it, keeping close to the shelter of friendly walls. The street was deserted. She met no one. After a while the exhilaration of the adventure thrilled her. It was like a dream, she thought, a little scary, but fascinating. She was afraid she might wake up before she reached Yusef's.

Just here it occurred to her that the lambs might have run away of their own accord. That naughty Minnie might have pushed her way through the unlatched gate and Jemmy have followed. Daphne paused in despair. In that case she might never find them. But in a few minutes she stumbled on again.

The road widened. Daphne saw the great city walls looming darkly ahead of her, blotting out the stars near the horizon. There was noise in front and people; moving figures and the flickering light of camp fires here and there. Daphne's heart sank. She had forgotten that the gates closed at sunset. The crowd was waiting till morning with their flocks and merchandise to be admitted. Of course there was an opening for unencumbered pedestrians, but she knew she could not reach it unseen. Tears sprang to her eyes.

The night air hummed with the grunting of camels, the drone of muleteers, the bleating of bewildered sheep. Perhaps the lambs had heard that bleating as a flock passed by—heard, and had followed! Perhaps they were there now! She had a desperate idea. If she should "baa-a" the way she always did, perhaps the lambs would recognize it and come; and if not, well, her timid bleat might not be heard by the shepherds, used to the soft commotion of their own flocks. Crouching back into the shadow, she called quaveringly, and again. Nothing answered.

And then her quick ears caught a solitary bleat, near at hand, distinct, familiar. Her heart pounding, she darted forward. "Baa-a!" A feebler one this time, like a small echo of the first. *It was the twins!* She crept nearer, "baa-ing" softly, hoping the Arabs would not hear. The lambs were in front of her, two small shadows against the night. Minnie was ahead, legs apart, wistful but wary. She moved her head uneasily as she bleated. Jemmy lagged behind, as usual. Sheeplike, he did what his sister did, bleated when she bleated, jumped when she jumped.

"Oh, lambies!" Forgetting her caution, Daphne sprang forward. She startled the lambs. They dodged. A shepherd rose from the outlying flocks!

Daphne's knees trembled. She felt as if she were in a nightmare where she wanted to run, and couldn't. She stumbled half-blindly after the lambs. They had turned aside and were bobbing up a shadowy hill. She looked back. The man was hesitating in the road. He had not seen her yet. A camp fire flared. It outlined his flowing headdress, the long slant of a gun across his back. Another man rose and joined him. They debated together.

Minnie bleated again.

The second figure strode forward, calling a hoarse guttural. Daphne gasped. She could not turn back now! Beyond her was a mass of shadow. She would have to hide there. She ran on. The lambs, bumping into each other, bobbed ahead of her. Something rose across her path. Her hands touched a wall. With a despairing sob she ran back and forth, feeling along it. Was she trapped at last? She glanced back. The men were still coming! The lambs, bewildered by her movements, rushed back and forth, bumping into her, tripping her. She sprawled forward, hands flung out instinctively. She touched loose stones. The wall was broken! Minnie put her little forelegs on it and peeped over. Daphne gave her a shove and she disappeared with a tiny sliding of pebbles. Jemmy was too big to lift, but Daphne dragged his stiff little body forward and pushed him over. There was a slip and a slide, a startled bleat, then silence. But she had no time to wonder where he had slid. She jumped over and down. Down! There was nothing under her feet. She flung out her arms and grabbed wildly. Leaves slipped through her fingers, she clung for an instant on the edge of a bank. Then she plunged on.

Presently she found herself staring upward at the stars. She did not feel like moving, somehow. Her ankle hurt so; it seemed to be doubled under her. She moved her arms cautiously, *they* did not hurt, anyway! Her fingers met something soft and warm. It stirred at her touch. Then she remembered. She had pushed Jemmy through the hole and he had fallen! She turned her head slowly. Where was Minnie? She became aware at that of voices, of two figures that moved back and forth along a black bank high up against the starry night. One of them seemed to have a queer hump on his shoulders—like—like— Why, her father had looked like that when he carried Minnie out of the Waddy Kelt! She understood then. The men who had followed her had caught Minnie and were taking her away to be a poor little Easter lamb! Daphne pushed Jemmy's head against the earth. At least they should not find him! She lay tense and still. Presently the voices died away. . . .

It was a garden she had fallen into. The scent of flowers was all about her, under her. She had dropped into a flower-bed! Violets, sweet William, roses, everything, filled the night with sweetness. Strange, how she did not feel like moving! She seemed to be rocking lightly away. What night was this? Oh, yes, Easter. She had been going to see the Holy Sepulchre again, on Easter, but her father had gone away. Fragments of thoughts danced crazily through her mind. Her father, the Holy Sepulchre, the lambs, Easter! That last made her think of a picture she'd seen in her Child's Bible: an angel sitting beside a door and two men stooping down to look in. Who were they? Oh, yes, Peter and John! Peter and John! Peter and— A light shone across her eyelids. She opened them. But there was no angel above her, his great pinions dripping light, only a lantern that waved redly, outlining two figures that stooped to look. Peter and John! They were picking her up now, and Peter, why Peter was talking to her in old Yusef's voice, and old Yusef's face, with no laugh-wrinkles under its beard, was squinting anxiously into hers!

. . . . . .

"He said he knew me, the way I 'baa-ed,' daddy!" Two days later Daphne snuggled under her father's arm as he sat on the edge of her bed. "And he knew the lambs because I had bows round their necks! He said one of those shepherds was an old friend of his, that's why he was there with them."

"It's a good thing for you he was, young lady! And that he had sense enough to keep on looking for you after he'd found Minnie! You can thank him that you got off with nothing worse than a sprained ankle and the sniffles."

"And that I've still got the twins," added Daphne meekly. "Jemmy's tougher than you'd have thought!" Presently she sighed, "Here we were going to go round and see everything this week, and I had to go and do this."

Professor Pollack stroked her dejected head. "Cheer up, Daffy! Don't you know what you fell into? Do you remember my telling you about a place I knew you'd love—oh, so much better than any Church of the Holy Sepulchre—a garden, Daffy? Well, it was that garden you fell into. They call it the Garden of the Resurrection, because some one a little while ago discovered an old tomb there that was different from other Jewish tombs. It had never been used, for one thing, and it had a slab at the head and foot where a mourner, or an angel, could sit, and outside was a great stone that had been rolled away. Some day we'll go to see it together. Think what you've got to write home, Daphne!

You spent Easter night in the Garden of the Empty Tomb!"

"And," added Daphne, practically, after a few minutes, "poor Jemmy and Minnie weren't Easter lambs after all!"

"Are you so sure of that?" asked her father, and smiled.

CAROL RYRIE BRINK

DAFFODILS OUT OF THE DARK

It was the day before Easter in Paris and the *foire aux jambons,* or "ham fair," was in full swing. The parkway in the center of the Boulevard Richard-Lenoir was filled for miles with little booths where everything could be bought from antique chairs and miniatures to rusty nails and horse-meat sausages. A great crowd of people surged up and down the street, but the crowd was most dense near the corner of the Rue St. Sabin where two young acrobats and a white dog were performing their tricks. The tall, dark-eyed boy could walk on his hands and twist his legs behind his head with the skill of a contortionist. The little curly-headed sister turned cart wheels and backward somersaults; and the dog rolled over, begged, and ran the gamut of ordinary canine performance. There were sword swallowers and contortionists scattered through the fair all the length of the Boulevard Richard-Lenoir, but something about the youth and freshness of these two acrobats, even in their dingy tights and spangles, drew the loiterers to watch them.

In the ring of spectators were two people who had watched them many times before. One was the slouching figure of a dark, heavy-faced man, who always returned when the crowd had dispersed and took the sous and francs which the girl had collected in her brother's ragged cap. When the spectators had not been generous and there were only a few sous in the cap, the man was very angry with them and the three performers often went supperless to bed.

The other person who had watched the show before was a rosy-cheeked country girl named Céleste Arnot. Whenever she heard the roll of the little drum by which the acrobats announced the beginning of their act, she left the booth where her father displayed his fine country hams and flew to watch her friends. It was Céleste who applauded most loudly and laughed most delightedly. Céleste had never been in Paris before in her life, although she lived only a few miles outside the limits of the great city. The *foire aux jambons* seemed to her the most marvelous sight she had ever seen, and marvel of marvels were the young acrobats who had come to be her friends. When the girl passed her brother's cap for sous, Céleste caught her arm and whispered in her ear:

"Come to the booth, when you have finished, Francine. Father will give you each a piece of sausage." Francine nodded and smiled. Sausage was better than sous, for, if one ate it quickly, the slouching man with the heavy face could not put it in his pocket and carry it away. Francine whispered to Jacques, and he smiled and nodded, too. As if he understood, Toto, the dog, jumped and barked. They gathered up the drum and their ragged coats and slipped through the crowd after Céleste.

"Tell us about your farm, Céleste," cried Francine as they ran along.

"Oh, I have told you so many times," laughed Céleste.

"We used to live on a farm, did we not, Jacques?" said Francine. "But I can scarcely remember. You must tell us what it is like so that we shall not forget."

"Oh, it is not half so gay as this," protested Céleste. "There are no booths or merry-go-rounds or crowds of people."

"I should like that," said Francine. "I am tired of fairs."

"Then why do you go about to them?" asked Céleste.

"Duval makes us," said the boy, glancing back over his shoulder as if he expected to see the slouching man behind them. "He works us for what we can bring him. It was he who taught us our tricks, but we have much more than repaid him for what he has done for us. When I am a little stronger, he shall not dare to treat us the way he does." Céleste was surprised to see the boy's clenched fists and tense face. Toto leaped up, whining, and licked his master's hand as if he understood.

Behind the booth of M. Arnot was a little tent where Céleste and her father were camped during the week of the fair. With the roar of the crowds and the tumult of city traffic rushing by them all day, they were as calm and secure as birds in a nest. Céleste pulled out some boxes for her guests to sit on, and cut thick slices of bread while her father cut rounds of sausage. There was a spicy smell from the home-cured meats and the fresh evergreen boughs which decorated the little booth.

Spring was late that year, and a cold mist hung in the air. After their violent activity, the acrobats shivered in their ragged coats, and Jacques drew Toto close to him for warmth and sympathy. M. Arnot beamed at them over a great link of sausage. He had a large, warm heart which was roomy enough for all of Céleste's friends.

"They are shivering, Céleste," he cried. "Give them that *café au lait* which I was warming on the oil stove. Now for a piece of country sausage—none of your horse flesh here, *mes enfants!* When you eat this, you eat the best!" They set their chattering teeth into the welcome food, and Francine said:

"Monsieur, you are very kind to us. Few people care what becomes of us when our act is over."

"*Eh bien,* where are your parents then?" inquired the good farmer.

"O papa, you must not ask them that!" cried Céleste. "Their father was killed in the War when they were babies. Their mother died sometime after, and this M. Duval is nothing to them but a hard master."

"Indeed? Indeed?" said M. Arnot. "And what would mamma say to such a story?"

"She would be very sad," said Céleste.

"It shall not be so with us always," said Jacques fiercely,

giving the remainder of his food to Toto and straightening his shoulders. "I am old enough now to take care of my sister and myself, if Duval would not follow us and take our money from us." As he was speaking Toto uttered a deep growl and the hair along his mane and clipped back stiffened. M. Duval came around the corner of the booth and laid his hand heavily on the boy's shoulder.

"You thought you would run away from me, did you?" he asked with an unpleasant smile. "You thought you could lose Duval in the crowd, eh? While you spent my money to fill your stomachs, eh?"

"No, monsieur!" cried Jacques, springing to his feet. "We have not spent a cent of the money. It is all here in my pocket."

"Ah, how shall I know that, eh? How shall I know?"

"Monsieur, you may take my word for it, if you will not take his," said M. Arnot, "although I think I have never seen a boy with a more honest face." Jacques counted the coppers out of his pocket into Duval's hand. Toto, growling and with his white fangs bared, stood close beside Jacques.

"That dog!" cried Duval. "It was I who beat the tricks into him by which he earns his living, and yet he would leap at my throat and kill me, if ever he got the chance. He adds nothing to the act. I think I shall sell him for what I can get."

"No!" cried Francine, throwing her arms about Toto's neck. "No! No!"

"The next time he leaps at my back as he did last night," said Duval, "he shall be sold. Now I go to the café where

I have promised to meet an old friend. When I return in fifteen minutes you will give another show."

In silence they watched him go slouching through the crowd and out into the busy street. Jacques was pale and trembling with fear and anger. The white dog stood beside him, his lip still curled in a snarl. Suddenly he leaped forward to overtake the man who had inspired him with so much hatred.

"Oh!" screamed Francine. "He will catch Duval! Duval will sell him!" Before she had finished speaking Jacques had darted after the dog, wildly calling his name. He rushed out into the street with only one thought in his mind —to save the dog who was their dearest possession. A taxi driver swerved to miss hitting the white dog which suddenly dashed from the curb, and struck instead the young acrobat. Jacques lay where he fell, crumpled and white.

Time seems to run more slowly in a hospital than in any other place. To those who lie on tumbled beds and gaze at the familiar walls, the hours seem doubled. But no clock can measure the uncertain anguish of those who sit and wait for news of life or death. To the two girls who waited in the corridor of the hospital with their dog, the night seemed endless. Doctors and nurses came and went on silent feet. Sometimes a cry of pain escaped through an opening door, but for the most part the night was silent and heavy with suspense. Dim night lights burned up and down the corridor and no one paid any attention to the two girls huddled in the shadows, waiting for word of Jacques.

At the far end of the corridor hung a cross. Céleste began to tell the old familiar Easter story as she had heard it ever since she could remember, hoping to comfort Francine. But somehow it was difficult to get beyond the crucifixion with the cross before her eyes and Francine's fitful sobbing in her ears. When she had finished, Francine said:

"Tell it again, Céleste. I shall try not to cry. I have not heard it since very long ago, when my mother told it to me."

Céleste told it again, wishing her own good mother were here now to comfort Francine. When she had finished, she talked of the country, and at last Francine, worn out by the troubles of the day, fell asleep with her head against Céleste's shoulder. At their feet Toto slept uneasily, opening his eyes at every noise as if he expected to see his young master.

Presently a little streak of early-morning light came through the half-closed shutter. Then a door opened and M. Arnot and the doctor came out together. Céleste sat up quickly and Francine and Toto were wide-awake in an instant. Good M. Arnot came toward them, his round face less ruddy than usual, but smiling.

"He is going to recover, my little one," he said, lifting Francine's tearful face. "He is sleeping now, and you must go and get some breakfast. Later on, when he awakes, you may see him for a moment. Here, Céleste, is some money for your breakfast. I have some business which must be seen to."

Stiff and dazed from the long vigil, but full of hope, the two girls put on their coats and went slowly out of the hospital. The night lights were still burning in the corridor, but outside the great square was sparkling with early sunshine. As they stood a moment, dazzled by the brilliance, the bells of the Cathedral of Notre Dame began to ring. Then they saw it just across the square. The ancient stones, which patient and inspired hands of long ago had carved into a lacework of figures and leaves and peering faces, were half in shadow, half in high relief, and from the two great towers came the singing of the joyful bells.

Toto began to leap and bark with joy at being free again.

"Francine," cried the country girl, "it is Easter morning! I had forgotten that today should be the day of Easter! See, the people are going to the early service. Let us go in only for a moment!" Unnoticed by the crowd of early worshipers, they slipped through one of the great doors and knelt a moment on the cold stones, covering their bare heads with their handkerchiefs and holding Toto sternly quiet. A great flood of light poured down from the rose windows, and flowers and tall white candles with flames of gold brightened the dark arches. Inside the cathedral the sound of the bells was lost in the pealing of the organ and the many happy voices singing: "He is risen! He is risen!" Céleste's eyes sparkled, for now the crucifixion seemed only the beginning of the Easter story and not the end. Francine clung to her and cried again, but only because she was happy.

When they came out into the sunshine, they almost skipped across the bridge to the Left Bank of the river Seine. There was a little café where they could get hot chocolate and fresh, crisp rolls. It was the first food they had tasted since their luncheon of bread and sausage had been interrupted the day before.

"I hear birds singing," said Céleste. "It sounds like the country." She finished her roll and stood up.

"It will be the bird market," said Francine. "Come, let us walk through it and return by the other bridge." All along the river bank between the two bridges were stalls filled with flowers and birds. It seemed as if the countryside had come to gray-stone Paris to make it bloom on Easter Sunday.

"Oh," said Céleste, "I have been away from home a whole week. The flowers will have blossomed while I was away." She was going to add: "Soon I shall return," but Francine caught her hand and fear and sorrow were in her face again. How could she bear to go home and leave Francine and Jacques to be ill-treated by M. Duval? "Look, Francine," she said, squeezing the thin hand, "here is a little pot of daffodils such as we have at home. It costs only two francs. See, I have money enough left to buy it."

Francine held the little flowerpot close against her heart as they returned to the hospital. The flowers kept nodding to her as she walked, and it was as if they said: "We sprang from the dark earth where there was only sorrow and despair. We are the flowers of hope."

M. Arnot, smiling more than ever, was there before them. In a moment the nurse took them to see Jacques. He looked strange and pale in his bandages, but still he smiled at them and at the pot of flowers which Francine put beside his bed. Then his face clouded.

"Where is Duval?" he whispered. "Did he sell our dog?"

"Ah," said M. Arnot, "that is what I wanted to tell you. Toto is safe. As for M. Duval, he will trouble you no more. When he heard of the accident, he was afraid that you would no longer be able to do the tricks he had taught you, and he was very willing to resign your guardianship to me."

"To you?" cried Céleste and Francine together.

"Yes," said M. Arnot, rubbing his hands together with pleasure, "and as soon as Jacques can be moved from here, we shall try what the country can do to make him well and strong and happy again."

"And Francine, too?" cried Céleste excitedly.

"Assuredly," said M. Arnot. "What will mamma say to having another daughter and son?"

"She will be so happy!" cried Céleste joyously. "She will be almost as glad as I am!" But Francine could say nothing; she could only hide her happy tears in the bright yellow daffodils.

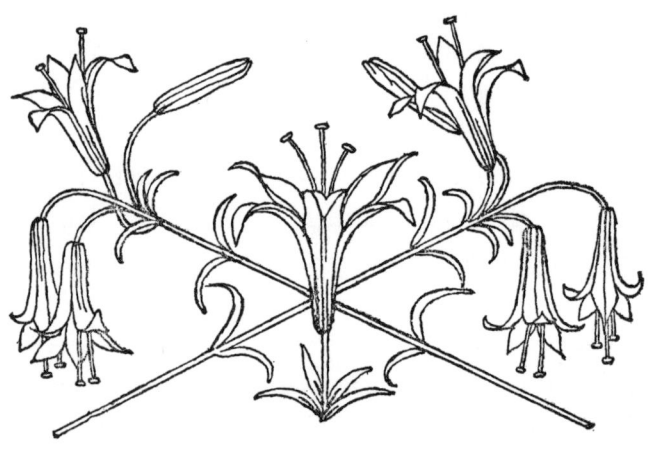

ANNE D. KYLE

EASTER CANDLE

"They are coming back!"

Fiametta, peering over the cliff at the soft Italian blue sea far below, saw the boat glide out and head for the tiny beach that lay like a white seashell caught between the two lonely promontories which formed the westernmost end of the island.

Yes, even the American Signora, whose name was Miss Vale, must have had enough for one day of the gloomy

Grotto with its dark waters hemmed by looming walls; its strange passageway that had been hewn apparently out of the rock itself only to stop abruptly in a blank wall. Sandro had taken Fiametta in there once in the early days before he had grown tired of supporting his orphaned girl-cousin. She was glad when she was out again. Better to tend Sandro's goats all day upon the sunny island hills than to explore a stuffy cavern whose silence was broken only by the ominous moaning of the sea outside! The American Signora, however, when she had come, hadn't minded that. Daily, at her direction, Sandro picked and hammered at the rocky barrier which ended the corridor.

"She is quite mad," Sandro told his wife Lisa, "but what matter so long as I get good money? Besides," he added, a sly look coming into his ferret face, "Florio in the village has told me that there is a man in Naples who sells old things, even to broken glass and headless statues, to mad foreigners, for large prices. If the Signora should chance to find something like that behind the wall . . . I may be able to take a little for myself . . . on the quiet."

Was the wall broken through yet? Was there anything beyond it? Fiametta wondered as she picked up the faded handkerchief in which she kept the lace she had just finished, and scrambled to her feet. Her sudden movement startled a goat which browsed jerkily among the broom nearby and it gave a jump and skipped off sidewise on delicate hoofs. There was a sudden crash, a frightened bleat and its hindquarters vanished as if the earth had swallowed them.

"Nanni!" Fiametta dropped her work and it caught on

a wild rose thorn. She sprang forward. There was indeed a yawning hole where only a moment before Jack-in-the-Pulpits had raised their little spotted canopies. Luckily for the goat, a slight projection in the rocky shaft had stopped its fall. Fiametta stooped and grabbed its forelegs but the little goat was too heavy for her to lift.

"Sandro!" He would be in by this time.

A surly shout answered from the beach. "I am busy. What is it?"

"Sandro, come quick! It is Nanni—"

Sandro's head appeared reluctantly over the top of the slope.

"What are you doing here? Now what thing is this?" For he had heard Nanni's frightened bleat. He strode over, shoved Fiametta aside and hauled Nanni up to solid ground. Then he turned on the panting girl. "So, you let my goats fall into holes!" He pulled her over to him and raised his hand to strike her across the face.

A cool voice intervened. "Let her alone, Sandro."

It was the Signora Miss Vale. Fiametta, in spite of her fear, managed to give a shy stare upward through her tangle of bright hair. This was the first time she had seen the Signora close at hand, though she had heard many strange things about her appearance—that she cut her hair shorter than Sandro's, for instance, who wore a wavy black fan on top of his head; and that she had big round glasses that were like frog's eyes. This was all true, Fiametta saw—but there was more also. For the Signora's mouth was firm and kind and the blue eyes behind the frog glasses looked as if they smiled often in spite of the fact that now there was fire in them that scorched Sandro until he cringed.

"But, Signora, I have warned her it was dangerous to bring the goats here! . . . Who knows how many have already fallen into that hole?" He dropped on his knees to peer mournfully into the aperture in which moaned a low hollow sound such as lies in the heart of a seashell.

"No, no!" Fiametta objected. "Nanni was the only one. And how should I know there was a hole hidden beneath the grass?"

"Why did you come up here, child?" Miss Vale interrupted her gently. "Was there no other place to pasture?" She spoke Italian well, the Signora.

"It was because . . . because . . . I wished to watch for you, Signora." Fiametta looked up timidly. "I thought perhaps you would buy the lace collar I make . . . and now it is all torn." Her eyes filled as she saw the forlorn crumple below the rose-bush. Miss Vale picked it up.

"But it can be easily mended. Fix it, child, and when I return from Naples—after Easter—"

"It was . . . for Easter . . . that I wanted the money." Fiametta cast a wary glance at Sandro who was still crouched beside the crevice, a puzzled look on his sly face. "For the 'festa' on Easter Eve," she added, dropping her voice. Everyone must have a Candle, you see, Signora, a beautiful Candle to light from his neighbor's when the bells ring out that Easter is here again, and everyone cries, 'Happy Easter!' —Buon Pascale. It is the greatest Festa in the whole year, Signora, and—and . . ." She bit at her lip to hold it stiff and pushed at a Jack with one bare brown foot. "Oh, Signora, when my mother lives I have always a Candle, but now . . . there is no money to waste on Candles . . . for me. . . ."

"I doubt if it would break him," commented Miss Vale in English, eyeing Sandro.

Fiametta looked bewildered. "How? I did not understand."

"Never mind. I was only thinking aloud. Take your kerchief and the lace, child. How much would it be if it were done?"

"I thought . . . perhaps . . . five lire?" said Fiametta timidly. "It is not fine as my mother would have made it. But I had only this thread left over—"

Miss Vale took out her purse and opened it. Fiametta paused, fascinated. Imagine having all those lire to carry around!

"Ecco!" Miss Vale held out a shiny five-lire piece and Fiametta's small peaked face glowed as though someone had held a candle to it. "If I pay for it now, will you finish it for me afterwards?"

"Oh, si—si—si—si, Signora!" Fiametta put out her hand for the money. It was pushed aside.

"If the Signora," suggested Sandro, his white teeth gleaming, "will give *me* the money to keep. . . ."

"Put your hand away, Sandro." Something clicked, like a pair of sharp scissors, in Miss Vale's voice. She laid the coin in the girl's warm palm and closed her fingers over it. "Keep it carefully," she warned her.

Fiametta breathed quickly and peeped at Sandro, from whose face the smile had dropped. But he only shrugged and turned to snap his fingers at the goats as if five lire meant nothing to him. The Signora observed him thoughtfully.

"Hm," she said, more to herself than to Fiametta. "What is your name, child, and where," as a light south wind tossed the girl's hair to the color of a flickering candle-flame, "where in South Italy did you ever get a head that shade?"

"Fiametta," answering the first question. As for the second: "There has always been hair like this in our family, Signora. Old nonna—my father's mother—had it also—"

"Why, you might almost be descended from those red-haired Goths that came down here with Odoacer! Well, if you are, you're the only sign of them I've seen yet, though if it wasn't for Easter, who knows—I might have found some before the week was up. That wall sounded pretty thin today! Well, addio, Fiametta. Have a good time at your festa—"

"Oh, Signora—if you would only stay and see for yourself how lovely it is—"

"Wish I could." Miss Vale, laying a kind hand on Fiametta's arm, thoughtfully fingered the deep cuff where Fiametta had turned the sleeve up because the dress, being one of her mother's, was too long for her thin young arm. "I've never heard of one quite like it here in Italy." She relapsed again into English. "If the Tylers decide to go straight to Rome, I might— Fiametta, will you wear this dress to the festa on Saturday?"

"I have no other, Signora," wonderingly.

"Then be sure and look hard at your cuffs before you go."

Fiametta had little time to puzzle over that strange bit of

advice, for Miss Vale was barely out of sight when Sandro spun round.

"The money," he commanded. "Give it to me!"

"No, it is mine. The Signora said it was mine!" Fiametta hugged her clenched fist tight against her breast.

"The Signora is a fool not to know I would have it sooner or later. Give me that money, I say!" And he forced her hand open.

"No, no, Sandro, it is mine! Give it back to me." She flung her frail body against his, her fingers tugging at his impassive hand. "Please, Sandro, it is for an Easter Candle—"

"Easter Candle, indeed! It will pay for a little of the spaghetti you eat! A very little, too. Go away, I am busy."

He shoved her arms back rudely and the jerk sent something fluttering lightly to the ground. It was a smudgy bit of paper,—a ten-lire note! Fiametta instinctively put her foot over it. Sandro had not noticed. He had already turned his back on her. Fiametta's heart leaped joyously; she understood.

So that was what the Signora had meant! That was why she had fingered the shabby cuff so long! She had known very well that Sandro would take the five lire the minute she was gone, and so she had quietly left more in its place. Ten lire, too—double the amount! That would buy the loveliest candle on the whole island! And she, Fiametta, need not miss the festa which thrilled her yearly with its starry beauty; which always seemed to make something,—what, she did not know,—bloom anew within her heart like the Easter Lilies that burst each spring from their brown hard bulbs. Surely this year, alone and unwanted, she needed that Resurrection Miracle more than ever.

"The good Signora! If only there was something I could do to thank her! I might make her another piece of lace, but that is nothing, really." Fiametta sighed as she lifted the money cautiously between her toes, her eyes still on Sandro's back. Later she would slip it within the hem of her dress for safe-keeping.

"Are you still there?" Sandro said impatiently over his shoulder. "Take the goats home at once. Tonight I shall give you that beating I refrained from out of deference to the Signora."

But at night, when he came in rather earthy and breathless, he had forgotten all about it. He sat and chuckled over his spaghetti until Lisa, his wife, asked him tartly what the joke was.

"Nothing," he told her, adding, "tonight I go to the village to see Florio and tomorrow I shall—very likely—go to Naples."

"It is Good Friday and a Holy Day," she warned him. "It will be bad luck to do business." But he only grinned.

Fiametta ran swiftly down the dusty road. It was Saturday and a fair day. She hummed a little tune as she ran. Her ten lire were safe in her hand and Lisa was off visiting a sick sister. As for Sandro, he was away on business as mysterious as that which had taken him yesterday to Naples. The astonished goats were locked safely in their pen, and Fiametta, the old handkerchief tied over her bright hair,—lest she stop at the church,—was on her way to the village.

But once there she wandered irresolutely from candle-shop to shop. So lovely were all their waxy wares, she could not make up her mind. But at last she selected a tall slim candle decorated with tiny gold roses and an angel blowing a golden trumpet. Her eyes were misty with delight as the storekeeper handed it to her. She held it carefully lest her warm hands mar its beautiful perfection. She darted across the Square through the crowd that had just poured off the morning boat from Naples.

All at once she stopped. Sandro was coming toward her accompanied by a fat stranger with a toothpick mustache. Fiametta shrank into a nearby doorway. Presently the two turned aside and sat down at a table outside Florio's restaurant. Fiametta breathed again. She slid out of her doorway, into the safety of an alley just this side of Florio's, whose patrons were protected from public gaze by a thick trellis of bougainvillea. Fiametta saw the two men dimly through the leaves. She was about to break into a run when Sandro's voice brought her to a startled halt.

"I confess that if the Signora were not in Naples I would never dare to touch them. She has an Evil Eye, that woman! She can turn your knees to water with a look."

The Signora? What things? Fiametta flattened herself against a wall and listened.

The stranger ordered two cups of coffee. "I am sorry I was not in yesterday, but it being a 'festa'—"

"It does not matter, since you have come today."

"Then let us talk business. What have you?"

"Nothing, Signore . . . with me . . . but before night, if we agree, you shall have as much as you want. Listen!"

Sandro dropped his voice and Fiametta edged an inch nearer. "After the Signora left on Thursday, I went back. I broke through the wall and squeezed myself in. Beyond, even as the Signora thought, there was another cave . . . hewn out . . . and crowded with such things as I have never laid eyes on before. They must have been hidden there long ago and then a stone placed cunningly to make the corridor appear blind. There was gold . . . and silver . . . lying about for the picking. But I had to leave it for my taper was almost gone. I swear that no one knows of all this but me. And, as I say, the Signora is gone! Think of her chagrin when she returns!"

Fiametta waited to hear no more. She sped down the alley and out of the village. There she leaned against a garden wall to catch her breath and think.

There was evil afoot for the Signora! The Signora who had been so good to her that Fiametta prayed night and morning for some way by which she might repay her. Was this the answer? Then, for awhile, Fiametta stood very still, staring at a little lizard who sunned himself head downward on the wall. Once or twice her gaze faltered to the candle, the beautiful candle, all roses and an Easter angel! She would never have another like it again! Could she . . . even for the Signora—? She dashed her hand across her eyes and walked on, her small chin firm. Once only she paused to ask a passing peasant, who puffed at his long pipe as he drove his donkey into town, if he had a match. He gave her two wax ones grudgingly.

Presently she reached the lonely white beach. Sandro's boat was still drawn up on the sand. She pushed and panted until at last it floated free. She scrambled in and picked up the oars. Her hands were shaking, but it was not because she was afraid of a boat. She was not island born for nothing. Besides the sea was satin smooth. No, it was the thought of what she was going to do that made her shake. Nevertheless, she did not hesitate. She sent the boat skimming toward the face of the cliff. At least, Sandro could not follow her when she had his boat! Before he could run back to town and borrow another she would be out again. And after that? Resolutely she kept her mind centered on present problems. She was determined, somehow, to forestall Sandro's thieving. The future would work itself out.

The tunnel in the cliff was directly ahead of her. She drew in her oars and slid to the bottom of the boat as it shot through. When she sat up she was rocking gently in a vast dim pool. Through the tunnel entrance daylight glimmered on the murky water. She struck one of her matches. It's head shot off sputtering,—if the other went out, too . . . but it did not. She cupped her hands around its pinpoint of flame until the candle caught and flared into a firm yellow light. Propping the candle between her knees she picked up the oars and sent the boat back into the gloomy depths of the cave. Presently its keel scraped upon an unseen beach. She held the candle high and looked around doubtfully. Was this the right place? With relief, she made out a darker mass among the eerie shadows beyond her candle-light. That must be the beginning of the corridor. She beached the boat and walked toward it, the candle pushing the reluctant darkness back. Behind her it closed in again promptly,—darkness and silence, broken only by the steady muffled hum of the sea. It made her ears ring,— filled them with strange, inexplicable sounds.

"What was that?" She paused, looking over her shoulder. Nothing, of course! For an instant she fancied a faint ray of light far off among the shadows. It was her imagination; —the only light in all that vast cave came from her own candle and that far glimmering arc across the pool. Reassured, she felt her way up the corridor, until the barrier that blocked it loomed out of the dark ahead. There was the jagged hole in it. She shoved the candle through, stuck it upright in some hot grease, and crept through the opening after it.

She found herself in a small octagonal room, chiseled out of the solid rock. At one end was a single stone altar. Above, on the wall, a face stared at her benignly. It was of a young Man, beardless, smiling, three fingers raised in blessing. More frescoes, dimmed by time and dampness, appeared here and there. One, almost faded out, was a curious procession of women dancing with hairy-hoofed goatmen. What a queer place! Sinister, too. The goaty men frightened her. She could not know that this had been a pagan shrine before the Christians sanctified it as a church, secret, underground, like the Catacombs of Rome.

Nor had she any way of knowing that all the chests, the bronze vases, the marble basins and statues, which lay in mouldy heaps about her feet, had been brought here in frantic haste by people long, long dead, hoping no doubt to save them from the thieving hands of those marauders who had just sacked Rome. She only knew that someone else was plotting to steal them now, and it was up to her to save them.

Feverishly she looked about her. Sandro had mentioned gold and—yes, there was a box over in the corner, in which yellow gleamed. She tried to lift it and it fell to pieces spilling its jeweled contents on the floor. Crosses and candlesticks; cups and plates; rings and other articles of jewelry,—all jumbled together. How was she to gather them up? She stared down at them, worried and nervous.

At last she untied the handkerchief from her head and spread it out. Good! Its ample folds would hold everything. She heaped it up and knotted the corners together, lifted it and then set the bundle down near the hole, while she turned once more to see what else she could manage.

And then, in the dark and the silence, she heard a sound! Near at hand, too. She spun around and the blood chilled in her veins. *A face was staring at her from the hole*—Sandro's face! Suddenly, his arm glided toward her, silent as a snake. With a scream, she shut her eyes, expecting to feel a blow sting across her face. But it did not come and at last she opened her eyes fearfully. She was alone! The face had disappeared! She could have believed it had never been there,—but for one thing.

The bundle by the door had disappeared!

With that, she came back to life. She regained the corridor and raced along it.

"I must stop him somehow!" she gasped. "I *must!*" If only she could reach the town first; persuade the one policeman they had to detain him with the goods until the Signora came back. Other plans raced desperately through her mind and all the time she wondered how soon she would feel Sandro's hands reach out for her. . . .

Nevertheless, she reached the beach unhindered and there she stopped, at last, incredulous and horror-struck. The boat was no longer there!

She stared in numb despair across the pool to where the distant arc marked the way to safety and to day. An object appeared in the center of it, as a little cloud floats across the face of a half-moon. It was her boat! And Sandro was in it! It hung poised an instant against the light, and then it vanished, shooting out into the sunny sea. While she . . . she was left behind alone, a dying candle in her nerveless hand. Oh, what was she to do? Frightened sobs shook her from head to foot. In her hand the candle flame flickered lower . . . lower. . . .

It seemed like hours that she stood there, the small waves licking at her bare feet, before the light went out abruptly and there was nothing to relieve the darkness but that glimmering distant arc. Nothing except . . . she turned away from its mocking glare . . . and once again she saw a faint slanting ray in the cavern depths. Impossible! And yet,—it was there, growing stronger, more distinct now that there was no nearer candle-gleam to dazzle her eyes.

It was day! Surely it was day! Her heart gave a bound. There was another entrance to the Grotto then. That explained how Sandro had gotten in without a boat. She began to grope her way toward it, scarcely daring yet to hope.

But when at last she stood herself within that ray of light, she found that she was still a prisoner. Far above, the blue sky shone and grasses waved in the slight soft breeze. But how was she to get out? She stared at the shaft of rock with sinking heart. If she called would anyone hear her? Where did that chimney lead? All at once she had a suspicion: Could it be the one that Nanni slipped into two days ago? Surely that was somewhere near! And if it was . . . Fiametta examined the sides again more carefully, and saw that there were niches cut into the rock at regular intervals to form a sort of precarious ladder. It was on one of these that Nanni's feet had found support. The shaft, so old, so long unused that the grass had spanned it, had been the landward entrance to the chapel underground!

"Fiametta! Are you a flower, that you sprout up from the earth?"

It was the Signora, Miss Vale! Fiametta, safe at last, stared at her incredulously.

"But, but," she stammered, and suddenly tears brightened her eyes and spilled down her wan cheeks. "Oh, Signora," she sobbed, "I tried . . . I did my best. . . ." She stumbled through her tragic tale. "It's all gone . . . all!"

"But look," said the Signora gently when she had finished —and there was the knotted handkerchief itself lying nearby beside a strange paper package. "I met Sandro," she explained, "running down the path with it. I recognized it as the one you wrapped your lace in and I stopped him. 'Sandro, what are you doing with that?' He stared as if he had seen a ghost! 'If you are taking what is not yours,' I told him sternly, 'I shall have the law on you.' And at that he shook all over, threw the bundle into a cactus hedge, and ran off. I fished it out and came on to find you. When I met you nowhere else I came here, thinking you might have disobeyed again. And I see you rise up out of the ground."

"Oh, Signora!" Fiametta kept her eyes on the bundle as if afraid it might disappear again. "They were for you, those golden things and—"

"They are not mine, 'Mettina mia,' they belong to your country—to Italy—which likes to learn what it can of the people . . . like you . . . who used to live in it. That is why it sent me down to see what I could find about the people who were here before the barbarians came, fourteen hundred years ago. The man Sandro talked to,—he is a notorious smuggler, Fiametta, who would have stolen all these things from the government and sold them out to foreigners for his own profit. So you see,—now let's talk of something pleasanter! I have brought you something from Naples, Fiametta, for the 'festa' tonight!" She lifted the paper package from the grass and put it into Fiametta's wondering hands. "It is for you to wear," she explained, as Fiametta opened it. "That was how I happened to meet Sandro."

It was a dress, a girl's dress, made to fit, not cut down from a larger! And it was blue and soft and shiny as the Madonna's robe. Fiametta laid the cool folds to her cheek in a rapture of delight.

"In America, it is the custom," Miss Vale told her twinkling, "to wear new clothes at Easter. If we go to the 'festa' together tonight, you and I,—will you help me choose two nice candles?—you must be like an American girl,—isn't that right? And after tonight"—she paused—"I fancy you will not be so welcome now at Sandro's even if he hasn't run away for good. Would you like to come and stay with me? I am going to rent a little house, for there will be much work to do in the Grotto, and—"

"Oh, Signora," cried Fiametta, starry-eyed, "if only I could do something . . . beautiful, for you!" and she told herself, "Another piece of lace, perhaps. Yes, I will do that, though it's nothing, really."

ANNIE TRUMBULL SLOSSON

A CHILD'S EASTER

Had I been there, when Christ, our Lord, lay sleeping
Within that tomb in Joseph's garden fair,
I would have watched all night beside my Saviour,—
    Had I been there.

Close to the hard, cold stone my soft cheek
    pressing,
I should have thought my head lay on His breast;
And dreaming that His dear arms were about me,
    Have sunk to rest.

All thro' the long, dark night when others
    slumbered,
Close, close beside Him still I would have stayed,
And, knowing how He loved the little children,
    Ne'er felt afraid.

"To-morrow," to my heart I would have
    whispered,
"I will rise early in the morning hours,
And wand'ring o'er the hillside I will gather
    The fairest flowers.

"Tall, slender lilies (for my Saviour loved them,
And tender words about their beauty spake),
And golden buttercups, and glad-eyed daisies,
    But just awake.

" 'Grass of the field' in waving, feath'ry beauty,
He clothed it with that grace, so fair but brief,
Mosses all soft and green, and crimson berry,
    With glossy leaf.

"While yet the dew is sparkling on the blossoms
I'll gather them, and lay them at His feet,

And make the blessed place where He is sleeping
    All fair and sweet.

"The birds will come, I know, and sing above
    Him,
The sparrows whom He cared for when awake,
And they will fill the air with joyous music
    For His dear sake."

And, thinking thus, the night would soon be
    passing,
Fast drawing near that first, glad Easter light.
Ah, Lord, if I could but have seen Thee leaving
    The grave's dark night,

I would have kept so still, so still, and clasping
My hands together as I do in prayer,
I would have knelt, rev'rent, but oh, so happy!—
    Had I been there.

Perhaps He would have bent one look upon me;
Perhaps, in pity for that weary night,
He would have laid on my uplifted forehead
    A touch so light;

And all the rest of life I should have felt it,
A sacred sign upon my brow imprest,
And ne'er forget that precious, lovely vigil,
    So richly blest.

Dear Lord, thro' death and night I was not near
   Thee;
But in Thy risen glory can rejoice,
So, loud and glad in song this Easter morning,
   Thou'lt hear my voice.

AMELIA W. SWAYNE

IVAN'S EASTER SERVICE

Ivan was a little Russian boy, who lived in the city of St. Petersburg. It was the day before Easter, and he was very happy, because he was to be allowed to go to the great church for the midnight service. His sister, Sonia, who was older than he was, had gone the year before and remembered much of what had happened.

As they set out from their home, Ivan asked, "Why is the church so dark when we go in?"

"Because people are remembering the time when everyone thought Jesus was dead," said his mother.

"That was a very dark time," said his father. "People thought the light of the world had gone out. The darkness of the church is to remind us of that time."

Soon they came to the church. As they went in, each one was given a candle. Ivan carried his very carefully, and sat down quietly beside his father. He could hear the soft music, but he could not see the great organ. Up on the altar a low light burned. The priest was beginning the service. He sang many parts of it, and the choir replied from time to time. Ivan could not understand all they were saying, but the music was very beautiful and he was glad to be sitting there, close to his father.

The priest finished his prayer, and with the other priests and the choir walked down the aisle. Ivan could hear the swish of their robes as they passed him. They left the church, and now all was very, very quiet, and very, very dark. Ivan sat as still as he could, and tried to think how the world would be if no one remembered the things that Jesus had taught.

Suddenly the great bells rang out, and the whole church seemed to become full of light. Easter Day had come! The priests and choir marched in singing joyfully, "He is risen," and everyone seemed very happy. A priest held out a shining taper, and Ivan reached up to it to light his candle. He now saw that the church was crowded with people all lighting candles. Soon after they had done this, the service ended, and everyone started home, carrying his light carefully.

"Christ is risen!" said Ivan's father.

"He is risen indeed!" replied his mother.

"Christ is risen!" said Sonia.

"He is risen indeed!" said Ivan.

Ivan was very happy. He was glad that he had gone to the church. He was glad that he could carry home his bright candle.

"It would still be dark, if we were not carrying our lights, wouldn't it?" he said.

SELMA LAGERLÖF

THE SACRED FLAME

I

A great many years ago, when the city of Florence had only just been made a republic, a man lived there named Raniero di Raniero. He was the son of an armorer, and had learned his father's trade, but he did not care much to pursue it.

This Raniero was the strongest of men. It was said of him that he bore a heavy iron armor as lightly as others wear a silk shirt. He was still a young man, but already he had given many proofs of his strength. Once he was in a house where grain was stored in the loft. Too much grain had been heaped there; and while Raniero was in the house one of the loft beams broke down, and the whole roof was about to fall in. He raised his arms and held the roof up until the people managed to fetch beams and poles to prop it.

It was also said of Raniero that he was the bravest man that had ever lived in Florence, and that he could never get enough of fighting. As soon as he heard any noise in the street, he rushed out from the workshop, in hopes that a fight had arisen in which he might participate. If he could only distinguish himself, he fought just as readily with humble peasants as with armored horsemen. He rushed into a fight like a lunatic, without counting his opponents.

Florence was not very powerful in his time. The people were mostly wool spinners and cloth weavers, and these asked nothing better than to be allowed to perform their tasks in peace. Sturdy men were plentiful, but they were not quarrelsome, and they were proud of the fact that in their city better order prevailed than elsewhere. Raniero often grumbled because he was not born in a country where there was a king who gathered around him valiant men, and declared that in such an event he would have attained great honor and renown.

Raniero was loud-mouthed and boastful; cruel to animals,

harsh toward his wife, and not good for any one to live with. He would have been handsome if he had not had several deep scars across his face which disfigured him. He was quick to jump at conclusions, and quick to act, though his way was often violent.

Raniero was married to Francesca, who was the daughter of Jacopo degli Uberti, a wise and influential man. Jacopo had not been very anxious to give his daughter to such a bully as Raniero, but had opposed the marriage until the very last. Francesca forced him to relent, by declaring that she would never marry any one else. When Jacopo finally gave his consent, he said to Raniero: "I have observed that men like you can more easily win a woman's love than keep it; therefore I shall exact this promise from you: If my daughter finds life with you so hard that she wishes to come back to me, you will not prevent her." Francesca said it was needless to exact such a promise, since she was so fond of Raniero that nothing could separate her from him. But Raniero gave his promise promptly. "Of one thing you can be assured, Jacopo," said he—"I will not try to hold any woman who wishes to flee from me."

Then Francesca went to live with Raniero, and all was well between them for a time. When they had been married a few weeks, Raniero took it into his head that he would practice marksmanship. For several days he aimed at a painting which hung upon a wall. He soon became skilled, and hit the mark every time. At last he thought he would like to try and shoot at a more difficult mark. He looked around for something suitable, but discovered nothing except a quail that sat in a cage above the courtyard gate. The bird belonged to Francesca, and she was very fond of it; but, despite this, Raniero sent a page to open the cage, and shot the quail as it swung itself into the air.

This seemed to him a very good shot, and he boasted of it to any one who would listen to him.

When Francesca learned that Raniero had shot her bird, she grew pale and looked hard at him. She marveled that he had wished to do a thing which must bring grief to her; but she forgave him promptly and loved him as before.

Then all went well again for a time.

Raniero's father-in-law, Jacopo, was a flax weaver. He had a large establishment, where much work was done. Raniero thought he had discovered that hemp was mixed with the flax in Jacopo's workshop, and he did not keep silent about it, but talked of it here and there in the city. At last Jacopo also heard this chatter, and tried at once to put a stop to it. He let several other flax weavers examine his yarn and cloth, and they found all of it to be of the very finest flax. Only in one pack, which was designed to be sold outside of Florence, was there any mixture. Then Jacopo said that the deception had been practised without his knowledge or consent, by some one among his journeymen. He apprehended at once that he would find it difficult to convince people of this. He had always been famed for honesty, and he felt very keenly that his honor had been smirched.

Raniero, on the other hand, plumed himself upon having succeeded in exposing a fraud, and he bragged about it even in Francesca's hearing.

She felt deeply grieved; at the same time she was as

astonished as when he shot the bird. As she thought of this, she seemed suddenly to see her love before her; and it was like a great piece of shimmery gold cloth. She could see how big it was, and how it shimmered. But from one corner a piece had been cut away, so that it was not as big and as beautiful as it had been in the beginning.

Still, it was as yet damaged so very little that she thought: "It will probably last as long as I live. It is so great that it can never come to an end."

Again, there was a period during which she and Raniero were just as happy as they had been at first.

Francesca had a brother named Taddeo. He had been in Venice on a business trip, and, while there, had purchased garments of silk and velvet. When he came home he paraded around in them. Now, in Florence it was not the custom to go about expensively clad, so there were many who made fun of him.

One night Taddeo and Raniero were out in the wine shops. Taddeo was dressed in a green cloak with sable linings, and a violet jacket. Raniero tempted him to drink so much wine that he fell asleep, and then he took his cloak off him and hung it upon a scarecrow that was set up in a cabbage patch.

When Francesca heard of this she was vexed again with Raniero. That moment she saw before her the big piece of gold cloth—which was her love—and she seemed to see how it diminished, as Raniero cut away piece after piece.

After this, things were patched up between them for a time, but Francesca was no longer so happy as in former days, because she always feared that Raniero would commit some misdemeanor that would hurt her love.

This was not long in coming, either, for Raniero could never be tranquil. He wished that people should always speak of him and praise his courage and daring.

At that time the cathedral in Florence was much smaller than the present one, and there hung at the top of one of its towers a big, heavy shield, which had been placed there by one of Francesca's ancestors. It was the heaviest shield any man in Florence had been able to lift, and all the Uberti family were proud because it was one of their own who had climbed up in the tower and hung it there.

But Raniero climbed up to the shield one day, hung it on his back, and came down with it.

When Francesca heard of this for the first time she spoke to Raniero of what troubled her, and begged him not to humiliate her family in this way. Raniero, who had expected that she would commend him for his feat, became very angry. He retorted that he had long observed that she did not rejoice in his success, but thought only of her own kin. "It's something else I am thinking of," said Francesca, "and that is my love. I know not what will become of it if you keep on in this way."

After this they frequently exchanged harsh words, for Raniero happened nearly always to do the very thing that was most distasteful to Francesca.

There was a workman in Raniero's shop who was little and lame. This man had loved Francesca before she was married, and continued to love her even after her marriage. Raniero, who knew this, undertook to joke with him before all who sat at a table. It went so far that finally the man could no longer bear to be held up to ridicule in Francesca's hearing, so he rushed upon Raniero and wanted to fight with him. But Raniero only smiled derisively and kicked him aside. Then the poor fellow thought he did not care to live any longer, and went off and hanged himself.

When this happened, Francesca and Raniero had been married about a year. Francesca thought continually that she saw her love before her as a shimmery piece of cloth, but on all sides large pieces were cut away, so that it was scarcely half as big as it had been in the beginning.

She became very much alarmed when she saw this, and thought: "If I stay with Raniero another year, he will destroy my love. I shall become just as poor as I have hitherto been rich."

Then she concluded to leave Raniero's house and go to live with her father, that the day might not come when she should hate Raniero as much as she now loved him.

Jacopo degli Uberti was sitting at the loom with all his workmen busy around him when he saw her coming. He said that now the thing had come to pass which he had long expected, and bade her be welcome. Instantly he ordered all the people to leave off their work and arm themselves and close the house.

Then Jacopo went over to Raniero. He met him in the workshop. "My daughter has this day returned to me and begged that she may live again under my roof," he said to his son-in-law. "And now I expect that you will not compel her to return to you, after the promise you have given me."

Raniero did not seem to take this very seriously, but answered calmly: "Even if I had not given you my word, I would not demand the return of a woman who does not wish to be mine."

He knew how much Francesca loved him, and said to himself: "She will be back with me before evening."

Yet she did not appear either that day or the next.

The third day Raniero went out and pursued a couple of robbers who had long disturbed the Florentine merchants. He succeeded in catching them, and took them captives to Florence.

He remained quiet a couple of days, until he was positive that this feat was known throughout the city. But it did not turn out as he had expected—that it would bring Francesca back to him.

Raniero had the greatest desire to appeal to the courts, to force her return to him, but he felt himself unable to do this because of his promise. It seemed impossible for him to live in the same city with a wife who had abandoned him, so he moved away from Florence.

He first became a soldier, and very soon he made himself commander of a volunteer company. He was always in a fight, and served many masters.

He won much renown as a warrior, as he had always said he would. He was made a knight by the Emperor, and was accounted a great man.

Before he left Florence, he had made a vow at a sacred image of the Madonna in the Cathedral to present to the Blessed Virgin the best and rarest that he won in every battle. Before this image one always saw costly gifts, which were presented by Raniero.

Raniero was aware that all his deeds were known in his

native city. He marveled much that Francesca degli Uberti did not come back to him, when she knew all about his success.

At that time sermons were preached to start the Crusades for the recovery of the Holy Sepulchre from the Saracens, and Raniero took the cross and departed for the Orient. He not only hoped to win castles and lands to rule over, but also to succeed in performing such brilliant feats that his wife would again be fond of him, and return to him.

II

The night succeeding the day on which Jerusalem had been captured, there was great rejoicing in the Crusaders' camp, outside the city. In almost every tent they celebrated with drinking bouts, and noise and roystering were heard in every direction.

Raniero di Raniero sat and drank with some comrades; and in his tent it was even more hilarious than elsewhere. The servants barely had time to fill the goblets before they were empty again.

Raniero had the best of reasons for celebrating, because during the day he had won greater glory than ever before. In the morning, when the city was besieged, he had been the first to scale the walls after Godfrey of Boulogne; and in the evening he had been honored for his bravery in the presence of the whole corps.

When the plunder and murder were ended, and the Crusaders in penitents' cloaks and with lighted candles marched into the Church of the Holy Sepulchre, it had been announced to Raniero by Godfrey that he should be the first who might light his candle from the sacred candles which burn before Christ's tomb. It appeared to Raniero that Godfrey wished in this manner to show that he considered him the bravest man in the whole corps; and he was very happy over the way in which he had been rewarded for his achievements.

As the night wore on, Raniero and his guests were in the best of spirits; a fool and a couple of musicians who had wandered all over the camp and amused the people with their pranks, came into Raniero's tent, and the fool asked permission to narrate a comic story.

Raniero knew that this particular fool was in great demand for his drollery, and he promised to listen to his narrative.

"It happened once," said the fool, "that our Lord and Saint Peter sat a whole day upon the highest tower in Paradise Stronghold, and looked down upon the earth. They had so much to look at, that they scarcely found time to exchange a word. Our Lord kept perfectly still the whole time, but Saint Peter sometimes clapped his hands for joy, and again turned his head away in disgust. Sometimes he applauded and smiled, and anon he wept and commiserated. Finally, as it drew toward the close of day, and twilight sank down over Paradise, our Lord turned to Saint Peter and said that now he must surely be satisfied and content. 'What is it that I should be content with?' Saint Peter asked, in an impetuous tone. 'Why,' said our Lord slowly, 'I thought that you would be pleased with what you have seen today.' But Saint Peter did not care to be conciliated.

'It is true,' said he, 'that for many years I have bemoaned the fact that Jerusalem should be in the power of unbelievers, but after all that has happened today, I think it might just as well have remained as it was.' "

Raniero understood now that the fool spoke of what had taken place during the day. Both he and the other knights began to listen with greater interest than in the beginning.

"When Saint Peter had said this," continued the fool, as he cast a furtive glance at the knights, "he leaned over the pinnacle of the tower and pointed toward the earth. He showed our Lord a city which lay upon a great solitary rock that shot up from a mountain valley. 'Do you see those mounds of corpses?' he said. 'And do you see the naked and wretched prisoners who moan in the night chill? And do you see all the smoking ruins of the conflagration?' It appeared as if our Lord did not wish to answer him, but Saint Peter went on with his lamentations. He said that he had certainly been vexed with that city many times, but he had not wished it so ill as that it should come to look like this. Then, at last, our Lord answered, and tried an objection: 'Still, you can not deny that the Christian knights have risked their lives with the utmost fearlessness,' said He."

Then the fool was interrupted by bravos, but he made haste to continue.

"Oh, don't interrupt me!" he said. "Now I don't remember where I left off—ah! to be sure, I was just going to say that Saint Peter wiped away a tear or two which sprang to his eyes and prevented him from seeing. 'I never would have thought they could be such beasts,' said he. 'They have murdered and plundered the whole day. Why you went to all the trouble of letting yourself be crucified in order to gain such devotees, I can't in the least comprehend!' "

The knights took up the fun good-naturedly. They began to laugh loud and merrily. "What, fool! Is Saint Peter so wroth with us?" shrieked one of them.

"Be silent now, and let us hear if our Lord spoke in our defense!" interposed another.

"No, our Lord was silent. He knew of old that when Saint Peter had once got a-going, it wasn't worth while to argue with him. He went on in his way, and said that our Lord needn't trouble to tell him that finally they remembered to which city they had come, and went to church barefooted and in penitents' garb. That spirit had, of course, not lasted long enough to be worth mentioning. And thereupon he leaned once more over the tower and pointed downward toward Jerusalem. He pointed out the Christians' camp outside the city. 'Do you see how your knights celebrate their victories?' he asked. And our Lord saw that there was revelry everywhere in the camp. Knights and soldiers sat and looked upon Syrian dancers. Filled goblets went the rounds while they threw dice for the spoils of war and—"

"They listened to fools who told vile stories," interpolated Raniero. "Was not this also a great sin?"

The fool laughed and shook his head at Raniero, as much as to say, "Wait! I will pay you back."

"No, don't interrupt me!" he begged once again. "A poor fool forgets so easily what he would say. Ah! it was this: Saint Peter asked our Lord if He thought these people were much of a credit to Him. To this, of course, our Lord had to reply that He didn't think they were.

" 'They were robbers and murderers before they left home, and robbers and murderers they are even to-day. This undertaking you could just as well have left undone. No good will come of it,' said Saint Peter."

"Come, come, fool!" said Raniero in a threatening tone. But the fool seemed to consider it an honor to test how far he could go without some one jumping up and throwing him out, and he continued fearlessly.

"Our Lord only bowed His head, like one who acknowledges that he is being justly rebuked. But almost at the same instant He leaned forward eagerly and peered down with closer scrutiny than before. Saint Peter also glanced down. 'What are you looking for?' he wondered."

The fool delivered this speech with much animated facial play. All the knights saw our Lord and Saint Peter before their eyes, and they wondered what it was our Lord had caught sight of.

"Our Lord answered that it was nothing in particular," said the fool. "Saint Peter gazed in the direction of our Lord's glance, but he could discover nothing except that our Lord sat and looked down into a big tent, outside of which a couple of Saracen heads were set up on long lances, and where a lot of fine rugs, golden vessels, and costly weapons, captured in the Holy City, were piled up. In that tent they carried on as they did everywhere else in the camp. A company of knights sat and emptied their goblets. The only difference might be that here there were more drinking and roystering than elsewhere. Saint Peter could not comprehend why our Lord was so pleased when He looked down there, that His eyes fairly sparkled with delight. So many hard and cruel faces he had rarely before seen gathered around a drinking table. And he who was host at the board and sat at the head of the table was the most dreadful of all. He was a man of thirty-five, frightfully big and coarse, with a blowsy countenance covered with scars and scratches, calloused hands, and a loud, bellowing voice."

Here the fool paused a moment, as if he feared to go on, but both Raniero and the others liked to hear him talk of themselves, and only laughed at his audacity. "You're a daring fellow," said Raniero, "so let us see what you are driving at!"

"Finally, our Lord said a few words," continued the fool, "which made Saint Peter understand what He rejoiced over. He asked Saint Peter if He saw wrongly, or if it could actually be true that one of the knights had a burning candle beside him."

Raniero gave a start at these words. Now, at last, he was angry with the fool, and reached out his hand for a heavy wine pitcher to throw at his face, but he controlled himself that he might hear whether the fellow wished to speak to his credit or discredit.

"Saint Peter saw now," narrated the fool, "that, although the tent was lighted mostly by torches, one of the knights really had a burning wax candle beside him. It was a long, thick candle, one of the sort made to burn twenty-four hours. The knight, who had no candle-stick to set it in, had gathered together some stones and piled them around it, to make it stand."

The company burst into shrieks of laughter at this. All pointed at a candle which stood on the table beside Raniero, and was exactly like the one the fool had described. The blood mounted to Raniero's head; for this was the candle which he had a few hours before been permitted to light at the Holy Sepulchre. He had been unable to make up his mind to let it die out.

"When Saint Peter saw that candle," said the fool, "it dawned upon him what it was that our Lord was so happy over, but at the same time he could not help feeling just a little sorry for Him. 'Oh,' he said, 'it was the same knight that leaped upon the wall this morning immediately after the gentleman of Boulogne, and who this evening was permitted to light his candle at the Holy Sepulchre ahead of all the others.' 'True!' said our Lord. 'And, as you see, his candle is still burning.'"

The fool talked very fast now, casting an occasional sly glance at Raniero. "Saint Peter could not help pitying our Lord. 'Can't you understand why he keeps that candle burning?' said he. 'You must believe that he thinks of your sufferings and death whenever he looks at it. But he thinks only of the glory which he won when he was acknowledged to be the bravest man in the troop after Godfrey.'"

At this all Raniero's guests laughed. Raniero was very angry, but he, too, forced himself to laugh. He knew they would have found it still more amusing if he hadn't been able to take a little fun.

"But our Lord contradicted Saint Peter," said the fool. "'Don't you see how careful he is with the light?' asked He. 'He puts his hand before the flame as soon as any one raises the tent-flap, for fear the draught will blow it out. And he is constantly occupied in chasing away the moths which fly around it and threaten to extinguish it.' "

The laughter grew merrier and merrier, for what the fool said was the truth. Raniero found it more and more difficult to control himself. He felt he could not endure that any one should jest about the sacred candle.

"Still, Saint Peter was dubious," continued the fool. "He asked our Lord if He knew that knight. 'He's not one who goes often to Mass or wears out the prie-dieu,' said he. But our Lord could not be swerved from His opinion.

" 'Saint Peter, Saint Peter,' He said, earnestly. 'Remember that henceforth this knight shall become more pious than Godfrey. Whence do piety and gentleness spring, if not from my sepulchre? You shall see Raniero di Raniero help widows and distressed prisoners. You shall see him care for the sick and despairing as he now cares for the sacred candle flame.' "

At this they laughed inordinately. It struck them all as very ludicrous, for they knew Raniero's disposition and mode of living. But he himself found both the jokes and laughter intolerable. He sprang to his feet and wanted to reprove the fool. As he did this, he bumped so hard against the table—which was only a door set up on loose boxes—that it wabbled, and the candle fell down. It was evident now how careful Raniero was to keep the candle burning. He controlled his anger and gave himself time to pick it up and brighten the flame, before he rushed upon the fool. But when he had trimmed the light the fool had already darted out of the tent, and Raniero knew it would be useless to pursue him in the darkness. "I shall probably run across him another time," he thought, and sat down.

Meanwhile the guests had laughed mockingly, and one of them turned to Raniero and wanted to continue the jesting. He said: "There is one thing, however, which is certain, Raniero, and that is—this time you can't send to the Madonna in Florence the most precious thing you have won in the battle."

Raniero asked why he thought that he should not follow his old habit this time.

"For no other reason," said the knight, "than that the most precious thing you have won is that sacred candle flame, which you were permitted to light at the church of the Holy Sepulchre in presence of the whole corps. Surely you can't send that to Florence!"

Again the other knights laughed, but Raniero was now in the mood to undertake the wildest projects, just to put an end to their laughter. He came to a conclusion quickly, called to an old squire, and said to him: "Make ready, Giovanni, for a long journey. To-morrow you shall travel to Florence with this sacred candle flame."

But the squire said a blunt no to this command. "This is something which I don't care to undertake," he said. "How should it be possible to travel to Florence with a candle flame? It would be extinguished before I had left the camp."

Raniero asked one after another of his men. He received the same reply from all. They scarcely seemed to take his command seriously.

It was a foregone conclusion that the foreign knights who

were his guests should laugh even louder and more merrily, as it became apparent that none of Raniero's men wished to carry out his order.

Raniero grew more and more excited. Finally he lost his patience and shouted: "This candle flame shall nevertheless be borne to Florence; and since no one else will ride there with it, I will do so myself!"

"Consider before you promise anything of the kind!" said a knight. "You ride away from a principality."

"I swear to you that I will carry this sacred flame to Florence!" exclaimed Raniero. "I shall do what no one else has cared to undertake."

The old squire defended himself. "Master, it's another matter for you. You can take with you a large retinue but me you would send alone."

But Raniero was clean out of himself, and did not consider his words. "I, too, shall travel alone," said he.

But with this declaration Raniero had carried his point. Every one in the tent had ceased laughing. Terrified, they sat and stared at him.

"Why don't you laugh any more?" asked Raniero. "This undertaking surely can't be anything but a child's game for a brave man."

III

The next morning at dawn Raniero mounted his horse. He was in full armor, but over it he had thrown a coarse pilgrim cloak, so that the iron dress should not become overheated by exposure to the sun's rays. He was armed with a sword and battle-club, and rode a good horse. He held in his hand a burning candle, and to the saddle he had tied a couple of bundles of long wax candles, so the flame should not die out for lack of nourishment.

Raniero rode slowly through the long, encumbered tent street, and thus far all went well. It was still so early that the mists which had arisen from the deep dales surrounding Jerusalem were not dispersed, and Raniero rode forward as in a white night. The whole troop slept, and Raniero passed the guards easily. None of them called out his name, for the mist prevented their seeing him, and the roads were covered with a dust-like soil a foot high, which made the horse's tramp inaudible.

Raniero was soon outside the camp and started on the road which led to Joppa. Here it was smoother, but he rode very slowly now, because of the candle, which burned feebly in the thick mist. Big insects kept dashing against the flame. Raniero had all he could do guarding it, but he was in the best of spirits and thought all the while that the mission which he had undertaken was so easy that a child could manage it.

Meanwhile, the horse grew weary of the slow pace, and began to trot. The flame began to flicker in the wind. It didn't help that Raniero tried to shield it with his hand and with the cloak. He saw that it was about to be extinguished.

But he had no desire to abandon the project so soon. He stopped the horse, sat still a moment, and pondered. Then he dismounted and tried sitting backwards, so that his body shielded the flame from the wind. In this way he succeeded in keeping it burning; but he realized now that the journey would be more difficult than he had thought at the beginning.

When he had passed the mountains which surround Jerusalem, the fog lifted. He rode forward now in the greatest solitude. There were no people, houses, green trees, nor plants—only bare rocks.

Here Raniero was attacked by robbers. They were idle folk, who followed the camp without permission, and lived by theft and plunder. They had lain in hiding behind a hill, and Raniero—who rode backwards—had not seen them until they had surrounded him and brandished their swords at him.

There were about twelve men. They looked wretched, and rode poor horses. Raniero saw at once that it would not be difficult for him to break through this company and ride on. And after his proud boast of the night before, he was unwilling to abandon his undertaking easily.

He saw no other means of escape than to compromise with the robbers. He told them that, since he was armed and rode a good horse, it might be difficult to overpower him if he defended himself. And as he was bound by a vow, he did not wish to offer resistance, but they could take whatever they wanted, without a struggle, if only they promised not to put out his light.

The robbers had expected a hard struggle, and were very happy over Raniero's proposal, and began immediately to plunder him. They took from him armor and steed, weapons and money. The only thing they let him keep was the coarse cloak and the two bundles of wax candles. They sacredly kept their promise, also, not to put out the candle flame.

One of them mounted Raniero's horse. When he noticed what a fine animal he was, he felt a little sorry for the rider. He called out to him: "Come, come, we must not be too cruel toward a Christian. You shall have my old horse to ride."

It was a miserable old screw of a horse. It moved as stiffly, and with as much difficulty, as if it were made of wood.

When the robbers had gone at last, and Raniero had mounted the wretched horse, he said to himself: "I must have become bewitched by this candle flame. For its sake I must now travel along the roads like a crazy beggar."

He knew it would be wise for him to turn back, because the undertaking was really impracticable. But such an intense yearning to accomplish it had come over him that he could not resist the desire to go on. Therefore, he went farther. He saw all around him the same bare, yellowish hills.

After a while he came across a goatherd, who tended four goats. When Raniero saw the animals grazing on the barren ground, he wondered if they ate earth.

This goatherd had owned a larger flock, which had been stolen from him by the Crusaders. When he noticed a solitary Christian come riding toward him, he tried to do him all the harm he could. He rushed up to him and struck at his light with his staff. Raniero was so taken up by the flame that he could not defend himself even against a goatherd. He only drew the candle close to him to protect it. The goatherd struck at it several times more, then he paused, astonished, and ceased striking. He noticed that Raniero's cloak had caught fire, but Raniero did nothing to smother the blaze, so long as the sacred flame was in danger. The goatherd looked as though he felt ashamed. For a long time he followed Raniero, and in one place, where the road was very narrow, with a deep chasm on each side of it, he came up and led the horse for him.

Raniero smiled and thought the goatherd surely regarded him as a holy man who had undertaken a voluntary penance.

Toward evening Raniero began to meet people. Rumors of the fall of Jerusalem had already spread to the coast, and a throng of people had immediately prepared to go up there. There were pilgrims who for years had awaited an opportunity to get into Jerusalem, also some newly-arrived troops; but they were mostly merchants who were hastening with provisions.

When these throngs met Raniero, who came riding backwards with a burning candle in his hand, they cried: "A madman, a madman!"

The majority were Italians; and Raniero heard how they shouted in his own tongue, "Pazzo, pazzo!" which means "a madman, a madman."

Raniero, who had been able to keep himself well in check all day, became intensely irritated by these ever-recurring shouts. Instantly he dismounted and began to chastise the offenders with his hard fists. When they saw how heavy the blows were, they took to their heels, and Raniero soon stood alone on the road.

Now Raniero was himself again. "In truth they were right to call me a madman," he said, as he looked around for the light. He did not know what he had done with it. At last he saw that it had rolled down into a hollow. The flame was extinguished, but he saw fire gleam from a dry grass-tuft close beside it, and understood that luck was with him, for the flame had ignited the grass before it had gone out.

"This might have been an inglorious end of a deal of trouble," he thought, as he lit the candle and stepped into the saddle. He was rather mortified. It did not seem to him very probable that his journey would be a success.

In the evening Raniero reached Ramle, and rode up to a place where caravans usually had night harbor. It was a large covered yard. All around it were little stalls where travelers could put up their horses. There were no rooms, but folk could sleep beside the animals.

The place was overcrowded with people, yet the host found room for Raniero and his horse. He also gave fodder to the horse and food to the rider.

When Raniero perceived that he was well treated, he thought: "I almost believe the robbers did me a service when they took from me my armor and my horse. I shall certainly get out of the country more easily with my light burden, if they mistake me for a lunatic."

When he had led the horse into the stall, he sat down on a sheaf of straw and held the candle in his hands. It was his intention not to fall asleep, but to remain awake all night.

But he had hardly seated himself when he fell asleep. He was fearfully exhausted, and in his sleep he stretched out full length and did not wake till morning.

When he awoke he saw neither flame nor candle. He searched in the straw for the candle, but did not find it anywhere.

"Some one has taken it from me and extinguished it," he said. He tried to persuade himself that he was glad that all was over, and that he need not pursue an impossible undertaking.

But as he pondered, he felt a sense of emptiness and loss. He thought that never before had he so longed to succeed in anything on which he had set his mind.

He led the horse out and groomed and saddled it.

When he was ready to set out, the host who owned the caravansary came up to him with a burning candle. He said in Frankish: "When you fell asleep last night, I had to take your light from you, but here you have it again."

Raniero betrayed nothing, but said very calmly: "It was wise of you to extinguish it."

"I have not extinguished it," said the man. "I noticed that it was burning when you arrived, and I thought it was of importance to you that it should continue to burn. If you see how much it has decreased, you will understand that it has been burning all night."

Raniero beamed with happiness. He commended the host heartily, and rode away in the best of spirits.

IV

When Raniero broke away from the camp at Jerusalem, he intended to travel from Joppa to Italy by sea, but changed his mind after he had been robbed of his money, and concluded to make the journey by land.

It was a long journey. From Joppa he went northward along the Syrian coast. Then he rode westward along the peninsula of Asia Minor, then northward again, all the way to Constantinople. From there he still had a monotonously long distance to travel to reach Florence. During the whole journey Raniero had lived upon the contributions of the pious. They that shared their bread with him mostly were pilgrims who at this time traveled *en masse* to Jerusalem.

Regardless of the fact that he nearly always rode alone, his days were neither long nor monotonous. He must always guard the candle flame, and on its account he never could feel at ease. It needed only a puff of breeze—a raindrop—and there would have been an end to it.

As Raniero rode over lonely roads, and thought only about keeping the flame alive, it occurred to him that once before he had been concerned with something similar. Once before he had seen a person watch over something which was just as sensitive as a candle flame.

This recollection was so vague to him at first that he wondered if it was something he had dreamed.

But as he rode on alone through the country, it kept recurring to him that he had participated in something similar once before.

"It is as if all my life long I had heard tell of nothing else," said he.

One evening he rode into a city. It was after sundown, and the housewives stood in their doorways and watched for their husbands. Then he noticed one who was tall and slender, and had earnest eyes. She reminded him of Francesca degli Uberti.

Instantly it became clear to him what he had been pondering over. It came to him that for Francesca her love must have been as a sacred flame which she had always wished to keep burning, and which she had constantly feared that

Raniero would quench. He was astonished at this thought, but grew more and more certain that the matter stood thus. For the first time he began to understand why Francesca had left him, and that it was not with feats of arms he should win her back.

. . . .

The journey which Raniero made was of long duration. This was in part due to the fact that he could not venture out when the weather was bad. Then he sat in some caravansary, and guarded the candle flame. These were very trying days.

One day, when he rode over Mount Lebanon, he saw that a storm was brewing. He was riding high up among awful precipices, and a frightful distance from any human abode. Finally he saw on the summit of a rock the tomb of a Saracen saint. It was a little square stone structure with a vaulted roof. He thought it best to seek shelter there.

He had barely entered when a snowstorm came up, which raged for two days and nights. At the same time it grew so cold that he came near freezing to death.

Raniero knew that there were heaps of branches and twigs out on the mountain, and it would not have been difficult for him to gather fuel for a fire. But he considered the candle flame which he carried very sacred, and did not wish to light anything from it, except the candles before the Blessed Virgin's Altar.

The storm increased, and at last he heard thunder and saw gleams of lightning.

Then came a flash which struck the mountain, just in front of the tomb, and set fire to a tree. And in this way he was enabled to light his fire without having to borrow of the sacred flame.

· · · · · ·

As Raniero was riding on through a desolate portion of the Cilician mountain district, his candles were all used up. The candles which he had brought with him from Jerusalem had long since been consumed; but still he had been able to manage because he had found Christian communities all along the way, of whom he had begged fresh candles.

But now his resources were exhausted, and he thought that this would be the end of his journey.

When the candle was so nearly burned out that the flame scorched his hand, he jumped from his horse and gathered branches and dry leaves and lit these with the last of the flame. But up on the mountain there was very little that would ignite, and the fire would soon burn out.

While he sat and grieved because the sacred flame must die, he heard singing down the road, and a procession of pilgrims came marching up the steep path, bearing candles in their hands. They were on their way to a grotto where a holy man had lived, and Raniero followed them. Among them was a woman who was very old and had difficulty in walking, and Raniero carried her up the mountain.

When she thanked him afterwards, he made a sign to her that she should give him her candle. She did so, and several others also presented him with the candles which they carried. He extinguished the candles, hurried down the steep path, and lit one of them with the last spark from the fire lighted by the sacred flame.

· · · · · · ·

One day at the noon hour it was very warm, and Raniero had lain down to sleep in a thicket. He slept soundly, and the candle stood beside him between a couple of stones. When he had been asleep a while, it began to rain, and this continued for some time, without his waking. When at last he was startled out of his sleep, the ground around him was wet, and he hardly dared glance toward the light, for fear it might be quenched.

But the light burned calmly and steadily in the rain, and Raniero saw that this was because two little birds flew and fluttered just above the flame. They caressed it with their bills, and held their wings outspread, and in this way they protected the sacred flame from the rain.

He took off his hood immediately, and hung it over the candle. Thereupon he reached out his hand for the two little birds, for he had been seized with a desire to pet them. Neither of them flew away because of him, and he could catch them.

He was very much astonished that the birds were not afraid of him. "It is because they know I have no thought except to protect that which is the most sensitive of all, that they do not fear me," thought he.

· · · · · · ·

Raniero rode in the vicinity of Nicæa, in Bithynia. Here he met some western gentlemen who were conducting a party of recruits to the Holy Land. In this company was Robert Taillefer, who was a wandering knight and a troubadour.

Raniero, in his torn cloak, came riding along with the candle in his hand, and the warriors began as usual to shout,

"A madman, a madman!" But Robert silenced them, and addressed the rider.

"Have you journeyed far in this manner?" he asked.

"I have ridden like this all the way from Jerusalem," answered Raniero.

"Has your light been extinguished many times during the journey?"

"Still burns the flame that lighted the candle with which I rode away from Jerusalem," responded Raniero.

Then Robert Taillefer said to him: "I am also one of those who carry a light, and I would that it burned always. But perchance you, who have brought your light burning all the way from Jerusalem, can tell me what I shall do that it may not become extinguished?"

Then Raniero answered: "Master, it is a difficult task, although it appears to be of slight importance. This little flame demands of you that you shall entirely cease to think of anything else. It will not allow you to have any sweetheart —in case you should desire anything of the sort—neither would you dare on account of this flame to sit down at a revel. You can not have aught else in your thoughts than just this flame, and must possess no other happiness. But my chief reason for advising you against making the journey which I have weathered is that you can not for an instant feel secure. It matters not through how many perils you may have guarded the flame, you can not for an instant think yourself secure, but must ever expect that the very next moment it may fail you."

But Robert Taillefer raised his head proudly and answered: "What you have done for your sacred flame I may do for mine."

. . . .

Raniero arrived in Italy. One day he rode through lonely roads up among the mountains. A woman came running after him and begged him to give her a light from his candle. "The fire in my hut is out," said she. "My children are hungry. Give me a light that I may heat my oven and bake bread for them!"

She reached for the burning candle, but Raniero held it back because he did not wish that anything should be lighted by that flame but the candles before the image of the Blessed Virgin.

Then the woman said to him: "Pilgrim, give me a light, for the life of my children is the flame which I am in duty bound to keep burning!" And because of these words he permitted her to light the wick of her lamp from his flame.

Several hours later he rode into a town. It lay far up on the mountain, where it was very cold. A peasant stood in the road and saw the poor wretch who came riding in his torn cloak. Instantly he stripped off the short mantle which he wore, and flung it to him. But the mantle fell directly over the candle and extinguished the flame.

Then Raniero remembered the woman who had borrowed a light of him. He turned back to her and had his candle lighted anew with sacred fire.

When he was ready to ride farther, he said to her: "You say that the sacred flame which you must guard is the life of your children. Can you tell me what name this candle's flame bears, which I have carried over long roads?"

"Where was your candle lighted?" asked the woman.

"It was lighted at Christ's sepulchre," said Raniero.

"Then it can only be called Gentleness and Love of Humanity," said she.

Raniero laughed at the answer. He thought himself a singular apostle of virtues such as these.

· · · · · ·

Raniero rode forward between beautiful blue hills. He saw he was near Florence. He was thinking that he must soon part with his light. He thought of his tent in Jerusalem, which he had left filled with trophies, and the brave soldiers who were still in Palestine, and who would be glad to have him take up the business of war once more, and bear them on to new conquests and honors.

Then he perceived that he experienced no pleasure in thinking of this, but that his thoughts were drawn in another direction.

Then he realized for the first time that he was no longer the same man that had gone from Jerusalem. The ride with the sacred flame had compelled him to rejoice with all who were peaceable and wise and compassionate, and to abhor the savage and warlike.

He was happy every time he thought of people who labored peacefully in their homes, and it occurred to him that he would willingly move into his old workshop in Florence and do beautiful and artistic work.

"Verily this flame has recreated me," he thought. "I believe it has made a new man of me."

V

It was Eastertide when Raniero rode into Florence.

He had scarcely come in through the city gate—riding backwards, with his hood drawn down over his face and the burning candle in his hand—when a beggar arose and shouted the customary "Pazzo, pazzo!"

At this cry a street gamin darted out of a doorway, and a loafer, who had had nothing else to do for a long time than to lie and gaze at the clouds, jumped to his feet. Both began shouting the same thing: "Pazzo, pazzo!"

Now that there were three who shrieked, they made a good deal of noise and so woke up all the street urchins. They came rushing out from nooks and corners. As soon as they saw Raniero, in his torn coat, on the wretched horse, they shouted: "Pazzo, pazzo!"

But this was only what Raniero was accustomed to. He rode quietly up the street, seeming not to notice the shouters.

Then they were not content with merely shouting, but one of them jumped up and tried to blow out the light. Raniero raised the candle on high, trying at the same time to prod his horse, to escape the boys.

They kept even pace with him, and did everything they could to put out the light.

The more he exerted himself to protect the flame the more excited they became. They leaped upon one another's backs, puffed their cheeks out, and blew. They flung their caps at the candle. It was only because they were so numerous and crowded on one another that they did not succeed in quenching the flame.

This was the largest procession on the street. People stood at the windows and laughed. No one felt any sympathy with a madman, who wanted to defend his candle flame. It was church hour, and many worshipers were on their way to Mass. They, too, stopped and laughed at the sport.

But now Raniero stood upright in the saddle, so that he could shield the candle. He looked wild. The hood had fallen back and they saw his face, which was wasted and pale, like a martyr's. The candle he held uplifted as high as he could.

The entire street was one great swarm of people. Even the older ones began to take part in the play. The women waved their head-shawls and the men swung their caps. Everyone worked to extinguish the light.

Raniero rode under the vine-covered balcony of a house. Upon this stood a woman. She leaned over the lattice-work, snatched the candle, and ran in with it. The woman was Francesca degli Uberti.

The whole populace burst into shrieks of laughter and shouts, but Raniero swayed in his saddle and fell to the street.

As soon as he lay there stricken and unconscious, the street was emptied of people.

No one wished to take charge of the fallen man. His horse was the only creature that stopped beside him.

As soon as the crowds had got away from the street, Francesca degli Uberti came out from her house, with the burning candle in her hand. She was still pretty; her features were gentle, and her eyes were deep and earnest.

She went up to Raniero and bent over him. He lay senseless, but the instant the candle light fell upon his face, he moved and roused himself. It was apparent that the candle flame had complete power over him. When Francesca saw that he had regained his senses, she said: "Here is your candle. I snatched it from you, as I saw how anxious you were to keep it burning. I knew of no other way to help you."

Raniero had had a bad fall, and was hurt. But now nothing could hold him back. He began to raise himself slowly. He wanted to walk, but wavered, and was about to fall. Then he tried to mount his horse. Francesca helped him. "Where do you wish to go?" she asked when he sat in the saddle again. "I want to go to the cathedral," he answered. "Then I shall accompany you," she said, "for I'm going to Mass." And she led the horse for him.

Francesca had recognized Raniero the very moment she saw him, but he did not see who she was, for he did not take time to notice her. He kept his gaze fixed upon the candle flame alone.

They were absolutely silent all the way. Raniero thought only of the flame, and of guarding it well these last moments. Francesca could not speak, for she felt she did not wish to be certain of that which she feared. She could not believe but that Raniero had come home insane. Although she was almost certain of this, she would rather not speak with him, in order to avoid any positive assurance.

After a while Raniero heard some one weep near him. He looked around and saw that it was Francesca degli Uberti, who walked beside him; and she wept. But Raniero saw her only for an instant, and said nothing to her. He wanted to think only of the sacred flame.

Raniero let her conduct him to the sacristy. There he dismounted. He thanked Francesca for her help, but looked all the while not upon her, but on the light. He walked alone up to the priests in the sacristy.

Francesca went into the church. It was Easter Eve, and all the candles stood unlighted upon the altars, as a symbol of mourning. Francesca thought that every flame of hope which had ever burned within her was now extinguished.

In the church there was profound solemnity. There were many priests at the altar. The canons sat in a body in the chancel, with the bishop among them.

By and by Francesca noticed there was commotion among the priests. Nearly all who were not needed to serve at Mass arose and went out into the sacristy. Finally the bishop went, too.

When Mass was over, a priest stepped up to the chancel railing and began to speak to the people. He related that Raniero di Raniero had arrived in Florence with sacred fire from Jerusalem. He narrated what the rider had endured and suffered on the way. And he praised him exceeding much.

The people sat spellbound and listened to this. Francesca had never before experienced such a blissful moment. "O God!" she sighed, "this is greater happiness than I can bear." Her tears fell as she listened.

The priest talked long and well. Finally he said in a strong, thrilling voice: "It may perchance appear like a trivial thing now, that a candle flame has been brought to Florence. But I say to you: Pray God that He will send Florence many bearers of Eternal Light; then she will become a great power, and be extolled as a city among cities!"

When the priest had finished speaking, the entrance doors of the church were thrown open, and a procession of canons and monks and priests marched up the center aisle toward the altar. The bishop came last, and by his side walked Raniero, in the same cloak that he had worn during the entire journey.

But when Raniero had crossed the threshold of the cathedral, an old man arose and walked toward him. It was Oddo, the father of the journeyman who had once worked for Raniero, and had hanged himself because of him.

When this man had come up to the bishop and Raniero, he bowed to them. Thereupon he said in such a loud voice that all in the church heard him: "It is a great thing for Florence that Raniero has come with sacred fire from Jerusalem. Such a thing has never before been heard of or conceived. For that reason, perhaps, there may be many who will say that it is not possible. Therefore, I beg that all the people may know what proofs and witnesses Raniero has brought with him, to assure us that this is actually fire which was lighted in Jerusalem."

When Raniero heard this he said: "God help me! how can I produce witnesses? I have made the journey alone. Deserts and mountain wastes must come and testify for me."

"Raniero is an honest knight," said the bishop, "and we believe him on his word."

"Raniero must know himself that doubts will arise as to this," said Oddo. "Surely, he can not have ridden entirely alone. His little pages could certainly testify for him."

Then Francesca degli Uberti rushed up to Raniero. "Why need we witnesses?" said she. "All the women in Florence would swear on oath that Raniero speaks the truth!"

Then Raniero smiled, and his countenance brightened for a moment. Thereupon he turned his thoughts and his gaze once more upon the candle flame.

There was great commotion in the church. Some said that Raniero should not be allowed to light the candles on the altar until his claim was substantiated. With this many of his old enemies sided.

Then Jacopo degli Uberti rose and spoke in Raniero's behalf. "I believe every one here knows that no very great friendship has existed between my son-in-law and me," he said; "but now both my sons and I will answer for him. We believe he has performed this task, and we know that one who has been disposed to carry out such an undertaking is a wise, discreet, and noble-minded man, whom we are glad to receive among us."

But Oddo and many others were not disposed to let him taste of the bliss he was yearning for. They got together in a close group and it was easy to see that they did not care to withdraw their demand.

Raniero apprehended that if this should develop into a fight, they would immediately try to get at the candle. As he kept his eyes steadily fixed upon his opponents, he raised the candle as high as he could.

He looked exhausted in the extreme, and distraught. One could see that, although he wished to hold out to the very last, he expected defeat. What mattered it to him now if he were permitted to light the candles? Oddo's word had been a death-blow. When doubt was once awakened, it would spread and increase. He fancied that Oddo had already extinguished the sacred flame forever.

A little bird came fluttering through the great open doors into the church. It flew straight into Raniero's light. He hadn't time to snatch it aside, and the bird dashed against it and put out the flame.

Raniero's arm dropped, and tears sprang to his eyes. The first moment he felt this as a sort of relief. It was better thus than if human beings had killed it.

The little bird continued its flight into the church, fluttering confusedly hither and thither, as birds do when they come into a room.

Simultaneously a loud cry resounded throughout the church: "The bird is on fire! The sacred candle flame has set its wings on fire!"

The little bird chirped anxiously. For a few moments it fluttered about, like a flickering flame, under the high chancel arches. Then it sank suddenly and dropped dead upon the Madonna's Altar.

But the moment the bird fell upon the Altar, Raniero was standing there. He had forced his way through the church, no one had been able to stop him. From the sparks which destroyed the bird's wings he lit the candles before the Madonna's Altar.

Then the bishop raised his staff and proclaimed: "God willed it! God hath testified for him!"

And all the people in the church, both his friends and opponents, abandoned their doubts and conjectures. They cried as with one voice, transported by God's miracle: "God willed it! God hath testified for him!"

Of Raniero there is now only a legend, which says he enjoyed great good fortune for the remainder of his days, and was wise, and prudent, and compassionate. But the people of Florence always called him Pazzo degli Ranieri, in remembrance of the fact that they had believed him insane. And this became his honorary title. He founded a dynasty, which was named Pazzi, and is called so even to this day.

It might also be worth mentioning that it became a custom in Florence, each year at Easter Eve, to celebrate a festival in memory of Raniero's home-coming with the sacred flame, and that, on this occasion, they always let an artificial bird fly with fire through the church. This festival would most likely have been celebrated even in our day had not some changes taken place recently.

But if it is true, as many hold, that the bearers of sacred fire who have lived in Florence and have made the city one of the most glorious on earth, have taken Raniero as their model, and have thereby been encouraged to sacrifice, to suffer and endure, this may here be left untold.

For what has been done by this light, which in dark times has gone out from Jerusalem, can neither be measured nor counted.

WINIFRED KIRKLAND

THE EASTER PEOPLE

The approach to old Salem of the old South is commonplace enough. Thirty miles of motoring roll away beneath our wheels. Prosperous fields to right and left spread to woody reaches that circle the horizon. The hesitant leaves of an early spring blur the stark outlines of trunk and branch.

Gnarled orchard boughs are all in milk-white flower. Against dusky wood spaces the Judas tree hangs its veils of deep pink, and the dogwood is just beginning to show the glint of silver disks. Other cars go honking past us. On the railroad parallel to us a train thunders by. We mount a hill and the twin city of Winston-Salem lies before us. We dip down the slope, then climb again, and abruptly we are in another world, we are in old Salem. I shall never again forget that the word Salem means peace.

After two heavy, gray days, the sun, at noon of Good Friday, comes riding forth clear of all cloud. The boxwood in old gardens is crisp and glistening. House walls of ancient brick, freshened by the rain, yield their full of mellow colour. As we roll up South Main Street, my companion points out this and that place of interest, for she is one of the many far-scattered Southern women who once were schoolgirls in the old Moravian Female Academy. The word Moravian has up to this time been merely a word to me, a term associated with quaint, long-persistent customs, but in a few brief days that word is to become potent with a significance that I feel inadequate to express, as hesitatingly and gratefully I try to set down the impressions of one chance visitor. In every recurrent springtime thousands and thousands of such visitors push into the old city, and at every Easter-tide by some strange contagion of reverence, quiet Salem has the power to subdue these alien crowds to the very spirit of its own piety. Such is the alchemy of influence possessed by the people who have made Easter the pivot of all the year, the very heart of all their faith and all their conduct.

Almost at once as we enter the town I am aware of an atmosphere vibrant with expectancy. Windows are being polished, and dooryards clipped, and faces lifted to us brighten with unspoken welcome. Old houses abut directly on the pavement, so that their modern occupants must have thick curtains for privacy, curtains now snowy starched for Easter. Some of the roomy dwellings have nestling beside them the little shops where once the master kept his business close to home. Externally most of the houses remain exactly as they were when first built, in the later eighteenth century. We pass the old Butner Tavern, standing just as it stood in 1781 when Washington occupied that now famous northeast chamber. In the museum there is still exhibited the harpsichord by which he was entertained, and the story runs that a little girl selected to play, broke down, and was kissed and comforted by the great first president himself.

We turn to our right at the time-worn Square, a stretching rectangle of towering water oaks crossed by diagonal paths. At opposite sides of the corner at which we enter are buildings that recall the deep community fellowship characteristic of the Moravian practice, for one of the two is the Widows' House, and the other, with its red-tiled roof and deep windows, is the House of the Single Brothers, where, for many years, before it became the present museum, they had their school for boys. We are facing now the long, unbroken brick façade that forms the entire east side of the Square. In the middle is the Academy, with its high white pillars, and at the south the Sisters' House with its two rows of dormer windows. At the north stands the old Home Church, with its staunch ancient walls dull red beneath bright ivy, its hooded door, its unfailing clock face in the gable beneath the domed white belfry. At the church we turn northward and get out of our car to search for the little cottage where we are to have rooms. Our motor cannot go farther, for all cars are barred from the long quiet avenue that lies before us. My friend is looking sadly for the great shaggy trees familiar to her girlhood, those towering ancient guardians of the dead that gave Cedar Avenue its name. But now those old trees themselves are dead, and their place taken by slim young poplars freshly green with spring. To me, the newcomer, Cedar Avenue is beautiful enough as it is today, a broad white gravelled path lined by the swaying green shafts of the poplars, and bordered on our left by a low stone wall, and on the right by a high picket fence, almost covered by ivy, and broken by white-arched gateways, on which, above the green-leaved pillars, are blazoned triumphant Easter texts. Within those portals in sunshine that is dappled by the shadows of cedar and boxwood stretches row after row of little flat white gravestones all exactly alike. Here is no distinction of persons nor of families, but merely of groups, married men together, married women, single men and boys and boy babies, single women and girls and girl babies. This green spot is the center of Salem; it is the center of the Moravian faith. This is the graveyard where, near and dear and instant in the memory of the living, the dead lie, asleep in sunny peace.

Nestling close to the graves is the little cottage, cheery with nodding tulips and bright hyacinths, where we are to stay with Miss Dorcas Reitzer, and her niece, Miss Bertha. Both are of old Moravian stock, readily tracing all their ancestors back to German Herrnhut of 1722. Miss Dorcas is eighty, her feet are slow with rheumatism, but her mind and heart are alert for one more exultant Easter. Along the gravel path beyond her door people are constantly passing on their way to the green and white graveyard, for the houses of the dead as well as the houses of the living must be shining clean and flower-trimmed for Easter morning.

On this day, Good Friday, there was a service of "deep, pervasive joyousness" and on Saturday, the "Great Sabbath," the graveyard was a place of pilgrimage and there were visits to the archive house of Salem and to the Sisters' House, the beautiful home of the retired teachers of Salem Academy and Salem College.

These three visits on this "Great Sabbath," to the archive house where the dead founders are still valiantly alive, to the Sisters' House where past and present are one, to the Bethabara graveyard where the trees of two centuries are once more green with youth, these three visits have put my spirit in tune for the Easter vigil. That vigil is ushered in by the gathering twilight, in which we sit with Miss Dorcas on her porch, watching the few late visitors still busy in the graveyard. Laden down with wreaths and bouquets, which she has spent all afternoon in arranging, Miss Bertha has gone to "my graves," as Miss Dorcas calls them. One friend after another drops in to chat awhile with us seated there on the dusky porch, while the gold of the sunset fades gently to gray, and the stars steal forth. There are children bobbing about, laughing, rolling on the green stretches in the happy evening, all talking of the mysterious antics of the Easter rabbit expected to make his rounds tomorrow morning. Miss Dorcas speaks in tranquil comment, "You think so much about the dead today, don't you? I am getting so old I shall be going any time now." Her words chime with the Bishop's who when someone asked him who was to conduct the Easter services, answered smiling, "I *say* that I shall, but when a man is eighty, he cannot know." True Moravians who have seen so many glad Easters cannot face death with any shudder, for they know their going will be told in music on the evening wind, that their graves on every Easter will be jocund with flowers, that their memories will be kept radiant in the fellowship of the living with the dead.

A young nephew of my friend's, blowing in upon her for a breezy greeting, says, "So near the graveyard? Aren't you afraid of ghosts?" then adds, "But I never heard of a Moravian ghost." If they could come back, Moravian ghosts, they would be sweet, dim visitants whom no one could fear,— that is my thought as I look out on their quiet sleeping place just before I get into bed.

Full of preparations, Miss Bertha has bustled us off to sleep early, but before we go upstairs she has made Miss Dorcas comfortable for the night, and has also arranged the couch for the little neighbour, Margaret Anne, who is to stay here tonight in order to go with us to the early service. Both fall asleep all eager expectancy, eight years old and eighty, side by side.

Miss Bertha is briskly winding her alarm clock when we say goodnight. She assures us that she will call us in good time for coffee and sugar cake with her at five.

Our sleep is fitful. Old Salem does not expect to sleep much on Easter Even. All night, steps crunch the gravel outside our windows. All night motor cars pour into the old streets from all the country round. Dreamily the noises drift in to me and now and then I start up for a brief wakeful moment at the chiming of the church clock. It is half past one when my friend's eager whisper rouses me, makes me hurry to kneel beside her at the dark window, for we must not miss the gathering of the trombone bands who shall go forth through all the sleeping streets announcing Easter. In the deep sky the Easter stars are shining, white above the dim squares in the long lines in the graveyard. One great window glows forth in the surrounding dark, the window of the room in the old Beloe House where they have been giving the band members coffee before their march. Just below us near the church, a mellow voice is speaking directions. There is moving to and fro of shadowy forms assembling. Through the gloom bob the ruddy orbs of torches, the night is too still for any flaring streamers of light. The shapes of men and boys are indistinct, but the torch glow shines clear on the metal of the long horns. Every Moravian boy knows how to play the trombone. There are fathers and sons and uncles in the groups mustering now. Boys too small to sound a horn may carry a torch. They are all gathering quietly, reverently. The voice of the director sounds low and clear through the Square, as one by one he dismisses a band of a score on its appointed march. Each band will have its particular tunes, its particular places for playing them. At exactly the same corner beneath our window Miss Dorcas has for forty years heard the same tune played. The cherished stanza to which her memory fits those measures she has had Miss Bertha write down for us. As two o'clock chimes from the dim belfry in the dark sky the trombones ring out on the stillness. Somewhere down in the silent house below us, Miss Dorcas is listening, whispering the words for which the music is the accompaniment:

> "Thy majesty, how vast it is,
>   And how immense the glory,
> Which thou, O Jesus, dost possess,
>   Both heaven and earth adore thee;
> The legions of angels exult thy great name,
>   Thy glory and might are transcendent,
> And thousands and thousands thy praises proclaim,
>   Upon thee gladly dependent."

For some minutes we hear the measured beat of their steps as band after band goes out from the old Square. For two hours, sounding now here, now there, distant yet poignant and clear, the ancient horns will peal forth their message. From our window we watch one company march down Cedar Avenue. Beyond that quiet avenue, we can hear the clang and rush of trolleys, the barking of automobiles. We watch the gleaming torches and dim-lit brass as the company tramps past the ivied gate posts and the arches with their texts of hope, while, white in the dusk and the stars, the long ranks of the flowered gravestones keep their measured march step by step accompanying the living. The torches bob to the rise and fall of those rhythmic feet, successors of feet that once, mad with unearthly joy, sped through dark streets, to tell men grief-bowed in black Jerusalem, of a golden morning.

The sweet Easter music rings at intervals through the few hours of sleep left. It does not seem long before we hear Miss

Bertha stirring about, and presently we are on our way downstairs. The windows are still coal-black squares and we eat by electric light. The table is gay with red tulips. Margaret Anne bows her little square-cropped head to ask the old Moravian blessing.

"Come, Lord Jesus, our guest to be
And bless the gifts bestowed by thee."

It is still dark at half-past five when we go out into the street. As Miss Anna's guests we have the good fortune to be admitted within the ropes which bar all entrance to the Square and also cut off the streets leading up to the graveyard. Beyond the Square, from earliest morning there has been gathering a phalanxed crowd stretching for blocks. We wait close to the church among the members of the home congregation. Just across from us is the side wall and sloping roof-gable of an old brick house. Against this house wall in the dusk and shadow the trombone bands, returned two hours ago, are massed. Their torches glow orbed and ruddy, gleaming now on the polished shaft of a long horn, now on some face suddenly flashing forth against the dark. Above the house roof there is lacework of woven branches softened by their first leaf-shoots. Beyond the branches floats the silver wafer of the Pascal moon, shining through ravelled cloud.

We wait there with eyes glued to the hooded front of the old church door. "Watch!" whispers Miss Bertha, for we must not miss the opening of that door. At last an electric light flashes up within the arched entrance. No word is spoken anywhere. The doors swing in. First come the ushers, then the choir, next the pastors of all the Moravian churches of the city, and then the mayor. Still we wait, watching the door. It is as if all the congregation in the Square and all those close-packed thousands in the surrounding streets,—it is as if each of us drew a long breath, waiting. Suddenly, silently, he is there, an old man standing in the stream of light from the church entrance. For blocks and blocks of dark streets people will hear his voice, a beautiful voice now pushed to its uttermost,—"The Lord is risen! He is risen indeed!"

Unnoticed the whiteness of morning has become visible against the outlines of old roofs. The tension of expectancy slackens into the beauty of realization. As with one single spontaneous voice the old Square sings:

> "Hail, all hail, victorious Lord and Saviour,
>   Thou hast burst the bonds of death;
> Grant, as to Mary, the great favour
>   To embrace thy feet in faith:
> Thou hast in our stead the curse endured,
> And for us eternal life procured;
>   Joyful we with one accord,
>   Hail thee as our risen Lord."

The Easter liturgy is the affirmation of triumphant belief. One by one the Bishop reads first the statement of faith in the Father, and at the close the congregation proclaims assent,

"This I verily believe."

Then in low reverent murmur the Lord's prayer rises. Next the Bishop reads, sentence after sentence, the articles that embody the faith in God's Son, to which the congregation responds,

"This I most certainly believe."

The Bishop's voice rings last in the words of belief in the Holy Ghost, and a third time the congregation affirms its creed,

"This I assuredly believe."

The stanza of a hymn closes the service in the Square, which is now broken by the march to the graveyard, where the "Easter Morning Litany" will be completed. The Bishop now addresses "those of many faiths, from many places gathered here." He begs those far crowds, in the name of the risen Lord, to move quietly, each person mindful of each other's need, each preserving the Easter spirit, as all march, forming into fours, congregation and visitors all proceeding in long unbroken column to the graveyard. The Bishop leads the procession. He wears a black cap, a long black overcoat, which, buttoned to the throat, faintly suggests the outline of a black gown, but there is absolutely no insignia, no hint of ceremonial. The Bishop is but one of a great concourse whom he leads to celebrate the Resurrection.

The first trombone band follows just behind the Bishop. The others come at intervals. They play antiphonally, passing their music back along the line as runners might pass a torch. Day is brightening everywhere. The moon has become a dead gray wisp. The dim scene grows palpitant with colour, the bright emerald of poplars, the soft red of old brick, the dense green of boxwood, the black-green of ivy, and against an old buff wall the drooping lavender grace of wistaria. The procession passes along the wide gravel path of Cedar Avenue between the lines of poplars. The gray stone wall that, on our left, separates Cedar Avenue from the town, is alive with watching faces. A father balances a wondering baby on that low parapet. The head of a bright-turbanned black mammy shows at another point. Every twelve feet along the march there is stationed an usher, wearing a tiny bit of red and white ribbon in his lapel. There are a hundred and fifty of these ushers. They stand with bared heads and reverent faces. The great crowd obeys the slightest motion of an usher's hand. The simple, grave decorum is dominant everywhere. The Bishop enters at the middle gate, passing beneath the white arch inscribed, "I am the Resurrection and the Life." He takes his stand at the center of the graveyard. The crowd is massed solidly in the broad intersecting paths. There are no ropes to protect the graves, but yet not a foot transgresses on their privacy. At every entrance now the crowd flows in, in steady fours endlessly. As he passes beneath the lettered arches, every man bares his head. Within the graveyard all face toward the Bishop. In the long reverent waiting for all to assemble, there is a low hum of talk but no noise anywhere. The birds, jocund at seven of a radiant March morning, can be clearly heard in the budding branches over our heads. The service is always timed to take place exactly at sunrise, but today it has been impossible to calculate the length of time it will take the procession to enter. The sun shows first a burning rim, then climbs to balance a scarlet disk on the far horizon beyond the trees, and is mounting high above the hill line, while still the crowd streams into the graveyard, twenty thousand when they have finished.

As we wait, the air is sweet with the flowers upon the graves. I wonder if we stand there alone, we who call ourselves "the living." Perhaps there bend to us above the white stones gracious presences from long ago. Who shall fathom at any time the subtle interweaving of life with death? Here in the sunny graveyard little gray crumbled slabs bear the blithe names mothers once sang in the lullabies of long-dead babies. Today blithe, bubbly, living children crowd close upon the lichened stones. Margaret Anne's hand is warm in mine. This is her first sunrise service. When she goes home she will hunt for the gifts the Easter rabbit will have left for her.

Still we watch the in-pouring of that great crowd, until in the distance we hear the notes of the trombone band at the end of the procession, and at last all are gathered within the ivied portals, and there among the flower-heaped graves the beautiful Easter litany is completed. The old hymns float up above the branches. Far over the hushed concourse the Bishop's voice rings in the age-old words of deathless triumph:

"I have a desire to depart, and to be with Christ, which is far better: I shall never taste death; yea, I shall attain unto the resurrection of the dead: for the body which I shall put off, this grain of corruptibility, shall put on incorruption; my flesh shall rest in hope.

"And the God of peace that brought again from the dead our Lord Jesus, the great Shepherd of the sheep, through the blood of the everlasting covenant, shall also quicken these our mortal bodies if so be that the Spirit of God hath dwelt in them."

In deep murmured unison sounds the response, "We poor sinners pray, hear us, gracious Lord and God."

Then come words that express the inmost spirit of this graveyard service, words that embody the aspiration that has made Easter the key of the Moravian creed:

"And keep us in everlasting fellowship with those of our brethren and sisters who, since last Easter-day, have entered into the joy of their Lord, and with the whole church triumphant, and let us rest together in thy presence from our labours."

When the service is completed, the great crowd in silence pours forth again through the white-arched entrances, thridding the streets of the city in all directions, moving homeward. One cannot talk, going home from that Easter worship by the graves.

Even when, in the afternoon, we leave old Salem, we cannot talk much, for the peace of a beautiful memory holds our spirits too deeply for any words. The crowding, whizzing cars, returning, make the highway a blur of noise and dust, a highway leading away from Easter into the busy hum of every day. Days and weeks and months shall turn their swift wheels bearing me far from Salem. Yet always that word will have power to release memories as fragrant as flowers placed tenderly within the hands of happy sleepers, a memory of a baby girl cradled beneath a great tree on a windy hill top, a memory of an old man's voice, invincible in faith, that rings through dim streets upon an Easter dawn:

"The Lord is risen! He is risen indeed!"

**TRANSLATED FROM THE LATIN
BY JOHN MASON NEALE**

THE ALLELUIATIC SEQUENCE
CANTEMUS CUNCTI

The strain upraise of joy and praise, Alleluia.

To the glory of their King
Shall the ransom'd people sing
                                  Alleluia.
And the choirs that dwell on high
Shall re-echo through the sky
                                  Alleluia.

They through the fields of Paradise that roam,
The blessed ones, repeat through that bright home
>> Alleluia.

The planets, glitt'ring on their heavenly way,
The shining constellations, join, and say
>> Alleluia.

Ye clouds that onward sweep!
Ye winds on pinions light!
Ye thunders, echoing loud and deep!
Ye lightnings, wildly bright!
In sweet consent unite your
>> Alleluia.

Ye floods and ocean billows!
Ye storms and winter snow!
Ye days of cloudless beauty!
Hoar frost and summer glow!
Ye groves that wave in spring,
And glorious forests, sing
>> Alleluia.

First let the birds, with painted plumage gay,
Exalt their great CREATOR'S praise, and say
>> Alleluia.

Then let the beasts of earth, with varying strain,
Join in Creation's Hymn, and cry again
>> Alleluia.

Here let the mountains thunder forth, sonorous,
>> Alleluia.

There, let the valleys sing in gentler chorus,
>> Alleluia.

Thou jubilant abyss of ocean, cry
          Alleluia.
Ye tracts of earth and continents, reply
          Alleluia.
To God, Who all Creation made,
The frequent hymn be duly paid:
          Alleluia.
This is the strain, the eternal strain, the Lord of all
 things loves:
          Alleluia.
This is the song, the heav'nly song, that CHRIST
 Himself approves:
          Alleluia.
Wherefore we sing, both heart and voice awaking,
          Alleluia.
And children's voices echo, answer making,
          Alleluia.
Now from all men be out-pour'd
Alleluia to the LORD;
With Alleluia evermore
The SON and SPIRIT we adore.

Praise be done to the THREE in ONE,
 Alleluia! Alleluia! Alleluia! Alleluia!

AUTHOR UNKNOWN

AN EASTER WISH

May the glad dawn
   Of Easter morn
     Bring joy to thee.

May the calm eve
   Of Easter leave
     A peace divine with thee.

May Easter night
   On thine heart write,
     O Christ, I live for thee!

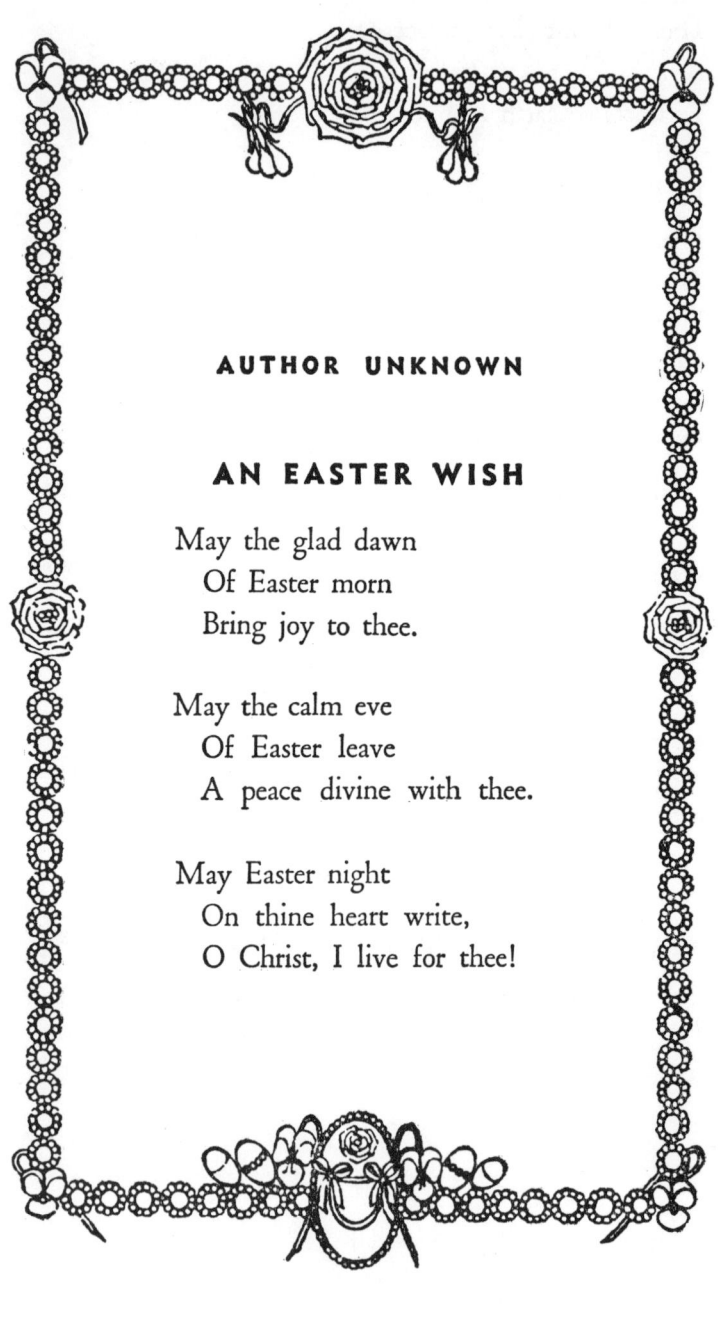

NOTES

EASTER MORNING: A PLAY OF THE RESURRECTION

STAGE DIRECTIONS AND SUGGESTIONS FOR COLOR-SCHEMES AND COSTUMES

The background is of gray, and made as conventionally as some old wood-cut or early religious painting. The door of the Tomb is narrow and just high enough for the figure to stand upright. Back of the door a black screen, or small enclosure of black screens, or curtains, will give the impression of the dark interior of the Tomb when the stone is rolled away. Against the entrance a large gray slab of rock is placed, with the seal of Caesar sealing it against the Tomb. A big rock can be placed at right of the entrance for the Centurion or Angel to sit upon.

The Centurions are dressed in Roman costume, with armor, shields, spears, short swords, etc., and different-colored togas— one in azure blue (not purple and not turquoise), the other in a soft green of the same value; both to be low in tone. These will look well with the gray background and silver armor, and keep the impression of the cool color of dawn, as warmer colors would not. Mary Magdalene is in red, a soft red, or rose color, and the two women at the Tomb in light blue and light green. A general impression of fairness in color is desired. Yellow and gold and white are reserved for the Angel and the figure of Christ. John is in purple, a gray purple, not too deep, and Peter in brown, a fisherman's costume. The two disciples of Emmaus are in gray cloaks. The figure of Christ is clothed in white, possibly with a gold ornament or pattern, and a halo of gold about the head. The actor impersonating Christ can have a thin veiling over the face, if desired, making the impression more elusive and suggestive. Light can be made to show on the figure of Christ, and the rest of the stage be kept in darkness, by having this actor stand back a little from the entrance of the Tomb and letting light in from the side of the enclosure making the Tomb. Very little light will be needed to make the distinction; if too great, the figures on the stage would lose in contrast.

The movement of the play, after the Centurions wake and find the angel, and after the women come in, is meant to be very rapid, though hushed, and full of low, but intense excitement. When the figure of Christ appears, it is the light that causes them all to turn in his direction, so that his "Peace be unto you" is given to them directly. After the last speech in the play, music is played a moment or two while the picture is held; then the music ceases and the curtain falls.

ALICE CORBIN HENDERSON

· · · · ·

APOLLON, A GARDENER

Whatever its present lacks or qualities, the story of "Apollon, A Gardener" is of noble if somewhat mixed descent. It centers around the old custom of playing hand-ball in the Cathedral of Auxerre at Easter, a custom which plays an important part in Walter Pater's "Denys of Auxerre," in his *Imaginary Portraits*. From this source was taken the idea of blending a Pagan spirit with the Mediaeval, also the idea of the gardener. Easter as the festival of the returning light of the sun after winter's darkness suggested the using of Apollo as the central figure. Certain charming details were found in the Catholic Encyclopedia's remarkable article on Easter customs. From there on, the story went its way.

KATHARINE GIBSON

· · · · ·

SAINT PATRICK AT TARA

The story of "Saint Patrick at Tara" has been adapted from three sources for purposes of this book only.

The text is in large part quoted from *Saint Patrick, his Writings and Life*, by Newport J. D. White, and represents selections from Dr. White's translation of Muirchu's *Life of Patrick*. It is given here with certain omissions and with interpolations from *The Tripartite Life of Patrick*, edited and translated by Whitley Stokes, and published by H. M. Stationery Office under the direction of the Master of the Rolls as one of the *Chronicles and Memorials of Great Britain and Ireland*. The stanza, "The Rune of St. Patrick," taken from Victor Branford's *St. Columba*, is a translation of "The Faedh; or, The Cry of the Deer," from *The Book of Hymns* (11th century) by Charles Mangan. It first appeared in *Lyra Celtica*, edited by E. A. Sharp and J. Matthay with Introduction and Notes by William Sharp.

ALICE I. HAZELTINE

. . . . .

THE FOUNTAIN OF YOUTH

COSTUMING

In "The Fountain of Youth" the Spaniards' costumes of silk, velvet, and armor—the former soiled and the latter dull—should be, if possible, hired from a costumer. In towns where a full range of costumes is not kept garments known as a "Captain John Smith" outfit may be substituted for the real thing. Be careful that they are not all alike in color. Other costumes may be copied from Eggleston's *Illustrated History of the United States*. These, of course, are the authentic ones. The Captain John Smith is of a much later period, and should only be used "when all signs fail." An excellent picture of Ponce de Leon will be found in *The History of the United States* by E. Benjamin Andrews. The Spirit of the Fountain should wear white Grecian robes of cotton crêpe or chiffon. Both hers and the costumes of The Daughters of the Dawn should be made according to the directions for The Powers of the Forest found in "The Pioneers." The Guardian of the Fountain also wears white stockings and silver sandals. The Daughters of the Dawn wear dawn-pink silkoline, both pale and rosy. Their hair is worn unbound. They have white stockings and pink sandals.

(From COSTUMING—under "The Pioneers")

... Silkoline (or cheese-cloth) will garb the Powers of the Forest ... See that it hangs in straight Grecian lines and is not bunchy. There should be bloomers and a straight underdress of silkoline wide enough to dance in, and then the overdress. It should be ankle-length, without a hem, and the material should not be cut too evenly. A prim look is not what is wanted ... On no account should high-heeled slippers be worn. They look ridiculous. Care should be taken to have the foot-gear as nearly alike as possible ... All the scarfs should be chiffon. Nothing else floats as delicately or can be whipped into expression as quickly and easily.

MUSIC

1. "Spring Song." Mendelssohn.
2. "Idyllo." Theodore Lack.

CONSTANCE D'ARCY MACKAY

INDEX OF AUTHORS

ABNEY, LOUISE
   Easter Morning 82
ANGELO, VALENTI
   Easter 244
BIANCHI, MARTHA GILBERT DICKINSON, translator
   An Easter Greeting 72
BRINK, CAROL RYRIE
   Daffodils Out of the Dark 285
   In All Things Beautiful 263
   Waking-Up Time 187
CARMAN, BLISS
   Daffodil's Return 56
CHAPMAN, EMILY D.
   An Easter Carol 83
CHARLES, ELIZABETH, translator
   Smile Praises, O Sky 67
CLEMENT, MARGUERITE
   Ys and Her Bells 115
COATSWORTH, ELIZABETH
   April 191
   The Sun Comes Dancing 77
COLUM, PADRAIC
   Brendan 163
CONE, HELEN GRAY
   An Easter Processional 75
CONKLING, HILDA
   Easter 86
COXE, ARTHUR CLEVELAND
   Tell Us, Gard'ner, Dost Thou Know? 6
DE ANGELI, MARGUERITE
   Aniela's Easter 199

DELAND, MARGARET
 Easter Music: Jonquils 61
DICKINSON, EMILY
 A Fuzzy Fellow 95
 The Waking Year 42
FROST, ROBERT
 A Prayer in Spring 107
GATTY, MARGARET
 A Lesson of Faith 97
GIBSON, KATHARINE
 Apollon, a Gardener 130
HENDERSON, ALICE CORBIN
 Easter Morning: a Play of the Resurrection 15
HINKSON, KATHARINE TYNAN
 Daffodil 57
 Love at Easter 80
HOUSMAN, A. E.
 The Lent Lily 59
 Loveliest of Trees 45
KERN, MARY ROOT
 Easter Rabbit 87
KILMER, JOYCE
 Easter 76
KIRKLAND, WINIFRED
 The Easter People 361
KYLE, ANNE D.
 Easter Candle 295
 Easter Lambs 268
LAGERLÖF, SELMA
 The Sacred Flame 322
LATHBURY, MARY A.
 Rise, Flowers, Rise 46
LOWERY, WOODBURY
 Ponce de Leon Finds the Land of Flowers (adapted) 167
MACKAY, CONSTANCE D'ARCY
 The Fountain of Youth 172
NEALE, JOHN MASON
 The World Itself 9

NEALE, JOHN MASON, *translator*
   The Alleluiatic Sequence 375
NICHOLSON, MARY A.
   Easter Flowers Are Blooming Bright 52
OXENHAM, JOHN
   Risen 11
PALMER, ALICE FREEMAN
   The Butterfly 105
PELZEL, HELENE
   A Happy Easter 210
PRESTON, MARGARET J.
   The First Te Deum 146
RICHARDS, LAURA E.
   Easter-Time 54
ROSSETTI, CHRISTINA GEORGINA
   An Easter Carol 70
SANGSTER, MARGARET E.
   Easter Flowers 48
SCOLLARD, CLINTON
   A Canticle 78
SEREDY, KATE
   Easter Eggs 234
SLOSSON, ANNIE TRUMBULL
   A Child's Easter 315
STRUTHER, JAN
   Sing, All Ye Christian People! 109
SWAYNE, AMELIA W.
   Ivan's Easter Service 319
THAXTER, CELIA
   A Song of Easter 111
TOWNE, CHARLES HANSON
   An Easter Canticle 91
TURNBULL, AGNES SLIGH
   The Maid of Emmaus 24
TURNER, NANCY BYRD
   Easter Again 41
UPJOHN, ANNA MILO
   Elena's *Ciambella* 227

WADDELL, HELEN, *translator*
   Saint Brendan and the White Birds 159
WIDDEMER, MARGARET
   A Child's Easter Song 64
YOUNG, ELLA
   Pasque 44

INDEX OF TITLES

ALLELUIATIC SEQUENCE, THE	375
John Mason Neale, *translator*	
ANIELA'S EASTER	199
Marguerite De Angeli	
APOLLON, A GARDENER	130
Katharine Gibson	
APRIL	191
Elizabeth Coatsworth	
BRENDAN	163
Padraic Colum	
BUTTERFLY, THE	105
Alice Freeman Palmer	
CANTEMUS CUNCTI *See* Alleluiatic Sequence, The	
CANTICLE, A	78
Clinton Scollard	
CHILD'S EASTER, A	315
Annie Trumbull Slosson	
CHILD'S EASTER SONG, A	64
Margaret Widdemer	
DAFFODIL	57
Katharine Tynan Hinkson	
DAFFODIL'S RETURN	56
Bliss Carman	
DAFFODILS OUT OF THE DARK	285
Carol Ryrie Brink	
EASTER	244
Valenti Angelo	
EASTER	86
Hilda Conkling	
EASTER	76
Joyce Kilmer	

EASTER AGAIN 41
  Nancy Byrd Turner
EASTER CANDLE 295
  Anne D. Kyle
EASTER CANTICLE, AN 91
  Charles Hanson Towne
EASTER CAROL 93
  Written for a French Carol Tune
EASTER CAROL, AN 83
  Emily D. Chapman
EASTER CAROL, AN 70
  Christina Georgina Rossetti
EASTER EGGS 234
  Kate Seredy
EASTER FLOWERS 48
  Margaret E. Sangster
EASTER FLOWERS ARE BLOOMING BRIGHT 52
  Mary A. Nicholson
EASTER GREETING, AN 72
  Martha Gilbert Dickinson Bianchi, *translator*
EASTER LAMBS 268
  Anne D. Kyle
EASTER MORNING 82
  Louise Abney
EASTER MORNING 15
  Alice Corbin Henderson
EASTER MUSIC: JONQUILS 61
  Margaret Deland
EASTER PEOPLE, THE 361
  Winifred Kirkland
EASTER PROCESSIONAL, AN 75
  Helen Gray Cone
EASTER RABBIT 87
  Mary Root Kern
EASTER SONG 62
  Author Unknown
EASTER-TIME 54
  Laura E. Richards

EASTER WISH, AN	378
Author Unknown	
ELENA'S *CIAMBELLA*	227
Anna Milo Upjohn	
FIRST TE DEUM, THE	146
Margaret J. Preston	
FLOWER CAROL	50
Translated from the Latin	
FOUNTAIN OF YOUTH, THE	172
Constance D'Arcy Mackay	
FUZZY FELLOW, A	95
Emily Dickinson	
HALLELUJAH	38
From the Messiah by George Frederick Handel	
HAPPY EASTER, A	210
Helene Pelzel	
HILARITER	69
Translated from the German	
IN ALL THINGS BEAUTIFUL	263
Carol Ryrie Brink	
IVAN'S EASTER SERVICE	319
Amelia W. Swayne	
LENT LILY, THE	59
A. E. Housman	
LESSON OF FAITH, A	97
Margaret Gatty	
LOVE AT EASTER	80
Katharine Tynan Hinkson	
LOVELIEST OF TREES	45
A. E. Housman	
MAID OF EMMAUS, THE	24
Agnes Sligh Turnbull	
PASQUE	44
Ella Young	
PLAUDITE COELI *See* Smile Praises, O Sky	
PONCE DE LEON FINDS THE LAND OF FLOWERS (Adapted)	167
Woodbury Lowery	

PRAYER IN SPRING, A 107
    Robert Frost
RISE, FLOWERS, RISE 46
    Mary A. Lathbury
RISEN 11
    John Oxenham
SACRED FLAME, THE 322
    Selma Lagerlöf
SAINT BRENDAN AND THE WHITE BIRDS 159
    Helen Waddell, *translator*
SAINT PATRICK AT TARA 149
    Adapted from Early Sources
SING, ALL YE CHRISTIAN PEOPLE! 109
    Jan Struther
SMILE PRAISES, O SKY 67
    Elizabeth Charles, *translator*
SONG OF EASTER, A 111
    Celia Thaxter
SONG OF PRAISE, A 85
    Adapted from an Ancient Canticle
SUN COMES DANCING, THE 77
    Elizabeth Coatsworth
TELL US, GARD'NER, DOST THOU KNOW? 6
    Arthur Cleveland Coxe
VERY EARLY IN THE MORNING 3
    Arranged from the Four Gospels. King James Version
WAKING YEAR, THE 42
    Emily Dickinson
WAKING-UP TIME 187
    Carol Ryrie Brink
WORLD ITSELF, THE 9
    John Mason Neale
YE HAPPY BELLS OF EASTER DAY 73
    Author Unknown
YS AND HER BELLS 115
    Marguerite Clement

Grant Public Library
Grant, NE 69140